ADOLESCENCE AND BODY IMAGE

Body image is a significant issue for the majority of adolescents. Anxieties relating to body image can be crippling across both genders, their debilitating effects sometimes leading to mental health problems. This important book is the first of its kind to focus specifically on adolescents, providing a comprehensive overview of the biological, psychological, and sociocultural factors relating to the development of body image. It also provides a detailed review of the measures that can be taken to address body dissatisfaction.

Discussing the role of culture, family, peers, schools, sport, and media in stimulating a negative body image, the book also examines the different challenges faced by girls and boys as they grow. Eating disorders and body change strategies are also addressed, as well as the challenges faced by youngsters affected by conditions causing visible differences, such as hair loss in cancer patients. The book presents original research, including the results from a large Australian study of the body image and associated health behaviours of adolescent boys and the results of a study of current teaching practices relating to body image.

Adolescence and Body Image will be ideal reading for students and researchers from a variety of fields, including developmental, health, and social psychology, sociology, and cultural and health studies. Professionals working with young people, whether in education, health promotion, or any other allied discipline will also find this book an invaluable resource.

Lina A. Ricciardelli is a Professor in the School of Psychology at Deakin University, Melbourne, Australia.

Zali Yager is a Senior Lecturer in the College of Education at Victoria University, Melbourne, Australia.

Adolescence and Society
Series Editor: John C. Coleman
Department of Education, University of Oxford

In the 20 years since it began, this series has published some of the key texts in the field of adolescent studies. The series has covered a very wide range of subjects, almost all of them being of central concern to students, researchers, and practitioners. A mark of its success is that several books have gone to second and third editions, illustrating their popularity and reputation.

The primary aim of the series is to make accessible to the widest possible readership important and topical evidence relating to adolescent development. Much of this material is published in relatively inaccessible professional journals, and the objective of the books has been to summarise, review, and place in context current work in the field so as to interest and engage both an undergraduate and a professional audience.

The intention of the authors is to raise the profile of adolescent studies among professionals and in institutions of higher education. By publishing relatively short, readable books on topics of current interest relating to youth and society, the series makes people more aware of the relevance of the subject of adolescence to a wide range of social concerns. The books do not put forward any one theoretical viewpoint. The authors outline the most prominent theories in the field and include a balanced and critical assessment of each. While some books may have a clinical or applied slant, the majority concentrate on normal development.

The readership rests primarily in two major areas: the undergraduate market, particularly in the fields of psychology, sociology, and education, and the professional training market, with particular emphasis on social work, clinical and educational psychology, counselling, youth work, nursing, and teacher training.

Also in this series:

ADOLESCENCE AND BODY IMAGE

From Development to Preventing Dissatisfaction

Lina A. Ricciardelli and Zali Yager

Routledge
Taylor & Francis Group

LONDON AND NEW YORK

First published 2016
by Routledge
2 Park Square, Milton Park, Abingdon, Oxon, OX14 4RN

and by Routledge
711 Third Avenue, New York, NY 10017

Routledge is an imprint of the Taylor & Francis Group, an informa business

British Library Cataloguing in Publication Data
A catalogue record for this book is available from the British Library

Library of Congress Cataloging in Publication Data

Ricciardelli, Lina A. (Lina Angela)
Adolescence and body image: from development to preventing dissatisfaction / Lina A. Ricciardelli and Zali Yager.
    pages cm
Includes bibliographical references and index.
    1. Body image in adolescence. 2. Body image. 3. Self-acceptance in adolescence. 4. Adolescent psychology. I. Yager, Zali. II. Title.
BF724.3.B55R53 2016
306.4'613—dc23   2015022108

ISBN: 978-1-84872-198-2 (hbk)
ISBN: 978-1-84872-199-9 (pbk)
ISBN: 978-1-31584-937-9 (ebk)

Typeset in Bembo
by codeMantra

CONTENTS

ACKNOWLEDGEMENTS

Many thanks to our editorial team, colleagues, students, friends and family, who have provided ongoing support and inspiration throughout the writing and production of this book.

A motivating force was Lucy Kennedy who provided assistance, encouragement and enthusiasm at every stage. There were a few times when our progress was slow and completing the book seemed daunting and unachievable but Lucy's emails were always reassuring and encouraging.

I am greatly indebted to Zali Yager who agreed to co-author this book. Her vision and drive kept the momentum going, and she was amazing in every way.

Thanks to all my colleagues, students, friends, and to my family (Mum, Dad, Carmela, Angelo, Leo and Ivanka). They have heard me talk about this book for a long time, and have supported me through some very difficult times. I would not have been able to keep living, working and achieving without them.

Finally, I have learnt so much about body image from my nieces, Laura, Alessia and Mia, and my nephew, Michael. Thank you for challenging many of my ideas and enriching my world.

1
INTRODUCTION

Our modern world places an inordinate emphasis on body image and appearance. It is everywhere and especially present in the lives of adolescents. Adolescence is a time of rapid development, and several factors during this period intensify adolescents' focus on physical appearance and their bodies. These include puberty, peer culture, an interest in dating, and identity formation. In addition, young people perceive immense pressure to meet the appearance ideals portrayed and transmitted via different forms of media (TV, movies, social networking sites). These concerns permeate many aspects of adolescents' lives and explain why body image concerns are rated among the most important issues affecting young people in today's society. Thus adolescence is a central place to commence studying the development of body image and target the prevention of body image concerns in girls and boys.

What Is Body Image?

Body image is a broad term that refers to a person's perceptions, thoughts, and feelings about his or her body (Cash, 2004; Grogan, 2008). There are four main elements:

The way we see our bodies (perceptual);
The way we feel about our bodies (affective);
The thoughts and beliefs we have about our bodies (cognitive);
The things we do because we are dissatisfied with our bodies (behavioural).

The majority of research in this area has focused on the construct of body dissatisfaction, and in particular dissatisfaction with body size, shape, or weight. Body dissatisfaction refers to the negative subjective evaluation of one's own body in relation to overall appearance, shape, and weight or specific body parts (Grogan, 2008). It may range from mild discomfort to feelings of abject revulsion, disgust, and hatred. Other aspects of body image and related terms include: body esteem, appearance orientation, appearance evaluation, body type preference, body surveillance, body shame, and appearance anxiety.

Having a positive body image is not simply the opposite of being dissatisfied with one's appearance, but rather involves a genuine appreciation of the body for its capabilities (Tylka, 2011). Those with a positive body image accept and value their bodies in a functional sense rather than what they look like. They have positive self-esteem, healthy attitudes towards food and eating, and are able to resist peer and media pressures to conform. On the other hand, those with body image concerns place an undue importance on their appearance, weight, size, or shape and avoid social and personal situations where they feel that they are being judged on their appearance. There is evidence to suggest that those with high levels of body image concerns engage in unhealthy weight control measures and may develop eating disorders and other associated behaviours such as steroid use.

Prevalence and Nature Body Image Concerns among Adolescents

Body image concerns are common among adolescents. In the largest survey of young people in Australia, body image was ranked third in the issues of personal concern, behind stress and school or study issues, among more than 15,000 young people aged 15 to 19. In total, 35.6% of adolescents, and more females (43%) than males (18.6%), indicated that body image was an important issue of personal concern (Mission Australia, 2012).

Girls

It is estimated that during preadolescence about 40 to 50% of girls report a preference to be thinner, and this increases to over 70% during adolescence (Wertheim & Paxton, 2011). Only about 10% of girls report a preference for a larger body size or weight, and most of these girls would want to be underweight (Wertheim & Paxton, 2011). In addition, several studies have examined the importance of being thin to adolescent girls, and this research shows that girls believe that being thinner makes them happier, healthier, better looking, and more successful with boys (Wertheim & Paxton, 2012).

Adolescent girls score higher than boys in terms of body surveillance (e.g., "During the day, I think about how I look many times"), body shame (e.g., "I feel like I must be a bad person when I don't look as good as I could"), and appearance anxiety (e.g., "I worry how others are evaluating how I look") (Slater & Tiggemann, 2010).

The focus for girls is also primarily on the aesthetic qualities of their bodies, which they universally evaluate more negatively than the functional qualities, and they express a greater desire to change these aspects than do males (Abbott & Barber, 2011). Interestingly, when girls are asked to focus on the functional aspects of their bodies, they make fewer negative evaluations and express lower body dissatisfaction (Abbott & Barber, 2011).

Among girls, studies consistently show that body dissatisfaction progressively increases throughout middle adolescence and into early adulthood (Bucchianeri, Arikian, Hannan, Eisenberg, Neumark-Sztainer, 2013; Calzo et al., 2012; Jones, 2004; Rosenblum & Lewis, 1999). Two large and longitudinal studies from the U.S. showed significant increases in body dissatisfaction over time among girls from 12 to 18 years of age (Calzo et al., 2012) and from 12 to 24 years of age (Bucchianeri et al., 2013). Similarly, a longitudinal study in Norway demonstrated an increase in body dissatisfaction to the age of 21 and a plateau until the age of 30 (Holsen, Jones, & Birkeland, 2012).

Boys

Studies show that 40 to 70% of adolescent boys are dissatisfied with their body size and/or specific parts of their body (Almeida, Severo, Araújo, Lopes, & Ramos 2012; Huenemann, Shapiro, Hampton, & Mitchell, 1966; Lawler & Nixon, 2011; McCabe & Ricciardelli, 2004). However, while the majority of adolescent girls desire a thinner body size, adolescent boys are more equally divided between those who want a thinner body size and those who want a larger body size. In addition, while girls are more dissatisfied with their thighs, hips, and waist, boys are more dissatisfied with biceps, shoulders, chests, and muscles (Huenemann et al., 1966; Ricciardelli, McCabe, & Ridge, 2006). It is also important to note that although boys often desire more muscularity, this is often lean muscularity.

Another difference with boys is that the focus is more on the functional aspects of the body rather than the aesthetic focus that we see among girls (Abbott & Barber, 2010). Boys often display dissatisfaction and place more importance on aspects of body image that are desirable for playing sports. These include 'size', 'height', 'speed', 'strength', 'fitness', 'stamina', 'endurance', and 'physical co-ordination' (Ricciardelli et al., 2006).

The age-related changes for boys' body image have been more variable. Some studies demonstrate that body dissatisfaction peaks at 13 to

14 years of age and then decreases as boys move through to later adolescence (Calzo et al., 2012), resulting in decreased body dissatisfaction levels among adolescent boys and young adult men aged 18 to 30 years (Eisenberg, Neumark-Sztainer, & Paxton, 2006; Holsen et al., 2012; Jones, 2004; Paxton, Eisenberg, & Neumark-Sztainer, 2006). Other research shows a consistent linear increase in body dissatisfaction from 12 to 24 years of age (Bucchianeri et al., 2013). This variability in findings is most likely due to the wide range of measures used to assess body image and to whether measures include an assessment of satisfaction with weight alone, muscularity alone, or both.

Adolescence as a Key Developmental Stage

Many researchers line up the commencement of adolescence with the start with puberty and mark the end of adolescence with legal adulthood, which is 18 years of age in Western countries (Hendry & Kloep, 2012; Slee, Campbell, & Spears, 2012; World Health Organisation, 2013). Other researchers feel that adolescence commences at the age of 12 or 13 years, which often corresponds with the start of secondary school (Gemelli, 1996; Hendy & Kloep, 2012). In addition, some conceptualise adolescence more broadly to span from 12 to 20 years; more recently this has been extended to the age of 25 years to encompass all of youth (Wise, 2000).

While researchers may not all agree with the definition of adolescence, all agree that a thorough understanding of adolescence requires integrating theories from a range of disciplines including anthropology, biology, education, ethology, history, psychology, and sociology. Importantly, adolescence is also viewed as the transition from childhood to adulthood and its cultural purpose as the preparation for adult roles. This involves the development of tasks such as achieving emotional independence, and choosing a career (Havighurst, 1953). There is also agreement that the majority of adolescents will move out of this stage at about 18 or 19 years with "an emancipated identity that is defined by the way in which he or she has cognitively processed the transactions between the biological, psychological, and social forces" (Gemelli, 1996, pp. 446–47).

Some researchers divide adolescence into an early phase, which includes the ages of 11/12 to 15 years, and a later phase, which includes the ages of 16 to 19 years (Cobb, 2010; Gemelli, 1996). Early adolescence is marked by the onset of puberty, changing gender roles, more autonomous relationships with parents, and more mature relationships with peers (Cobb, 2010). On the other hand, late adolescence is organised around the central task of achieving an identity, in which adolescents integrate their sexuality into their relationships, prepare for a career, and develop a personal set of beliefs (Cobb, 2010).

Throughout the last two centuries, adolescence has often been portrayed as a period of 'storm and stress' (Hall, 1904), and much of the focus has been on parent-adolescent conflict, emotional moodiness, and risk-taking behaviours (Slee et al., 2012). This portrayal of 'storm and stress' also underlies the psychoanalytic view of adolescence as summarised by Wise (2000, p. 7):

> Adolescence—when we are no longer children and have not yet reached adulthood—is a time of much disturbance, change and potential growth. The adolescent is confronted with a body that stretches, changes and grows in all directions, as does her or his mind. … Normal adolescent development includes unpredictable and sudden changes in the adolescent's mind, as he is confronted from the onset of puberty with inner turmoil, his emerging adolescent/adult sexuality and the constraints of his conscience. By contrast, fixed or inflexible feelings and behaviours are signs of psychopathology.

In addition to 'storm and stress' other main developmental theorists have focused on either the social or cognitive development of adolescents. For example, Erikson (1968) viewed the formation of an identity as one of the key tasks of adolescence. Erikson maintained that the adolescent's developing sense of identity was evident in his/her psychosocial well-being and also demonstrable "when 'at home' in one's body, family and social world" (Slee et al., 2012, p. 507). Thus, the development of a positive body image, which can be viewed as part of an adolescent's identity, is pivotal.

In contrast to Erikson, Piaget, another influential developmental theorist, put more emphasis on cognitive development. The 'formal operations' stage is critical for Piaget, and this begins at about 11 years of age. It is marked by the ability for an individual to reason in an abstract manner (Piaget & Inhelder, 1969). It is this advance in abstract reasoning that allows adolescents to more fully reflect on their own attributes and compare themselves with others, which then can lead to more body image concerns.

Physical Changes

In addition to the important psychosocial and cognitive changes that occur during adolescence, the physical changes that occur during this period are very significant. Marked physical changes occur in height, weight, body composition, and the distribution of fat across the body (Shroff & Ricciardelli, 2012; Stang & Story, 2005). Before the age of 9 to 13, boys are taller and heavier than girls. However, these growth indicators are reversed at puberty, as girls enter their growth spurt and puberty about two year earlier than boys.

Generally girls will experience puberty between 10 and 14 years, although between 8 and 15 years is still considered developmentally normal. One of the first noticeable changes is a growth spurt in height. On average the growth spurt for girls begins between the ages of 8 and 13 years, and girls reach their full adult height between the ages of 10 and 16 years. Girls on average gain between 7 and 25 kg (15 and 55 lb) of weight during puberty and experience a 120% increase in body fat. Girls will also experience a widening of hips and the development of breasts. Breasts begin to bud on average between the ages of 8 and 13 years, and breast development is completed on average, between 14 and 15 years of age. Pubic hair appears for girls between the ages of 8 and 14 years and reaches full development between the ages of 14 and 15. Underarm hair appears between the ages of 10 and 16 years, and other body hair becomes thicker and coarser during this time. Head hair also becomes coarser and thicker and may even darken in colour.

During puberty, boys gain between 7 and 30 kg (15 and 65 lb). Boys' peak weight gain occurs about the same time as their peak increase in height, that is, around 13.5 to 14 years of age. For boys there is also an increase in fat-free mass (muscle) with a minimal increment in fat mass, leading to a decrease in the percentage of body fat during the later stages of pubertal development. Overall, boys' fat-free body mass increases faster and for a longer period than girls'. Boys reach the fat-free body mass of a young man at about 19 to 20 years of age.

Other notable physical changes during puberty for boys include increases in testicles and penis size along with the first appearance of pubic hair. Pubic hair appears after genitalia start to develop. Pubic hair has been found to be visible as early 9.5 years, and it reaches full development between the ages of 13 and 17.5 years. It usually appears about 1.5 years later in boys than in girls. Other hair appears about two years after pubic hair in the following order: armpits, anus, upper lip, sideburns, nipples, middle of the chest, neck under the chin, rest of the chin and beard area, limbs and shoulders, back, and buttocks. However, not all males develop chest hair. Another physical change that occurs for boys is the deepening of the voice. The voice box or larynx is more distinct in boys than in girls, and this causes boys' voices to drop and deepen.

It is only natural that these physical changes during puberty will draw adolescents' focus to their bodies and make adolescents feel more self-conscious of their bodies (Slee et al., 2012). The changes are also likely to reinforce the notion of the 'imaginary audience', that is, that others are evaluating their appearance (Elkind, 1967). Moreover, many of these physical changes may intensify adolescents' body image concerns. The effects of puberty and pubertal timing on body image concerns are examined in Chapter 4.

Models and Theories of Body Image

There are implicit and explicit models and/or theories of body image; one is the biopsychosocial model. Many studies use this model to examine a range of factors that influence body image, including selected biological, psychological or individual, and sociocultural risk factors (e.g., Cafri, van den Berg, & Thompson, 2006; Paxton et al., 2006; McCabe & Ricciardelli, 2006; Smolak & Stein, 2006; Stice & Whitenton, 2002). In this book we specifically examine biological factors such as puberty and BMI (Chapter 4), sociocultural factors, which include the media (Chapter 5), peers (Chapter 6), the family (Chapter 7), and individual risk factors, which include self-esteem and perfectionism (Chapter 9). It is important to note that some factors that have been studied do not neatly fit into these groupings; however, some such as sexual orientation and gender roles involve aspects of biology, psychology, and culture.

Although we have primarily classified the factors influencing body image as 'biological', 'sociocultural', or 'individual', it is important to acknowledge that some researchers have classified the various factors differently, and these conceptualisations are also useful. Some researchers refer to factors as 'distal' or 'historical' (e.g., BMI, teasing history, and self-esteem) versus 'proximal' (e.g., everyday experiences such as current peer groups and recent media exposure). Other researchers have classified factors as 'fixed' (e.g., late pubertal timing, ethnicity, personality) versus 'modifiable' (e.g., negative affect, self-esteem, internalisation of the thin ideal). Furthermore, it is important to note that while the biopsychosocial model is designed to best summarise the available empirical data, further research is needed to study the mechanisms underlying these relationships and the interplay among the various biological, sociocultural, and individual factors (Ricciardelli & McCabe, 2004).

Sociocultural Theories

Several theories place the main focus on sociocultural factors (Striegel-Moore, Silberstein, & Rodin, 1986; Tiggemann, 2012). These include:

1. Social comparison theory
2. Social learning theory
3. The Tripartite Influence Model
4. Feminist theory
5. Self-objectification theory
6. Cultivation theory

Social Comparison Theory

Social comparison theory (Festinger, 1954) proposes that individuals evaluate their own values and capabilities by comparing themselves to others. These comparisons are especially important during the adolescent years (Jones, 2004), as young persons are developing their identity. Peer social comparisons are reviewed in Chapter 6.

Social Learning Theory

Bandura proposed that individuals learn from others (Bandura, 1986). Social learning theory explains the effects of the media, peers, and the family on body image by proposing that adolescents and adults learn about the meaning of attractiveness by watching others and that these sources are a dominant form of information. The impact of the media, peers, and the family on body image is examined fully in Chapters 5, 6, and 7, respectively.

Tripartite Influence Model

In line with social learning theory, the Tripartite Influence Model developed by Thompson, Heinberg, Altabe, and Tantleff-Dunn (1999) proposes that the media, peers, and family are the main sources of pressures that influence one's body image and appearance concerns. These influences are primarily examined separately in Chapters 5, 6, and 7; however, some comparisons across the three sources are evaluated in Chapter 7.

Feminist Theory

Underlying much of the research conducted on body image among girls and women is feminist theory, which highlights the increasing homogenisation of Western cultural images of female bodies (as young, white, thin, attractive, healthy, heterosexual, middle-class for example) and how women feel about and respond to such images (Coleman, 2008). Underlying these cultural images of female bodies are the themes of discrimination, objectification, oppression, patriarchy, and stereotyping, which are used to understand social relations and gender inequality.

More recently feminist theory has also been extended and applied to males from different cultural groups in order to explain why some men demonstrate greater body image problems and more disordered eating (Jung, Forbes, & Lee, 2009; Ricciardelli, McCabe, Williams, & Thompson, 2007). On the whole, studies suggest that being a male from a minority group and being a male in a new generation of a rapidly developing country carry negative social and health implications. These differences may in part reflect the changing status quo and power relations for males and/or the higher level of social isolation of men in minority groups when compared to the dominant cultural group(s). In particular, men more than women may be worse off in a climate of emerging acculturation and modernisation as they may have more to lose than they have to gain in social status with changing social structures. These views are examined further in Chapter 8.

Self-objectification Theory

Self-objectification theory is also proposed as an explanation for the high levels of body dissatisfaction among girls and women (Frederickson & Roberts, 1997). This theory focuses on the notion that women are predominantly valuable due to their role as sexual objects, to be admired and looked at rather than having any practical or intellectual purpose. The media is blamed for contributing to increased levels of self-objectification in women due to the number of sexualised images that are depicted across the broad spectrum of genres. Viewing these images is associated with increased self-objectification in college women (Harper & Tiggemann, 2008; Morry & Staska, 2001). Internalisation and self-objectification have also been linked to the development of body dissatisfaction and eating disorder symptomatology in college women (Calogero, 2004). However, research indicates that objectification theory may not be as applicable for men (Daniel & Bridges, 2009), and support for models seems to depend largely on the measures used for dissatisfaction with muscularity or adiposity. Daniel and Bridges (2009) found that objectification was not related to a drive for muscularity, whereas other studies found support for a relationship between objectification and disordered eating using measures of dissatisfaction with adiposity (Calogero, 2009; Tiggemann & Kuring, 2004) such as the Eating Disorder Inventory (Garner, 1991). Although most of the research regarding objectification, the media, and body image has been conducted among adult men and women, it is assumed that the process of objectification is initiated in adolescence due to developmental awareness of the gaze of others. A study by Slater and Tiggemann (2010) showed that self-objectification did impact on measures of body shame, appearance anxiety, and disturbed eating among adolescent boys and girls aged 12 to 16 years (Slater & Tiggemann, 2010). Other studies that examine self-objectification are reviewed in Chapter 5.

Cultivation Theory

Cultivation theory, developed in the media and communications literature, suggests that the images, attitudes, and themes presented in the media build up over time in the minds of consumers and influence perceptions of what is real and normal (Gerbner, Gross, Morgan, Signorielli, & Shanahan, 2002). In terms of body image, this means that the large number of images that feature a very narrow range of body sizes for men and women contribute to individuals' beliefs about normal, possible and desirable body shapes. This theory is usually used to explain the influence of television, and recent work has applied it to the body shapes that feature in video games (Martins, Williams, Ratan, & Harrison, 2010).

Overview of Book Chapters

Chapter 2

A large range of measures has been developed for assessing body image and body dissatisfaction among adolescents. Chapter 2 provides an overview of the types of measures and a brief description of those most commonly used in the body image research literature. This will provide a greater understanding of the results of much of the research discussed in the book and might inform those wishing to select measures for the assessment of body image and body dissatisfaction in adolescents.

Chapter 3

This chapter examines the range of body change strategies and negative health outcomes associated with body dissatisfaction among adolescents. These include disordered eating and weight loss strategies; body change strategies associated with the pursuit of muscularity; and the impact body dissatisfaction has on other aspects of adolescents' lives including mental health, academic performance, health-risk behaviours, and maintenance of obesity. Other practices that adolescents use to manage or modify their appearance include body hair removal, tanning behaviours, tattooing and body piercing, and more extreme methods such as cosmetic surgery.

Chapter 4

This chapter examines the relationship between the physical and biological factors of body weight and body image and puberty and body image and how they differ between girls and boys. Puberty is associated with important developmental changes in physical appearance, self-image, mood and interactions with others. We discuss pubertal timing and the implications of early and late maturation for body image in adolescent boys and girls. Theories such as the "the off-time hypothesis" will be explored. Increased weight, generally measured relative to height using the BMI, has been found to be the most robust predictor of body dissatisfaction. We explore this research and examine other related factors such as increased peer teasing about weight.

Chapter 5

Mass media provide a constant reminder of what is considered to be attractive, how important it is to look that way, and how to achieve that look and are often blamed directly for the development of body image problems and eating disorders. This chapter explores the basis for these claims and provides an overview of the correlational, longitudinal, and experimental research that has investigated the impact of the media on adolescents. Also discussed will be the trends in the presentation of male and female images over time, the impact of the Internet and social media, and the factors that might make some adolescents more or less vulnerable to this powerful influence.

Chapter 6

Peers play an important role in influencing adolescents' body image and appearance concerns, and they exert their influence in a range of ways. The influence of peers becomes more influential than parents during the adolescent period, heightening their potential impact. This chapter examines peer pressure and modelling, peer group norms, peer social comparisons, appearance-related teasing by peers, and the impact of appearance-based conversations among peers. We also differentiate the potential impact of close friends as opposed to all same-aged peers on body image.

Chapter 7

This chapter examines the role of family influences in the development of adolescents' body image concerns. Much of the research has focused primarily on direct and indirect messages transmitted by mothers, but several studies have also examined fathers. Parents and other family members primarily exert their influence directly via positive and negative messages. In addition, family members exert their influence indirectly via their own attitudes and behaviours, and these may then be modelled by adolescents. The nature of the relationship adolescents have with their family members is also important. Although adolescence is the time to become more independent physically, emotionally, and cognitively, adolescents continue to need a positive and secure family environment where they can get support, reassurance and guidance.

Chapter 8

The majority of studies prior to the 1990s focused on adolescent girls primarily from Western countries. Increasingly researchers are examining body image concerns among adolescent girls and boys from non-Western countries and among minority cultural groups living in non-Western countries. Chapter 8 provides a review of this research, and also examines other important sociocultural factors such as acculturation, socioeconomic status (SES), and gender roles.

Chapter 9

In addition to sociocultural factors, a range of individual factors have been found to be consistently associated with body image concerns among adolescents. These will be examined in Chapter 9 and include the internalisation of appearance ideals, negative affect and self-esteem, perfectionism, and sexual orientation. More of the research has been done with girls than boys, but increasingly studies are showing that similar factors are associated with body image concerns among boys, especially if measures that are more sensitive to boys' concerns are used.

This chapter will also provide a review of what we know about body image and appearance concerns among adolescents with visible differences. While negotiating body image and appearance concerns is a developmental task for all adolescents, it can prove even more challenging for adolescents who have visible differences. These may be the result of congenital conditions, chronic illnesses, injuries, or surgical interventions.

Chapter 10

The chapter examines how sport provides an important sociocultural context for studying adolescent body image, especially among boys. Sport is one of the main ways males demonstrate and strengthen various facets of masculinity that are closely aligned with the pursuit of muscularity. Although there is less focus on the importance of sport for girls, this chapter also examines the relationship between sport and body image for girls. Sport can promote an active, instrumental experience of the self with the focus being on what the body can do rather than what it looks like. However, some sports, with the emphasis on obtaining an optimal weight for athletic performance, promote a subculture with intensified pressures to be thin, and this increases adolescents' risk of developing disordered eating.

Chapter 11

Adolescents spend the majority of their time in schools with their peers, and therefore this setting can have a great deal of influence on body image and body dissatisfaction. This chapter outlines the way in which schools might contribute to the development of body image issues and how they might be involved in attempts to prevent the development of body dissatisfaction. Included is recent research on current school practice in terms of implementing a whole school approach to the promotion of positive body image and how teachers and researchers can work together to promote positive body image. A discussion of strategies that are not recommended in schools is also examined.

Chapter 12

Given that so many adolescents are affected by body image concerns and the serious implications of negative body image, prevention of these issues is considered to be a public health priority. This chapter examines the empirical evidence of the success of widespread public policy initiatives to promote positive body image. The chapter also provides an overview of the theoretical foundations of intervention programs that focus on the individual and a systematic review of the body image programs that have been conducted with adolescents in a range of settings. Some of the major issues are discussed, and answers to practical questions are provided.

Chapter 13

The final chapter provides suggestions for future research, including the use of participant-centred, qualitative, and participatory methods that will help to uncover more relevant and significant issues for adolescents. In addition, interviews and more in-depth qualitative studies are needed to further our understanding of the different factors that impact adolescent body image.

Conclusion

Adolescence is a time of rapid physical and emotional development, and these changes naturally draw young persons' attention to their body image and appearance. In this chapter we have highlighted the prevalence and nature of different body image concerns among girls and boys. In addition, we have introduced several models and theories of body image, which we will examine further throughout the book.

References

Abbott, B.D., & Barber, B.L. (2010). Embodied image: Gender differences in functional and aesthetic body image among Australian adolescents. *Body Image, 7,* 22–31.

Abbott, B.D., & Barber, B.L. (2011). Differences in functional and aesthetic body image between sedentary girls and girls involved in sports and physical activity: Does sport type make a difference? *Psychology of Sport and Exercise, 12,* 333–42.

Almeida, S., Severo, M., Araújo, J., Lopes, C., & Ramos, E. (2012). Body image and depressive symptoms in 13-year-old adolescents. *Journal of Paediatrics and Child Health, 48,* E165–E171.

Bandura, A. (1986). *Social foundations of thought and action: A social cognitive theory.* Englewood Cliffs, NJ: Prentice Hall.

Bucchianeri, M.M., Arikian, A.J., Hannan, P.J., Eisenberg, M.E., & Neumark-Sztainer, D. (2013). Body dissatisfaction from adolescence to young adulthood: Findings for a 10-year longitudinal study. *Body Image, 10,* 1–7.

Cafri, G., van den Berg, P., & Thompson, J.K. (2006). Pursuit of muscularity in adolescent boys: Relation among biopsychosocial variables and clinical outcomes. *Journal of Clinical and Adolescent Psychology, 35,* 283–91.

Calogero, R.M. (2004). A test of objectification theory: The effect of the male gaze on appearance concerns in college women. *Psychology of Women Quarterly, 28,* 16–21.

Calzo, J.P., Sonneville, K.R., Haines, J., Blood, E.A., Field, A.E., & Austin, S.B. (2012). The development of associations among body mass index, body dissatisfaction, and weight and shape concerns among adolescent boys and girls. *Journal of Adolescent Health, 5,* 517–23.

Cash, T.F. (2004). Body image: Past, present and future. *Body Image, 1,* 1–5.

Coleman, R. (2008). The becoming of bodies: Girls, media effects, and body image. *Feminist Media Studies, 8,* 163–79.

Cobb, N.J. (2010). *Adolescence* (7th ed.). Sunderland, MA: Sinauer Associates.

Daniel, S., & Bridges, S.K. (2009). The drive for muscularity in men: Media influences and objectification theory. *Body Image, 7,* 32–38.

Eisenberg, M.E., Neumark-Sztainer, D., & Paxton, S.J. (2006). Five-year change in body satisfaction among adolescents. *Journal of Psychosomatic Research, 61,* 521–27.

Elkind, D. (1967). Egocentrism in adolescence. *Child Development, 38,* 1025–34.

Erikson, E.H. (1968). *Identity, youth and crisis.* London: Faber.

Festinger, L. (1954). A theory of social comparison process. *Human Relations, 7,* 117–40.

Frederickson, B.L., & Roberts, T.A. (1997). Objectification theory: Toward understanding women's lived experiences and mental health risks. *Psychology of Women Quarterly, 21,* 173–206.

Gardner, R.M. (2011). Perceptual measures of body image for adolescents. In T. F. Cash & L. Smolak (Eds.), (2nd ed., pp. 146–53). *Body image: A Handbook of science, practice, and prevention.* New York, NY: Guilford Press.

Garner, D.M. (1991). *Eating Disorder Inventory-2. Professional Manual.* Odessa, FL: Psychological Assessment Resources.

Gemelli, R. (1996). *Normal child and adolescent development.* Washington, DC: American Psychiatric Press.

Gerbner, G., Gross, L., Morgan, M., Signorielli, N., & Shanahan, J. (2002). Growing up with television: Cultivation processes. In J. Bryant & D. Zillmann (Eds.), *Media effects: Advances in theory and research* (2nd ed., pp. 43–67). Mahwah, NJ: Lawrence Erlbaum.

Grogan, S. (2008). *Body image: Understanding body dissatisfaction in men, women, and children* (2nd ed.). London: Routledge.

Hall, G.S. (1904). *Adolescence: Its psychology and its relations to physiology, anthropology, sociology, sex, crime, religion and education* (Volume 1 & 2). New York, NY: Appleton.

Harper, B., & Tiggemann, M. (2008). The effect of thin ideal media images on women's self-objectification, mood, and body image. *Sex Roles, 58*, 649–57.

Havighurst, R. (1953). *Human development and education*. New York, NY: Longman.

Hendry, L.B., & Kloep, M. (2012). *Adolescence and adulthood: Transitions and transformations*. New York, NY: Palgrave Macmillan.

Holsen, I., Jones, D.C., & Birkeland, M.S. (2012). Body image satisfaction among Norwegian adolescents and young adults: A longitudinal study of the influence of interpersonal relationships and BMI. *Body Image, 9*, 201–208.

Huenemann, R.L., Shapiro, L.R., Hampton, M.D. & Mitchell, B.W. (1966). A longitudinal study of gross body composition and body conformation and association with food and activity in teenage population: Views of teenage subjects on body conformation, food and activity. *American Journal of Clinical Nutrition, 18*, 323–38.

Jones, D.C. (2004). Body image among adolescent girls and boys: A longitudinal study. *Developmental Psychology, 40*, 823–35.

Jung, J., Forbes, G.B., & Lee, Y. (2009). Body dissatisfaction and disordered eating among early adolescents from Korea and the US. *Sex Roles, 61*, 42–54.

Lawler, M., & Nixon, E. (2011). Body dissatisfaction among adolescent boys and girls: The effects of body mass, peer appearance culture and internalization of appearance ideals. *Journal of Youth and Adolescence, 40*, 59–71.

Martins, N., Williams, D.C., Ratan, R.A., & Harrison, K. (2010). Virtual Muscularity: A content analysis of male video game characters. *Body Image, 8*, 43–51.

McCabe, M.P., & Ricciardelli, L.A. (2004). Body image dissatisfaction among males across the lifespan: A review of past literature. *Journal of Psychosomatic Research, 56*, 675–85.

McCabe, M.P. & Ricciardelli, L.A. (2006). Prospective study of extreme weight change behaviors among adolescent boys and girls. *Journal of Youth and Adolescence, 35*, 425–34.

Mission Australia (2012). *Youth Survey 2012*. https://missionaustralia.com.au/what-we-do-to-help-new/young-people/understanding-young-people/annual-youth-survey.

Morry, M.M., & Staska, S.L. (2001). Magazine exposure: internalization, self-objectification, eating attitudes, and body satisfaction in male and female university students. *Canadian Journal of Behavioral Science, 33*, 269–79.

Paxton, S.J., Eisenberg, M.E., & Neumark-Sztainer, D. (2006). Prospective predictors of body dissatisfaction in adolescent girls and boys: A five-year longitudinal study. *Developmental Psychology, 42*, 888–99.

Piaget, J., & Inhelder, B. (1969). *The psychology of the child*. New York, NY: Basic Books.

Ricciardelli, L.A., & McCabe, M.P. (2004). A biopsychosocial model of disordered eating and the pursuit of muscularity in adolescent boys. *Psychological Bulletin, 130*, 179–205.

Ricciardelli, L.A., McCabe, M.P., & Ridge, D. (2006). The construction of the adolescent male body through sport. *Journal of Health Psychology, 11*, 577–87.

Ricciardelli, L.A, McCabe, M.P., Williams, R.J., & Thompson, J.K. (2007). The role of ethnicity and culture in body image and disordered eating among males. *Clinical Psychology Review, 27*, 582–606.

Rosenblum, G.D., & Lewis, M. (1999). The relations among body image, physical attractiveness and body mass in adolescence. *Child Development, 70*, 50–64.

Shroff, H.P., & Ricciardelli, L.A. (2012). Physical appearance changes during childhood and adolescence. In T. Cash (Ed.), *Encyclopedia of body image and human appearance. Volume 2* (pp. 608–14). London: Elsevier.

Slater, A., & Tiggemann, M. (2010). Body image and disordered eating in adolescent girls and boys: A test of objectification theory. *Sex Roles, 63*, 42–49.

Slee, P.T., Campbell, M., & Spears, B. (2012). *Child, adolescent and family development* (3rd ed.). Cambridge: Cambridge University Press.

Smolak, L., & Stein, J.A. (2006). The relationship of drive for muscularity to sociocultural factors, self-esteem, physical attributes, gender role, and social comparison in middle school boys. *Body Image, 3*, 121–29.

Stang J., & Story, M. (2005). (Eds.), *Guidelines for adolescent nutrition services*. Minneapolis, MN: Center for Leadership, Education and Training in Maternal and Child Nutrition, Division of Epidemiology and Community Health, School of Public Health, University of Minnesota.

Stice, E., & Whitenton, K. (2002). Risk factors for body dissatisfaction in adolescent girls: A longitudinal investigation. *Developmental Psychology, 38*, 669–78.

Striegel-Moore, R.H., Silberstein, L.R., & Rodin, J. (1986). Toward an understanding of risk factors for bulimia. *American Psychologist, 41*, 246–63.

Thompson, J.K., Heinberg, L., Altabe, M., & Tantleff-Dunn, S. (1999). *Exacting Beauty: Theory, assessment, and treatment of body image disturbance.* Washington, DC: American Psychological Association.

Tiggemann, M. (2012). Sociocultural perspectives on body image. In T.F. Cash, (Ed.), *Encyclopedia of body image and human appearance, Volume 2* (pp. 758–65). London: Elsevier.

Tiggemann, M., & Kuring, J.K. (2004). The role of body objectification in disordered eating and depressed mood. *British Journal of Clinical Psychology, 43*, 229–311.

Tylka, T.L. (2011). Positive psychology perspectives on body image. In T.F. Cash & L. Smolak (Eds.), *Body image: A Handbook of science, practice, and prevention* (2nd ed., pp. 56–64). New York, NY: Guilford Press.

Wertheim, E.H., & Paxton, S.J. (2011). Body image development in adolescent girls. In T.F. Cash & L. Smolak (Eds.), (2nd ed., pp. 76–84). *Body image: A Handbook of science, practice, and prevention.* New York, NY: Guilford Press.

Wertheim, E.H., & Paxton, S.J. (2012). Body image development: Adolescent girls. In T. F. Cash, (Ed.), *Encyclopedia of body image and human appearance, Volume 1* (pp. 187–93). London: Elsevier.

Wise, I. (2000). (Ed.), *Adolescence*. London: Institute of Psycho-Analysis.

World Health Organization (2013). http://www.who.int/topics/adolescent_health/en/ retrieved 14th March, 2015.

2
ASSESSMENT AND MEASUREMENT OF BODY IMAGE

In his article, "The (mis)measurement of body image", Thompson (2004) describes the explosion of body image research, and subsequent outbreak of body image measures developed to assess this multidimensional construct. At that time, he summarised over 50 measures that were available to assess body image. As this was 10 years ago, it is assumed that this number has continued to rise. However, only a few of these have been specifically designed for adolescents and/or have been validated for this age group (Menzel, Krawczyk, & Thompson, 2011). Of the 41 measures reviewed by Menzel et al. (2011), only five included adolescents in their validation sample. In this chapter, we focus primarily on the measures that have been validated for use among adolescents.

We provide an overview of the different types of body image measures that are most commonly used in the literature. Evaluative and attitudinal measures of trait body image are the most common, and we describe six of the most commonly used scales for adolescent boys and girls. We then describe state measures and figure rating scales, as well as perceptual and behavioural measures.

Types of Body Image Measures

Body image is a multidimensional construct that has four dimensions: cognitive, perceptual behavioural, and affective or evaluative (Hrabosky et al., 2009). The majority of measures capture only one or two of these dimensions. Abbott and Barber (2010) argue that the components need to be assessed separately in order to adequately capture the complexity of a construct such as body image.

Gender differences also need to be considered. A historical focus on body image as a female concern has meant that many measures that are still among the most popular do not consider the needs of males. Body image concerns among females generally focus on adiposity, while males are concerned with muscularity. In addition, the majority of measures initially designed for women tend to concentrate heavily on female-specific sites of body dissatisfaction, or on 'feeling fat', and therefore do not assess the spectrum of body image for young men.

Culture has a strong impact on body image (see Chapter 8) and needs to be reflected in the choice of measures for diverse populations. The majority of body image measures were developed in Western cultures in English. Cash (2002a) warns against the simple translation of the language of the measures without consideration to the change in meaning among different ethnic groups. The majority of measures we discuss below have been translated for use among other cultures, and psychometric data indicate that these scales are valid and reliable in other cultural contexts.

State Measures of Body Image

Body image is a dynamic construct. Therefore, while trait measures of body image are intended to assess body image as a stable construct (Thompson, 2004), state body image measures assess how participants feel 'at that moment in time' and are needed for assessing short-term change in body image (for example, after viewing media images). Most of the state measures of body image have not been validated among adolescents, so some examples of those used with college women are provided below.

- State Subscale of the Physical Appearance State and Trait Anxiety Scale [PASTAS] This measure requires participants to rate their level of anxiety with 16 particular areas of the body 'right now' (as opposed to 'in general' with the trait subscale of the same questionnaire). Areas of the body that are the focus of the questions can be divided into weight related (hips, thighs, stomach, legs, etc.) and non-weight related (ears, lips, wrists, etc.). The state scale can be used in response to certain scenarios to determine participants' physical anxiety in situations such as swimsuit shopping. This measure has good two-week test-retest reliability (.87), and convergent validity was established with the Eating Disorder Inventory but has only been validated among college women (Reed et al., 1991).
- Body Image States Scale [BISS] This six-item questionnaire taps into domains of 'body experience' including satisfaction with size, shape, and

weight, as well as feelings of attractiveness and evaluation of your own looks in relation to others. Participants respond on a 9-point bipolar Likert scale whereby participants are instructed to "check the box that best describes how you feel right now at this very moment" (Cash et al., 2002, p. 106). This scale was tested in the 'neutral context', as in just how participants are feeling at that moment, but they are also used in conjunction with short scenarios that ask participants to indicate how they would feel in positive or negative body image contexts such as being at the beach in a bathing suit or reading a magazine. The BISS has only been validated for use among college students, where internal consistency was .77 for women and .72 for men (Cash et al., 2002).

- State Visual Analogue Scales [VAS] This method of assessment requires participants to make a mark on a 10 cm line in response to a question such as "right now, how much do you like your body shape?" anchored at each end by "not at all" to "completely" to indicate their current level of body satisfaction or dissatisfaction to produce a score out of 100 (Humphreys & Paxton, 2004). This method originally required participants to indicate how they feel 'right now' and originally included four dimensions: Fat, Strong, Dissatisfaction with weight and shape, and Dissatisfaction with overall appearance (Hargreaves & Tiggemann, 2004; Heinberg & Thompson, 1995). While the actual items often vary between studies, the general response format remains the same. VAS scales are viewed favourably for their ease of use, as well as their sensitivity to change, which is needed in experimental research (McCormack, Horne, & Sheather, 1988). These scales are also viewed to be less prone to experimental demand, as participants are unlikely to be able to recall their responses from previous questionnaires (Heinberg & Thompson, 1995). Those that use multiple items of VAS scales often find that some items share a large proportion of common variance and so are generally combined to form one subscale. The VAS method has been found to have good convergent validity with the body dissatisfaction subscale of the Eating Disorders Inventory (Garner, Olmstead, & Polivy, 1983) when tested with undergraduates (Heinberg & Thompson, 1995) and adolescents (Durkin & Paxton, 2002). This scale has been demonstrated to have good convergent validity with the current ideal discrepancy score of the Figure Rating Scale (Fallon & Rozin, 1985) and to have discriminant validity from measures of depression and anxiety (Durkin & Paxton, 2002). The VAS method has also been used with males and females, adolescents and adults, online and in paper and pencil format (Durkin & Paxton, 2002; Hargreaves & Tiggemann, 2004).

Trait Measures of Body Image

Evaluative or Attitudinal Measures of Body Image

Evaluative or attitudinal measures assess the thoughts (cognitive) or feelings (affective) associated with our bodies (Cafri & Thompson, 2004). These measures typically originated from measures used for the assessment of eating disorders. The Eating Attitudes Test [EAT] (Garner & Garfinkel, 1979), Eating Disorder Inventory [EDI] (Garner et al., 1983), and Eating Disorder Examination [EDE] (Fairburn & Cooper, 1993) were all developed as screening and/or diagnostic tests for eating disorders, and the latter two have a body image component. The Body Dissatisfaction subscale of the EDI and the Shape and Weight Concerns subscales of the EDE are among the most popular body image measures used in evaluations of body image programs (Yager, Diedrichs, Ricciardelli, & Halliwell, 2013).

The most commonly used attitudinal measure of body image are described below.

- Body Dissatisfaction subscale of Eating Disorders Inventory [EDI] (Garner et al., 1983), EDI-2, and EDI-3 (Garner, 2004). This 9-item subscale requires that participants answer questions about four parts of the body (hips, thighs, stomach, buttocks) in both positive and negatively worded ways, and there is one question about satisfaction with body shape. Example items include: "*I think that my hips are too big*" or "*I think that my hips are just the right size*". Participants rate their response on a six-point scale from Never (0) to Always (6). Non-clinical scoring retains these values for scale totals, while clinical scoring involves giving the most anorectic score a 3, the next a 2, and the next a 1. The Body Dissatisfaction subscale of the EDI is arguably the most commonly used measure of body image, and yet there are no large studies publishing psychometric details of this scale for adolescents. The original validity and reliability studies were conducted among females with anorexia nervosa and female college students as a control group (Garner et al., 1983). One study with adolescent girls in Hong Kong revealed high internal consistency (Cronbach's Alpha = .87) (Leung, Wang, & Tang, 2004). Acceptable internal consistency of this subscale has also been reported among Western adolescent boys (Cronbach's Alpha = .86) and girls (Cronbach's Alpha = .91), although sample sizes in this study were low (Shore & Porter, 1990).
- As this scale was developed for women, it assesses predominantly female concerns. Some researchers have modified the items to include some male-relevant sites such as the chest and biceps, which have demonstrated adequate internal reliability (Cronbach's Alpha = .81 in

Ricciardelli & McCabe, 2001; Cronbach's Alpha = .89 in Jones, 2004) (Jones, 2004; Ricciardelli & McCabe, 2001).

- Weight and Shape Concerns subscale of the Eating Disorder Examination [EDE] (Fairburn & Cooper, 1993). The interview version of this measure is considered to be the gold standard in the assessment of eating disorders (Darcy & Hsiao-Jung Lin, 2012). In the questionnaire version, participants rate their response to questions such as: "*How dissatisfied have you felt about your weight*" on a seven-point scale from Not at All to Markedly. Validation studies have indicated that the interview version of the EDE has high internal consistency among adolescent males (Cronbach's Alpha = .93) and females (.95) (Darcy et al., 2012). However, a review of assessment measures for eating disorders indicates that the validity and reliability of both the child and adult versions of the EDE interview are questionable (Micali & House, 2011). Norms for 12- to 14-year-old adolescent girls were assessed for the self-report questionnaire version of the EDE (Carter, Stewart, & Fairburn, 2001). For this study, some modifications were made, such as reducing the 28-day timeframe to 14 days. However no psychometric data were reported (Carter et al., 2001). An intervention study using this measure among adolescents demonstrated internal consistency to be high (Cronbach's Alphas for boys = .92 and girls = .95) (Wilksch & Wade, 2009). However, there are no other psychometric data for this scale with adolescents.

- Body Esteem Scale for Adolescents and Adults. The authors of this measure characterise body esteem as the "self-evaluations of one's body or appearance" (Mendelson et al., 2001, p. 90). This 23-item questionnaire has three subscales. The Appearance subscale captures a general evaluation of, and feelings towards appearance (e.g., "*I like what I look like in pictures*"). The Weight subscale measures the level of satisfaction with weight (e.g., "*I really like what I weigh*"), and the Attribution subscale measures body esteem in terms of the evaluations from others (e.g., "*People my own age like my looks*"). Participants respond to these items on a four-point Likert scale from Never (0) to Always (4). Research conducted among adolescents aged 12 to 25 years found that the BES has convergent validity with the appearance subscale from a measure of Global Self Worth (Neeman & Harter, 1986).

Other attitudinal measures of body image also exist. These newer scales tend to be more gender neutral and are appropriate for use among male and female audiences, as they were not derived from diagnostic eating disorder measures.

- Body Image and Body Change Inventory (Ricciardelli & McCabe, 2000). The Body Image and Body Change Inventory was designed specifically for use among male and female adolescents and consists of seven scales: Body Image Satisfaction, Body Image Importance, Body Change Strategies to Decrease Weight, Body Change Strategies to Increase Weight, Body Change Strategies to Increase Muscles, and Food Supplements. A copy of the scales is included in Appendix 1 (at the end of this chapter).

The Body Image Satisfaction Scale consists of three items that measure adolescents' positive or negative subjective evaluations regarding their weight, body shape, and muscle size, which are usually examined as single items. There are seven additional items that focus on the respondents' attitudes to specific body parts. The scale includes body parts that have been shown to be more important to boys (e.g., "*shoulders*" and "*chest*") and others that are of more concern to girls (e.g., "*hips*" and "*thighs*") together with body parts, which are regarded as important to both boys and girls (e.g., "*abdominal region/stomach*"). Each item is rated on a five-point Likert scale ranging from Extremely Satisfied (1) to Extremely Dissatisfied (5). The Body Satisfaction Scale has high internal consistency for adolescent boys and girls (Cronbach's Alpha >.80) and has been validated by both exploratory and confirmatory factor analysis (Ricciardelli & McCabe, 2000).

The Body Image Importance Scale assesses cognitions and affective states associated with the amount of importance placed on body image. It includes three items that require the respondents to positively or negatively evaluate the importance of their weight, body shape, and muscular size. Additionally, there are seven items that focus on specific body parts that have been shown to be important to adolescent boys (e.g., "*shoulders*") and other body parts that are more important to girls (e.g., "*hips*") as well as body parts that are important to both boys and girls (e.g., "*abdominal region/stomach*"). Items are rated on a five-point Likert scale, which ranged from Not at All Important (1) to Extremely Important (5), with higher scores indicating higher levels of importance. Internal consistency has been shown to be adequate (Crobach's Alpha = .77 for males and females). Validity has been confirmed by both exploratory and confirmatory factor analysis (Ricciardelli & McCabe, 2000).

Three of the scales, known as the 'Body Change Inventory' were designed to evaluate the strategies utilised by adolescent boys and girls to decrease their weight, increase weight, and increase muscle size (Ricciardelli & McCabe, 2002).

The first is the Body Change Strategies to Decrease Weight, which includes 6 items that are rated on a five-point Likert scale, which ranges from Always (5) to Never (1). Questions on this scale include "*How often do you change your eating to decrease the size of your body".* The second scale is the Body Change Strategies to Increase Weight, which also consists of 6 items rated on a 5-point Likert scale in which the responses range from Always (5) to Never (1). Items on this scale include *"How often do you change your levels of eating to increase your body size?"* The last scale is the Body Change Strategies to Increase Muscle Scale and includes 6 questions scored on a 5-point Likert scale with responses that range from Always (5) to Never (1). Questions on this scale include *"How often do you worry about changing your levels of exercise to increase the size of your muscles?"* Scores for each of the subscales—decrease weight, increase weight, and increase muscle—range from 6 to 30 with higher scores on each indicating more strategies were being used to affect change.

The Body Change Inventory has demonstrated adequate levels of internal consistency (Cronbach's Alpha >.77, for all scales) for adolescent boys, and it has been validated by both exploratory and confirmatory factor analysis (Ricciardelli & McCabe, 2002). Concurrent validity for the Strategies to Lose Weight Scale has been demonstrated, for boys, by moderate correlations (r = .68) with Drive for Thinness scale from the EDI-2 (Garner, 1991), and the dieting factor (r = .53) of the Bulimia Test Revised, (BULIT-R) (Thelen, Farmer, Wonderlich, & Smith, 1991). Evidence of the scales' discriminant validity was less clear cut as there were modest correlations between the scales Strategies to Gain Weight and Strategies to Increase Muscle with the Drive for Thinness Scale and the BULIT-R dieting scale (Ricciardelli & McCabe, 2002).

The last scale, Food Supplements, was designed to specifically examine the use of special foods (e.g., vitamins, protein powders) and other supplements (e.g., steroids, creatine) to modify body weight (Ricciardelli & McCabe, 2000). The original version did not separate supplements that were used to either decrease weight or increase muscles, but our more recent version included in Appendix 1 at the end of this chapter does make this distinction.

- Embodied Image Scale (Abbott & Barber, 2010) Measures of body image are typically focused on the extent of satisfaction or dissatisfaction with appearance, and very few have attempted to determine the extent of satisfaction with the functionality of the body. However the Embodied Image Scale was designed to measure both the functional and aesthetic aspects of body image, which may be particularly critical for adolescent boys. This 19-item questionnaire has six subscales. It assesses body image from a cognitive (value), behavioural (investment), and affective (satisfaction) components for both aesthetic and functional body image separately. An example of an item assessing functional satisfaction is: "*How good I feel about my body depends a lot on what my body can do physically*", and an example from the aesthetic satisfaction subscale is: "*I feel really good about the way I look*". Participants respond on a five-point scale, from Very True for Me to Not at All True for Me. This relatively new scale has been validated among male and female Australian adolescents, where internal consistency was adequate (Cronbach's Alpha = .86).

Drive for Muscularity Scale (McCreary & Sasse, 2000) This 15-item scale assesses attitudes and behaviours relating to satisfaction with muscularity. A main strength of this measure is that it assesses attitudinal and behavioural components of body image specific to males (Cafri & Thompson, 2004). This measure was developed for adolescents and adults, and has demonstrated good internal consistency in male (.84) and female (.78) adolescents. Convergent validity was also established through high correlations between the number of weight training sessions per week and DMS scores. Discriminant validity was present between the DMS and measures of drive for thinness and Eating Attitudes Test. This scale has been used widely, particularly in male body image research, with adolescents and adults.

Measures Utilising Figure Rating Scales

Figure Rating Scales are often seen as both an attitudinal measure of absolute levels of body dissatisfaction and perceptual measure of current body size if they link perceived body size with actual participant BMI. Measures using figural stimuli generally present participants with a range of figures—either line drawings or modified photographs—that are scaled in terms of their adiposity (and sometimes muscularity). Participants are asked to identify which figure they think best represents their current body weight and shape and then which figure represents their ideal weight and shape. The discrepancy between the two is then recorded as an indicator of body dissatisfaction (Yanover & Thompson, 2009). In 1995, a review found 21 sets of figure rating scale measures, the majority of which were developed for adults or university students (Thompson & Gray, 1995). A subsequent review in 2010 found eight paper-and-pencil figure rating scales for use among children and adolescents and 11 for use among adults (Gardner, 2011). Here we will review two scales that have been used frequently and are well-validated among adolescents.

• Figure Rating Scales (Stunkard, Sorenson, & Schulsinger, 1983) This very early measure consists of nine figures that increase in adiposity for males and females. Although the figures are adults, this scale has been widely used among adolescents. Participants follow the protocol outlined above and indicate the number corresponding to the figure they believe represents their current figure, ideal figure, the figure that represents how they think they look, and the one that represents how they feel most of the time. Participants are also asked to select the figure that they think represents the male and female ideal. Test-retest reliability and convergent validity with other body image measures (EDI-BD) was first established among college students (Thompson & Altabe, 1991), and 4 to 5 week test-retest was high among a sample of adolescent girls (current figure $r = .87$, ideal figure $r = .83$) (Banasiak, Wertheim, Koerner, & Voudouris, 2001). Cohn and colleagues established psychometric properties with adolescents aged 10.5 to 15 years and found that current perceived body size was strongly correlated with actual weight for boys ($r = .61$, $p < .001$) and girls ($r = .71$, $p < .001$). Level of satisfaction according to Tanner stages of development was also considered (Cohn et al., 1987). Further research involved modifications to the original figures to make them more suitable for adolescent girls. This involved the development of two separate sets of figures suitable for 11-year-olds and 17-year-olds and tested among a small (n ~ 100) number of girls in each of those age groups (Sherman, Iacono, & Donnelly, 1995). The current figure selection by participants using the modified images were found to be highly correlated with the original Figure Rating Scale for 17-year-olds ($r = 0.85$).

- Contour Drawing Rating Scale [CDRS] (Thompson & Gray, 1995) This scale also includes nine figures that increase in adiposity; however, the graduations between the figures are considered to be finer than those in the Stunkard Scale. In addition, the CDRS allows for additional points to be used between the figures to increase the range of responses, and thus, the accuracy of the scale (Wertheim, Paxton, & Tilgner, 2004). Psychometric properties of this scale were tested among a large sample of adolescent girls aged 11.8 to 14.7 years (Wertheim et al., 2004). Test-retest reliability for the current figure was adequate at two ($r = .84$), six (.83), and 14 weeks (.77). Test-retest reliability for ideal figure was less reliable at two ($r = .78$), six (.78), and 14 weeks (.68). Concurrent validity was established, as current-ideal discrepancy was significantly correlated with the Body Dissatisfaction subscale ($r = .40$) and Drive for Thinness subscales ($r = .62$) of the EDI (Wertheim et al., 2004). In this study, it was also noted that the figure girls selected was also significantly correlated with their BMI ($r = .69$), indicating that adolescent girls could accurately estimate their weight using this measure.

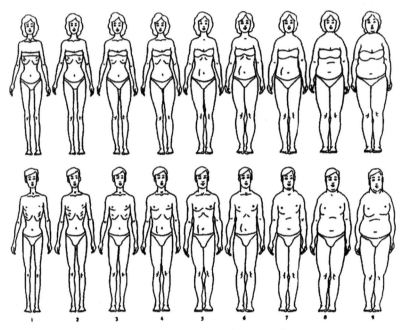

FIGURE 2.1 The Contour Drawing Rating Scale [CDRS].
Source: Development and Validation of a New Body-Image Assessment Scale. Marjorie A. Thompson and James J. Gray. Journal of Personality Assessment, 1995; 64 (2) reprinted by permission of the publisher (Taylor & Francis Ltd, http://www.tandfonline.com).

Contour drawings were originally presented as a relatively quick and straightforward method of measuring body image. However, the use of contour drawings and figures has fallen out of fashion among the body image research community in recent years, in favour of attitudinal assessment, following methodological concerns (Gardner & Brown, 2010; Gardner, Friedman, & Jackson, 1998). The limited number of figures and variability in graduations means that they are a particularly coarse measurement of body image (Gardner et al., 1998; Wertheim et al., 2004). These types of measures are also less reliable when used among adolescents as their own bodies are changing over time (Yanover & Thompson, 2009). Finally, the fact that the figures increase only in terms of adiposity limits the application of these scales among males, as they cannot accurately indicate dissatisfaction with muscularity (Cafri & Thompson, 2004). Although the somatomorphic matrix (Cafri, Roehrig, & Thompson, 2004) does include figures that increase on a dual axis of muscularity and adiposity, and is available for both genders in computerised and paper and pencil format (Shroff, Calogero, & Thompson,

2009), it has not been widely used among adolescents. In one unpublished study with adolescent boys aged between 12 and 16, the participants reported that they found this scale difficult to complete (Barton, 2006).

Perceptual Measures of Body Image

Perceptual measures of body image disturbance focus on determining individuals' capacity to accurately estimate their body size (Cafri & Thompson, 2004). These measures require participants to estimate their current body size and their ideal body size. Body distortion is then determined by the difference between perceived body size and actual body size. A range of measures has been used to determine body size distortion, and the two main categories are "whole image", and "body site estimation" techniques (Gardner, 2011). In "whole image" adjustment measures, participants view a real-life complete image of themselves and adjust the size according to their perceptions. This is similar to the use of figural drawings and silhouette scales but uses real, morphed images of the participant, with varying degrees of increased and decreased adiposity. New approaches utilise specially designed software and camera technologies such as laser full body scans for this purpose (e.g., Stewart et al., 2012). Researchers in Canada are among the only ones to use these techniques with adolescents. They first created a database of de-identified adolescent images of adolescents in a body suit from the front and side view (Aleong, Duchesne, & Paus, 2007). They then developed a morphing tool that allows participants to vary the size of 54 tagged body points on the images to represent their perceived body size and shape (Aleong et al., 2007). The discrepancy between the perceived current and actual figure is then determined and indicates the extent of the body distortion.

In measures using "body site estimation", participants are asked to visually estimate the size of certain body parts, for example, the hips and stomach. In early research in the 1970s, this was done using the 'movable caliper technique' (Slade & Russell, 1973), where participants used the arms of the caliper to estimate the width of their body at various sites. In the 1980s, projected light beams were used in the development of the 'Body Image Detection Device' [BIDD]. An overhead projector was utilised to project a horizontal beam of light onto a wall, and participants were asked to modify that width until it represented their perceived body sites (Ruff & Barrios, 1986). This device was later modified to project four beams of light corresponding with the cheeks, stomach, hips, and thighs to form the Adjustable Light Beam Apparatus [ALBA](Thompson & Spana, 1988). Due to the amount of equipment required, and individual testing conditions, perceptual measures of body image are relatively uncommon, particularly in research among adolescents.

Behavioural Measures of Body Image

Measures of the behavioural component of body image are designed to assess the level of importance placed on the body, investment in maintaining it, and behaviours associated with negative or positive body image (Cash, 2002b). Both Cash (1994) and Thompson (2004) recommend that the behavioural component of body image be assessed in order to represent the multidimensional nature of body image. However, the majority of behavioural measures actually assess weight change behaviours (Yanover & Thompson, 2009), which are arguably measuring a consequence of body dissatisfaction rather than body image itself (Banfield & McCabe, 2002). In order to measure the behavioural component of body image, scales should focus on body checking and avoidance behaviours (Yanover & Thompson, 2009).

Body checking involves a series of repeated, compulsive behaviours such as frequent weighing, pinching rolls of fat to determine size, and observation of body sites in mirrors and reflective surfaces (Shafran, Fairburn, Robinson, & Lask, 2004). These behaviours are considered to further reinforce body image issues and disordered eating as they encourage a hyper-vigilance with regard to minute changes in shape and weight and overemphasise identification of flaws and the importance of shape and weight. The Body Checking Questionnaire [BCQ](Rheas, Whisenhunt, Netemeyer, & Williamson, 2002) is a 23-item measure of body checking behaviours that also includes three related sub factors of checking related to overall appearance, checking of specific body parts, and idiosyncratic checking rituals. Psychometric testing was conducted with females whose age ranged from 16 to 56 years (mean = 20.8 years), so although adolescents were in the sample, the measure was not specifically designed or validated for them. The BCQ demonstrated high test–retest reliability (.94) and convergent validity with the Body Image Avoidance Questionnaire [BIAQ] (Rosen, Srebnik, Saltzberg, & Wendt, 1991), Body Shape Questionnaire [BSQ] (Rosen, Jones, Ramirez, & Waxman, 1996), and the Eating Attitudes Test [EAT] (Garner & Garfinkel, 1979).

At the other end of the spectrum from body checking, avoidance behaviours involve purposely evading situations that enhance individuals' concerns over their body or appearance. Examples include the avoidance of revealing the body by skipping activities such as swimming or going to the beach, avoiding tight clothes, and avoiding physical intimacy with partners. The Body Image Avoidance Questionnaire (Rosen et al., 1991) includes questions about these behaviours, as well as changes to diet that might indicate a behavioural component to body dissatisfaction. This measure has only been validated with female university students. Some experts have questioned the use of this measure as participants might indicate that they engage in some of the behaviours without doing so because of their body image (Cash, 2002a). Behavioural measures of body image such as body checking and avoidance have not generally been designed for, and are not commonly used among, adolescents.

Conclusion

Although a wide number of body image measures exist, only a few have demonstrated good psychometric properties when validated with adolescents, and these are all attitudinal measures. There could be scope for new measures to be developed to capture the attitudinal, perceptual, and behavioural components of body image in more concise, valid, and reliable ways. However, given the difficulty in comparing results from different measures, it would be useful if researchers continue to include at least one standard measure. Further development of measures of body image that involve few items and are quick and easy to administer may increase the chances that this construct will be measured as a part of other public health and health psychology research. We further recommend that researchers use only the measures that have been validated with adolescents. Finally, researchers need to ensure that the measures of body image that are used are appropriate and sensitive for both girls and boys, and that any gender bias needs to be fully acknowledged.

References

Abbott, B.D., & Barber, B.L. (2010). Embodied image: Gender differences in functional and aesthetic body image among Australian adolescents. *Body Image, 7*, 22–31.

Aleong, R., Duchesne, S., & Paus, T. (2007). Assessment of adolescent body perception: Development and characterisation of a novel tool for morphing images of adolescent bodies. *Behavior Research Methods, 39*(3), 651–66.

Banasiak, S.J., Wertheim, E.H., Koerner, J., & Voudouris, N.J. (2001). Test–retest reliability and internal consistency of a variety of measures of dietary restraint and body concerns in a sample of adolescent girls. *International Journal of Eating Disorders, 29*, 85–89.

Banfield, S., & McCabe, M.P. (2002). An evaluation of the construct of body image. *Adolescence, 37*(146), 373–93.

Barton, M. (2006). *The development of young adolescent boys' weight and shape concerns.* Unpublished doctoral thesis, Deakin University, Melbourne, Australia.

Cafri, G., Roehrig, M., & Thompson, K.J. (2004). Reliability assessment of the somatomorphic matrix. *International Journal of Eating Disorders, 35*, 597–600.

Cafri, G., & Thompson, J.K. (2004). Measuring male body image: A review of current methodology. *Psychology of men and masculinity, 5*(1), 18–29.

Carter, J.C., Stewart, D.A., & Fairburn, C. (2001). Eating disorder examination questionnaire: Norms for young adolescent girls. *Behaviour Research and Therapy, 39*(5), 625–32.

Cash, T.F. (2002a). Cognitive-behavioral perspectives on body image. In T.F. Cash & T. Pruzinsky (Eds.), *Body image: A handbook of theory, research, and clinical* practice (pp. 38–46). New York: Guilford Press.

Cash, T.F. (2002b). Crucial considerations in the measurement of body image. In T.F. Cash & T. Pruzinsky (Eds.), *Body image: A handbook of theory, research, and clinical practice* (pp. 129–37). New York, NY: Guilford Press.

Cash, T.F., Fleming, E.C., Alindogan, J., Steadman, L., & Whitehead, A. (2002). Beyond body image as a trait. The development and evaluation of the Body Image States Scale. *Eating Disorders: Journal of Treatment and Prevention, 10*, 103–13.

Cohn, L.D., Adler, N.E., Irwin, C.E., Millstein, S.G., Kegeles, S.M., & Stone, G. (1987). Body-figure preferences in male and female adolescents. *Journal of Abnormal Psychology, 96*(3), 276–79.

Darcy, A.M., Celio Doyle, A., Lock, J., Peebles, R., Doyle, P., & Le Grange, D. (2012). The Eating Disorders Examination in adolescent males: How does it compare to adolescent females? *International Journal of Eating Disorders, 45*, 110–14.

Darcy, A. M., & Hsiao-Jung Lin, I. (2012). Are we asking the right questions? A review of assessment of males with eating disorders. *Eating Disorders, 20*, 416–26.

Durkin, S., & Paxton, S. (2002). Predictors of vulnerability to reduced body image satisfaction and psychological wellbeing in response to exposure to idealized female media images in adolescent girls. *Journal of Psychiatric Research, 53*, 995–1005.

Fairburn, C., & Cooper, Z. (1993). The Eating Disorder Examination (12th Edition). In C. Fairburn & G. T. Wilson (Eds.), *Binge eating: Nature, assessment and treatment* (pp. 317–56). New York, NY: The Guilford Press.

Fallon, A.E., & Rozin, P. (1985). Sex differences in perceptions of desirable body shape. *Journal of Abnormal Psychology, 94*, 102–105.

Gardner, R.M. (2011). Perceptual measures of body image for adolescents and adults. In T.F.C.a.L.S. (Ed.), *Body image: A handbook of science, practice and prevention* (2nd ed., pp. 146–53). New York, NY: Guilford Press.

Gardner, R.M., & Brown, D.L. (2010). Body image assessment: A review of figural drawing scales. *Personality and Individual Differences, 48*(2), 107–11.

Gardner, R.M., Friedman, B.N., & Jackson, N.A. (1998). Methodological concerns when using silhouettes to measure body image. *Perceptual and motor skills, 86*, 387–95.

Garner, D.M. (1991). *Eating Disorder Inventory-2. Professional manual.* Odessa, FL: Psychological Assessment Resources.

Garner, D.M. (2004). *Manual for the Eating Disorders Inventory-3 (EDI-3).* Odessa, FL: Psychological Assessment Resources.

Garner, D.M., & Garfinkel, P.E. (1979). The Eating Attitudes Test: An index of the symptoms of anorexia nervosa. *Psychological Medicine, 9*, 273–79.

Garner, D.M., Olmstead, M.P., & Polivy, J. (1983). The Eating Disorder Inventory: A measure of cognitive-behavioural dimensions of anorexia nervosa and bulimia. In A. Liss (Ed.), *Anorexia nervosa: Recent developments in research.* New York, NY: LEA.

Hargreaves, D.A., & Tiggemann, M. (2004). Idealized media images and adolescent body image: "comparing" boys and girls. *Body Image, 1*(4), 351–61.

Heinberg, L., & Thompson, J.K. (1995). Body image and televised images of thinness and attractiveness: A controlled laboratory investigation. *Journal of Social and Clinical Psychology, 14*(4), 325–38.

Hrabosky, J.I., Cash, T.F., Veale, D., Neziroglu, F., Soll, E.A., Garner, D.M., ... Phillips, K. A. (2009). Multidimensional body image comparisons among patients with eating disorders, body dysmorphic disorder, and clinical controls: A multisite study. *Body Image, 6*(3), 155–63.

Humphreys, P., & Paxton, S. (2004). Impact of exposure to idealised male images on adolescent boys' body image. *Body Image, 1*, 253–66.

Jones, D.C. (2004). Body image among adolescent girls and boys: A longitudinal study. *Developmental Psychology, 40*(5), 823–35.

Leung, F., Wang, J., & Tang, C.W. (2004). Psychometric properties and normative data of the Eating Disorder Inventory among 12 to 18 year old Chinese girls in Hong Kong. *Journal of Psychosomatic Research, 57*(1), 59–66.

McCormack, H.M., Horne, D.J., & Sheather, S. (1988). Clinical applications of visual analogue scales: a clinical review. *Psychological Medicine, 18*, 1007–19.

McCreary, D., & Sasse, D. (2000). An exploration of the drive for muscularity in adolescent boys and girls. *Journal of American College Health, 48*(6), 297–304.

Mendelson, B.K., Mendelson, M.J., & White, D.R. (2001). Body Esteem Scale for adolescents and adults. *Journal of Personality Assessment, 76*, 90–106.

Menzel, J.E., Krawczyk, R., & Thompson, J.K. (2011). Attitudinal assessment of body image for adolescents and adults. . In T.F. Cash & L. Smolak (Eds.), *Body image: a handbook of science, practice, and prevention* (pp. 154–69). New York, NY: Guilford.

Micali, N., & House, J. (2011). Assessment measures for child and adolescent eating disorders: A Review. *Child and Adolescent Mental Health, 16*(2), 122–27.

Neeman, J., & Harter, S. (1986). *Manual for the Self-Perception Profile for College Students.* Denver, CO: University of Denver Press.

Reed, D.L., Thompson, J.K., Brannick, M.T., & Sacco, W.P. (1991). Development and validation of the Physical Appearance State and Trait Anxiety Scale (PASTAS). *Journal of Anxiety Disorders, 5*, 323–32.

Rheas, D.L., Whisenhunt, B.L., Netemeyer, R., & Williamson, D.A. (2002). Development of the Body Checking Questionnaire: A Self-Report Measure of Body Checking Behaviors. *International Journal of Eating Disorders, 31*, 324–33.

Ricciardelli, L.A., & McCabe, M.P. (2000). *Psychometric evaluation of the Body Image and Body Change Inventory: An assessment Instrument for adolescent boys and girls.* Unpublished manuscript, Deakin University, Melbourne, Australia.

Ricciardelli, L.A., & McCabe, M.P. (2001). Dietary restraint and negative affect as mediators of body dissatisfaction and bulimic behavior in adolescent girls and boys. *Behaviour Research and Therapy, 39*, 1317–28.

Ricciardelli, L.A., & McCabe, M.P. (2002). Psychometric evaluation of the Body Change Inventory: An assessment instrument for adolescent boys and girls. *Eating Behaviors, 3*, 45–59.

Rosen, J.C., Jones, A., Ramirez, E., & Waxman, S. (1996). Body Shape Questionnaire: Studies of validity and reliability. *International Journal of Eating Disorders, 20*(3), 315–19.

Rosen, J.C., Srebnik, D., Saltzberg, E., & Wendt, S. (1991). Development of a body image avoidance questionnaire. *Psychological Assessment, 3*, 32–37.

Ruff, G.A., & Barrios, B.A. (1986). Realistic assessment of body image. *Behavioral Assessment, 8*(3), 237–51.

Shafran, R., Fairburn, C.G., Robinson, P., & Lask, B.D. (2004). Body checking and its avoidance in eating disorders. *International Journal of Eating Disorders, 35*, 93–101.

Sherman, D.K., Iacono, W.G., & Donnelly, J.M. (1995). Development and validation of body rating scales for adolescent females. *International Journal of Eating Disorders, 18*(4), 327–33.

Shore, R.A., & Porter, J.E. (1990). Normative and reliability data for 11 to 18 year olds on the Eating Disorder Inventory. *International Journal of Eating Disorders, 9*(2), 201–207.

Shroff, H., Calogero, R.M., & Thompson, J.K. (2009). Assessment of body image. In D.B. Allison & M.L. Baskin (Eds.), *Handbook of assessment methods for eating behaviors and weight-related problems: Measures, theory, and research* (2nd ed., pp. 115–36). Thousand Oaks, CA: Sage.

Slade, P.D., & Russell, G.F.M. (1973). Experimental investigations of bodily perception in anorexia nervosa and obesity. *Psychotherapy and Psychosomatics, 22*, 359–63.

Stewart, A.D., Klein, S., Young, J., Simpson, S., Lee, A.J., Harrild, K., … Benson, P.J. (2012). Body image, shape, and volumetric assessments using 3D whole body laser scanning and 2D digital photography in females with a diagnosed eating disorder: Preliminary novel findings. *British Journal of Psychology, 103*(2), 183–202.

Stunkard, A., Sorenson, T., & Schulsinger, F. (1983). *Use of the Danish adoption register for the study of obesity and thinness.* In Kety, S., Roland, L., Sidman, R., Matthysse, S. (Eds.). *Genetics of Neurological and Psychiatric Disorders.* New York, NY: Raven Press.

Thelen, M.H., Farmer, J., Wonderlich, S., & Smith, M. (1991). A revision of the Bulimia Test: The BUILT-R. *Psychological Assessment: A Journal of Consulting and Clinical Psychology., 3*(1), 119–24.

Thompson, J.K. (2004). The (mis)measurement of body image: ten strategies to improve assessment for applied and research purposes. *Body Image, 1*(1), 7–14.

Thompson, J.K., & Altabe, T. (1991). Psychometric qualities of the figure rating scale. *International Journal of Eating Disorders, 10*, 615–19.

Thompson, J.K., & Gray, J. (1995). Development and validation of new body image assessment tool. *Journal of Personality Assessment, 64*, 258–69.

Thompson, J.K., & Spana, R.E. (1988). The adjustable light beam method for the assessment of size estimation accuracy: Descriptive, psychometric, and normative data. *International Journal of Eating Disorders, 7*(4), 521–26.

Thompson, M.A., & Gray, J.J. (1995). Development and validation of a new body image assessment tool. *Journal of Personality Assessment, 64*, 258–69.

Wertheim, E., Paxton, S., & Tilgner, L. (2004). Test-retest reliability and construct validity of Contour Drawing Rating Scale scores in a sample of early adolescent girls. *Body Image, 1*, 199–205.

Wilksch, S.M., & Wade, T.D. (2009). Reduction of shape and weight concern in young adolescents: A 30-month controlled evaluation of a media literacy program. *Journal of the American Academy of Child and Adolescent Psychiatry, 48*(6), 652–61.

Yager, Z., Diedrichs, P.C., Ricciardelli, L.A., & Halliwell, E. (2013). What works in secondary schools? A systematic review of classroom-based body image programs. *Body Image, 10*, 271–81.

Yanover, T., & Thompson, J.K. (2009). Assessment of body image in children and adolescents. In L. Smolak & J.K. Thompson (Eds.), *Body image, eating disorders, and obesity in youth: Assessment, prevention, and treatment (2nd Ed.)* (pp. 177–92). Washington, D.C: American Psychological Association.

APPENDIX 1

BODY IMAGE AND BODY CHANGE INVENTORY

Body Image Satisfaction

1. How satisfied are you with your **weight**?

Extremely Satisfied	Fairly Satisfied	In Between	Fairly Dissatisfied	Extremely Dissatisfied

2. How satisfied are you with your **body shape**?

Extremely Satisfied	Fairly Satisfied	In Between	Fairly Dissatisfied	Extremely Dissatisfied

3. How satisfied are you with your **muscle size**?

Extremely Satisfied	Fairly Satisfied	In Between	Fairly Dissatisfied	Extremely Dissatisfied

    The remainder of the questions in this section ask about your level of satisfaction with particular body parts.

4. Your hips.

Extremely Satisfied	Fairly Satisfied	In Between	Fairly Dissatisfied	Extremely Dissatisfied

5. Your thighs.

Extremely Satisfied	Fairly Satisfied	In Between	Fairly Dissatisfied	Extremely Dissatisfied

6. Your chest.

Extremely Satisfied	Fairly Satisfied	In Between	Fairly Dissatisfied	Extremely Dissatisfied

7. Your abdominal region/stomach.

Extremely Satisfied	Fairly Satisfied	In Between	Fairly Dissatisfied	Extremely Dissatisfied

8. The size/width of your shoulders.

Extremely Satisfied	Fairly Satisfied	In Between	Fairly Dissatisfied	Extremely Dissatisfied

9. Your legs.

Extremely Satisfied	Fairly Satisfied	In Between	Fairly Dissatisfied	Extremely Dissatisfied

10. Your arms.

Extremely Satisfied	Fairly Satisfied	In Between	Fairly Dissatisfied	Extremely Dissatisfied

Body Image Importance

1. How important to you is **what you weigh** compared to other things in your life?

Extremely Important	Fairly Important	In Between	Fairly Unimportant	Not Important At All

2. How important is the **shape of your body** compared to other things in your life?

Extremely Important	Fairly Important	In Between	Fairly Unimportant	Not Important At All

3. How important are the **size and strength of your muscles** compared to other things in your life?

Extremely Important	Fairly Important	In Between	Fairly Unimportant	Not Important At All

The remainder of the questions in this section ask about the importance of the appearance of different parts of your body.

4. Your hips.

Extremely Important	Fairly Important	In Between	Fairly Unimportant	Not Important At All

5. Your thighs.

Extremely Important	Fairly Important	In Between	Fairly Unimportant	Not Important At All

6. Your chest.

| Extremely Important | Fairly Important | In Between | Fairly Unimportant | Not Important At All |

7. Your abdominal region/stomach.

| Extremely Important | Fairly Important | In Between | Fairly Unimportant | Not Important At All |

8. The size/width of your shoulders.

| Extremely Important | Fairly Important | In Between | Fairly Unimportant | Not Important At All |

9. Your lepgs.

| Extremely Important | Fairly Important | In Between | Fairly Unimportant | Not Important At All |

10. Your arms.

| Extremely Important | Fairly Important | In Between | Fairly Unimportant | Not Important At All |

Body Change Strategies to Decrease Weight

1. How often do you feel like changing the types of foods you eat so that you can lose weight?

| Always | Almost Always | Frequently | Sometimes | Never |

2. How often do you change your eating to decrease your body size?

| Always | Almost Always | Frequently | Sometimes | Never |

3. How often do you change your levels of exercise to decrease your body size?

| Always | Almost Always | Frequently | Sometimes | Never |

4. How often do you think about changing your levels of exercise to decrease your body size?

| Always | Almost Always | Frequently | Sometimes | Never |

5. How often do you worry about changing your eating to decrease your body size?

| Always | Almost Always | Frequently | Sometimes | Never |

6. How often do you think about exercising to lose weight?

| Always | Almost Always | Frequently | Sometimes | Never |

Body Change Strategies to Increase Weight

1.   How often do you change your eating to increase your body size?

     Always   Almost Always   Frequently   Sometimes   Never

2.   How often do you change your levels of exercise to increase your body size?

     Always   Almost Always   Frequently   Sometimes   Never

3.   How often do you think about changing your eating to increase your body size?

     Always   Almost Always   Frequently   Sometimes   Never

4.   How often do you think about changing your levels of exercise to increase your body size?

     Always   Almost Always   Frequently   Sometimes   Never

5.   How often do you worry about changing your eating to increase your body size?

     Always   Almost Always   Frequently   Sometimes   Never

6.   How often do you worry about changing your levels of exercise to increase your body size?

     Always   Almost Always   Frequently   Sometimes   Never

Body Change Strategies to Increase Muscles

1.   How often do you change your levels of exercise to increase the size of your muscles?

     Always   Almost Always   Frequently   Sometimes   Never

2.   How often do you change your food supplements to increase the size of your muscles?

     Always   Almost Always   Frequently   Sometimes   Never

3.   How often do you think about changing your eating to increase the size of your muscles?

     Always   Almost Always   Frequently   Sometimes   Never

4.   How often do you think about changing your levels of exercise to increase the size of your muscles?

     Always   Almost Always   Frequently   Sometimes   Never

5. How often do you worry about changing your eating to increase the size of your muscles?

    |_____|_____|_____|_____|
    Always   Almost Always   Frequently   Sometimes   Never

6. How often do you worry about changing your levels of exercise to increase the size of your muscles?

    |_____|_____|_____|_____|
    Always   Almost Always   Frequently   Sometimes   Never

Food Supplements

1. How often do you take vitamins to change your body weight?

    |_____|_____|_____|_____|
    Always   Almost Always   Frequently   Sometimes   Never

2. How often do you take food supplements (for example, diet pills, sustagen) to change your body weight?

    |_____|_____|_____|_____|
    Always   Almost Always   Frequently   Sometimes   Never

3. If you could take steroids without them causing any harm to you, how frequently would you think about taking them?

    |_____|_____|_____|_____|
    Always   Almost Always   Frequently   Sometimes   Never

4. How often do you think about taking vitamins?

    |_____|_____|_____|_____|
    Always   Almost Always   Frequently   Sometimes   Never

5. How often do you feel like taking food supplements? (for example, diet pills, sustagen).

    |_____|_____|_____|_____|
    Always   Almost Always   Frequently   Sometimes   Never

6. How often do you feel like taking steroids?

    |_____|_____|_____|_____|
    Always   Almost Always   Frequently   Sometimes   Never

7. Have you ever taken steroids to change your body weight? ☐ YES   ☐ NO

8. How many times have you used steroids?

(a) In your lifetime

    |_____|_____|_____|_____|
    None   1–2 times   3–5 times   6–10 times   More than 10 times

(b) During the last 12 months

    |_____|_____|_____|_____|
    None   1–2 times   3–5 times   6–10 times   More than 10 times

(c) During the last month

| None | 1–2 times | 3–5 times | 6–10 times | More than 10 times |

9. How often do you take food supplements (for example, diet pills) to lose weight?

| Always | Almost Always | Frequently | Sometimes | Never |

10. How often do you feel like taking food supplements (for example, diet pills) to lose weight?

| Always | Almost Always | Frequently | Sometimes | Never |

11. How often do you think about taking food supplements (for example, diet pills) to lose weight?

| Always | Almost Always | Frequently | Sometimes | Never |

12. How often do you worry about taking food supplements (for example, diet pills) to lose weight?

| Always | Almost Always | Frequently | Sometimes | Never |

13. How often do you take food supplements (for example, sustagen) to increase your muscles?

| Always | Almost Always | Frequently | Sometimes | Never |

14. How often do you feel like taking food supplements (for example, sustagen) to increase your muscles?

| Always | Almost Always | Frequently | Sometimes | Never |

15. How often do you think about taking food supplements (for example, sustagen) to increase your muscles?

| Always | Almost Always | Frequently | Sometimes | Never |

3
BODY CHANGE STRATEGIES, APPEARANCE MANAGEMENT, AND HEALTH

In this chapter we will explore the range of body change strategies and negative health outcomes associated with body dissatisfaction among adolescents. These include disordered eating and weight loss strategies. Extreme weight loss strategies are viewed as part of disordered eating, and body dissatisfaction has been found to be the strongest predictor of disordered eating. Other body change strategies are associated with the pursuit of muscularity, and these are more frequently used by males. Other practices adolescents use to manage or modify their appearance will also be reviewed. These include widely accepted grooming practices such as body hair removal and tanning behaviours; other practices such as tattooing and body piercing that adolescents may use to visually express their individuality; and more extreme methods such as cosmetic surgery. In the last section we will examine the impact body dissatisfaction has on other aspects of adolescents' lives including mental health, health, academic performance, health-risk behaviours, and maintenance of obesity.

Disordered Eating and Weight Loss Strategies

Disordered eating is one of the main terms used to refer to problem-eating attitudes and behaviours that occur on a continuum ranging from extreme weight loss strategies, which include fasting, purging, excessive exercise, and binge eating to eating disorders such as anorexia and bulimia nervosa (Ricciardelli & McCabe, 2004). Other terms used by researchers include *eating pathology* and *eating disturbance*.

Numerous studies have shown that body dissatisfaction predicts increased disordered eating among adolescent girls and boys (Graber, Brooks-Gunn, Paikoff, & Warren, 1994; Neumark-Sztainer, Paxton, Hannan, Haines, & Story, 2006; Patton, Johnson-Sabine, Wood, Mann, & Wakeling, 1990; Stice, 2001; Stice, Marti, & Durant, 2011). In one study, adolescent girls who were in the upper 24% on measures of body dissatisfaction showed a 4.0-fold increased incidence of developing an eating disorder or more specifically a 24% chance of developing an eating disorder compared to only a 6% chance for those who were low on body dissatisfaction (Stice et al., 2011). In addition, improved body satisfaction has been found to predict the cessation of binge eating from late adolescence to early adulthood in a large sample of females and males (Goldschmidt, Wall, Loth, Bucchianeri, & Neumark-Sztainer, 2014).

The mechanisms by which body dissatisfaction leads to disordered eating are still not fully understood. One of the main views is that body dissatisfaction leads young people (and in particular girls) to employ weight-loss strategies in order to achieve thinness, and this can lead to progressively more extreme and unhealthy strategies (Crowther & Williams, 2011; Stice, 2002). The severe caloric restriction associated with fasting and skipping meals also initiates physiological processes that both decrease metabolism to reduce energy demands and inhibit the release of fat stores to be burned (Brownell, 1991). In addition, calorie deprivation can lead to craving and binge eating. The binge eating then leads to weight gain and higher levels of body dissatisfaction. Body dissatisfaction is also associated with negative affect which encompasses mood states such as depression, stress, and guilt (Watson, Clark, & Tellegen, 1988), and binge eating may be used to regulate and/or alleviate negative affect (Crowther & Williams, 2011; Stice, 2002). However, binge eating may also lead to increases in negative affect (Haedt-Matt & Keel, 2011).

Although fewer adolescent boys and adult men develop eating disorders, it is now recognised that 25% to 33% of eating disorder diagnoses are male (Hay, 1998; Madden, Morris, Zurynski, Kohn, & Elliot, 2009). Greater gender differences are found when estimates of the prevalence for the full syndrome of anorexia nervosa, bulimia nervosa, and binge eating disorder are considered. For adolescent girls and adult women these range from .3% to 2.2% for anorexia nervosa, .5% and 1.6% for bulimia nervosa, and 1.9% and 3.5% for binge eating disorder (Ricciardelli & McCabe, 2015). For adolescent boys and adult men these range from 0% to .3% for anorexia nervosa, .1% and .7% for bulimia nervosa, and .3% to 2.0% for binge eating disorder (Ricciardelli & McCabe, 2015). However, gender differences are less marked when estimates also include partial syndrome eating disorders in the case of anorexia (1.81% in women and .92% in men) and bulimia (3.16% in women and 1.08% in men) (Woodside et al., 2001). Moreover, in the case of binge eating disorder, when partial syndrome eating disorders are considered, gender differences are reversed with the prevalence being higher among men (1.9%) than among women (.6%) (Hudson, Hiripi, Pope, & Kessler, 2007). The inclusion of partial syndrome eating disorders may be a more accurate indicator of the prevalence of eating disorders for men, as assessment instruments designed to detect and evaluate disordered eating have been developed primarily for women and do not accurately assess disordered eating attitudes and behaviours that are more specific to men (Stanford & Lemberg, 2012).

The prevalence of specific weight loss strategies among adolescent girls and boys has also been examined. These include skipping meals or fasting, exercising, smoking, the use of diet pills and laxatives, and self-induced vomiting. Estimates of adolescent boys who skip meals to lose weight range between 7% and 23.3% as compared to 20% to 49% of girls (e.g., Ross & Ivis, 1999; Serdula et al., 1993; Whitaker et al., 1989; Vander Wal, 2011). A more frequently used weight loss strategy for both boys and girls is exercising to lose weight, with estimates ranging from 30% to 48% for boys compared to 51% to 71% for girls (e.g., Drewnowski, Kurth, & Krahn, 1995; Krowchuck, Kreiter, Woods, Sinal, & DuRant, 1998; Neumark-Sztainer, Story, Falkner, Beuhring, & Resnick, 1999; Ross & Ivis, 1999; Serdula et al., 1993; Utter et al., 2012). Other weight loss strategies, such as smoking, diet pill usage, laxatives, and self-induced vomiting are used less frequently by both boys and girls. It is estimated that between 1% and 5.6% of boys as compared 2.6% to 6.9% of girls smoke cigarettes to lose weight; .1% to 4.7% of boys as compared to .7% to 17% of girls use diet pills; .1% to 1.6% of boys as compared to .3% to 2% of girls use laxatives; and .4% to 1.7% of boys as compared to .3% to 8.3% of girls use self-induced vomiting as a weight loss strategy (e.g., Field et al., 1999; Krowchuck et al., 1998; López-Guimeró et al., 2013; Neumark-Sztainer et al., 1999; Ross & Ivis, 1999; Stephen et al., 2014; Whitaker et al., 1989; Vander Wal, 2011).

Body Change Strategies Associated with Pursuit of Muscularity

In recent years there has been an increasing appreciation that eating disorders are expressed differently among males (Ricciardelli & McCabe, 2015). Males are more likely to use less extreme weight control methods and engage in behavioural problems associated with the pursuit of muscularity (Ricciardelli & McCabe, 2004; 2015). In its most extreme form the pursuit of muscularity manifests as muscle dysmorphia. As in anorexia nervosa, muscle dysmorphia is characterised by an unrealistic perception of the body, but in contrast to anorexia nervosa, where there is a fear of being fat and a preoccupation that one's body is not sufficiently thin, the focus in muscle dysmorphia is on not being sufficiently lean and muscular, and there is a fear of being too small or inadequately muscular (Pope, Phillips, & Olivardia, 2000). Although muscle dysmorphia has been classified as a subtype of body dysmorphic disorder, there is increasing evidence that it might be better classified as a type of eating disorder (Darcy, 2011; Jones & Morgan, 2010; Murray et al., 2012; Ricciardelli & McCabe, 2004). Researchers have highlighted the similarities between muscle dysmorphia and eating disorders, as both involve body image disturbance, excessive exercise, rigid diet patterns, compensation behaviours, appearance-enhancing substance use, elaborate body checking, and avoidance of bodily exposure (Darcy, 2011; Murray et al., 2012). In addition, several of the risk factors associated with the pursuit of muscularity, more broadly, include the same factors associated with disordered eating (Connan, 1998; Ricciardelli & McCabe, 2004; Rodgers, Ganchou, Franko, & Chabrol, 2012).

One of the potential problems associated with adolescent boys wanting to become more muscular, gain body size and weight, and increase body strength is the increased likelihood of using anabolic steroids to achieve quick results. Estimates for the number of adolescent boys who have ever used steroids range from 1.2% to 12% as compared to .2% to 9% for girls (Harmer, 2010; Ricciardelli & McCabe, 2004). In a recent representative sample of secondary high school students in Australia, the lifetime use of steroids was reported by 2.4% of 12 to 17 year olds (Dunn & White, 2011). Regardless of age, being male, speaking a language other than English at home, not being at school on the previous day, and perception that one's schooling ability was below average were also associated with a greater likelihood of using steroids in one's lifetime and previous year (Dunn & White, 2011). In addition, those who reported using steroids also reported experimenting with other substances, including alcohol, tobacco, cannabis, cocaine, or heroin.

Other body change strategies that may be used to increase weight and/or muscles among adolescent boys include ingesting large amounts of food or overeating, exercise, and the use of food supplements (McCabe & Ricciardelli, 2001; Eisenberg, Wall, & Neumark-Sztainer, 2012). These strategies have been found to range from 21.2% to 47.0% for adolescent boys and from 6.3% to 36.5% for adolescent girls (Eisenberg et al., 2012; Krowchuck et al., 1998; Middleman, Vazquez, & DuRant, 1998; Neumark-Sztainer et al., 1999; Ricciardelli & McCabe, 2003). The most frequently used strategy for increasing muscles among both boys and girls is exercise (Eisenberg et al., 2012). This is used often by 40.9% of boys and by 27.3% of girls (Eisenberg et al., 2012).

Other food supplements used to increase weight, overall body build, and muscles are protein powders and bars, creatine, ephedrine, and adrenal hormones (Pope et al., 2000; Yager & O'Dea, 2014). Studies show that 7.9% to 23% of adolescent boys and .3% to 2% of girls have used creatine (Metzl, Small, Levine, & Gershel, 2001; Ray et al., 2001; Smith & Dahm, 2000).

Appearance Management Behaviours

In addition to the range of body change strategies used by adolescents to achieve the thin ideal by girls and the muscular ideal by boys, adolescents engage in a range of other practices to manage or modify their appearance and/or bodies. These include body hair removal, tanning, tattooing and body piercing, and cosmetic surgery. Although all of these behaviours may be used by adolescents to modify their appearance, they vary in acceptability and health risks posed.

Body Hair Removal

Body hair removal or *body depilation,* primarily on legs, underarms and face, is a common appearance management strategy among girls that is widely accepted and expected, as unwanted body hair is not seen as feminine (Boroughs, 2012). Over 90% of women remove hair from their legs and armpits for the main reason that this is in line with societal views that equate hairlessness with femininity (Terry & Braun, 2013). The removal of pubic hair for females is another frequent practice, with one study showing that 70.4% of females aged 12 to 20 years reported frequently shaving or waxing their pubic hair (Bercaw-Pratt et al., 2012).

Removing body hair is currently fashionable for males, with studies showing that between 60% and 80% of young adult men from the U.S., Australia, and N.Z. have engaged in body hair removal (below the neck) from some part of the body at least once (Boroughs & Thompson, 2014). No study that focused specifically on adolescent boys was located, but the recent survey of men by Boroughs and Thompson (2014), which included 18 to 19 year olds, showed that the primary sites for body depilation were the pubic area (72.8%), abdomen (44.5%) and chest (40.7%). Moreover, a third of the males engaged in body depilation of the pubic area and the chest at weekly intervals or more regularly.

As found among women, many males view the removal of body hair as a grooming norm (Terry & Baum, 2013). However, many men also use body depilation to improve their attractiveness and appearance in terms of sex appeal, body definition, and muscularity (Boroughs & Thompson, 2014; Martins, Tiggemann, & Churchett, 2008). Although body depilation is becoming more common and prevalent among males, they are more likely to commence body hair removal during the later adolescent years (17 to 18 years) in comparison to girls who commence at the average age of 12 years (Terry & Braun, 2013).

Tanning Behaviour

Tanning behaviour is another widespread practice many adolescents use to improve their appearance and body image (Asvat, Cafri, Thompson, & Jacobsen, 2010; Holman & Watson, 2013; Gillen & Markey, 2012; Prior, Fenwick, & Peterson, 2014), but this practice comes with the high risk of developing skin cancer (Prior et al., 2014). Tanning behaviour includes outdoor tanning, often referred to as *sunbathing*, the use of fake tanning products, and indoor tanning. Indoor tanning includes the use of sunlamps, sunbeds, and tanning booths. Given the direct exposure to ultraviolet radiation when adolescents engage in either outdoor or indoor tanning, the use of fake tanning products is often considered a safer practice and promoted as a harm minimisation strategy (Williams, Jones, Caputi, & Iverson, 2011). However, the use of fake tanning products is associated with decreased sun protective behaviours such as not wearing a hat and the reduced use of both upper and lower body protective clothing, thus its health risks are often underestimated (Williams et al., 2011).

Estimates for the prevalence of outdoor tanning range from 49% to 75.5% among females and 26% to 27.7% for males (Gillen & Markey, 2012; Robinson, Rademaker, Sylvester, & Cook, 1997; Yoo, 2009). Estimates for the prevalence for indoor tanning range from 22% to 73.3% among females and from 6.7% to 39% for males (Blashill, 2013; Gillen & Markey, 2012; Guy, Tai, & Richardson, 2011; Yoo, 2009). Use of fake tanning products has been primarily studied among girls with the prevalence ranging from 19% to 34.5% (Williams et al., 2011).

Although adolescent girls and young adult females are more likely to report both outdoor and indoor tanning than males, the appearance-related motivations are the same (Gillen & Markey, 2012; Prior et al., 2013). These include tanning to improve one's general attractiveness and to feel more confident about one's appearance; tanning to look leaner, more toned and fitter, and also tanning to cover acne-related scars (Cafri et al., 2008).

Tattooing and Body Piercing

Tattooing and body piercing are two other body-modification practices that are frequently acquired before the age of 17 (Carroll, Riffenburgh,

Roberts, & Myhre, 2002). Although tattoos and body piercing have come to be viewed as fashion accessories, they are also viewed as acts of self-expression and self-identity and are closely associated with the "drive to aesthetically improve one's physical appearance" (Kent, 2011, p. 390). Thus they may be used by adolescents to visually express their individuality.

Estimates for tattooing are fairly similar among girls and boys with rates ranging between 3.5% and 16.6% for girls, and 8.8% and 10.1% for boys (Bercaw-Pratt et al., 2012; Carroll et al., 2002; Yoo, 2009). However, the prevalence of body piercing has been found to higher among girls with estimates ranging between 36.7% and 57.1% in comparison to estimates ranging between 10.1% and 13.7% for boys (Bercaw-Pratt et al., 2012; Carroll et al., 2002; Yoo, 2009). Health risks are also associated with tattooing and body piercing, as these may be performed by unlicensed personnel, and in the case of body piercing even by peers (Marcoux, 2000). Some of the main health risks include bacterial infections, viral hepatitis, and adverse skin reactions (Grogan, 2008; Marcoux, 2000).

Cosmetic Surgery

Cosmetic surgery, defined as surgery to improve a normal appearance, is an appearance-management behaviour that is becoming frequently used among women (Zuckerman & Abraham, 2008), as it is viewed as normal and accessible (Grogan, 2008). It is also increasingly being used by men (Grogan, 2008). There is no clear agreement among clinicians as to when cosmetic surgery is appropriate and necessary among adults; however, cosmetic surgery is generally not viewed as appropriate for adolescents given that their bodies and body image are still developing (de Vries, Peter, Nikken, & de Graff, 2014). Nevertheless, many adolescents have positive attitudes towards cosmetic surgery (Lunde, 2013; Zuckerman & Abraham, 2008), and the number of procedures with adolescents has increased since the 1990s. For example, in 1996 there were only 14,000 cases of adolescents who had cosmetic surgery in the U.S. (Zuckerman & Abraham, 2008), but in 2005 and 2013 there were 77,229 and 83,823 cases, respectively (American Society of Plastic Surgeons, 2013). Although 90% of adolescents who have had cosmetic surgery are girls (Zuckerman & Abraham, 2008), a similar portion of girls (10.8%) and boys (7.4%) report that they would undergo cosmetic surgery if it was offered to them for free (de Vries et al., 2014).

Adolescents' investment in or the importance they attach to their physical appearance has been found to be related to the desire to undergo cosmetic surgery (de Vries et al., 2014). However, dissatisfaction with specific body features rather than general appearance concerns predicted actual cosmetic surgery in a representative survey of Norwegian adolescent girls aged 12 to 17 (von Soest, Kvalem, & Wichstrom, 2012). In this study, which tracked girls over a 13-year period, 4.9% underwent cosmetic surgery. This included breast augmentations (26.8%), breast reductions (19.5%), breast lifts (4.9%), liposuctions (15.9%), ear operations (7.3%), rhinoplasties (4.9%), birth mark operations (4.9%), abdominoplasties (2.4%), scar corrections (2.4%), and eyelid operations (2.4%). Moreover, the study highlighted the need to consider cosmetic surgery in relation to mental health and health-risk behaviours more broadly. A range of mental health symptoms and health risk behaviours predicted cosmetic surgery, including depression and anxiety, a history of deliberate self-harm, para-suicide, and illicit drug use. In addition, girls who underwent surgery during the course of the study experienced greater increases in depressive and anxiety symptoms, eating problems, and alcohol use.

Body Dissatisfaction and Impact on Other Aspects of Adolescent Lives

Mental health outcomes and health-risk behaviours have also been shown to be directly associated with body dissatisfaction. For example, body dissatisfaction has been found to predict negative affect in adolescents (Rierdan, Koff, & Stubbs, 1989; Stice & Bearman, 2001; Stice, Hayward, Cameron, Killen, & Taylor, 2000). Specifically in one study body dissatisfaction uniquely predicted depressive mood and low self-esteem in girls between 12 and 17 years of age and among boys between the ages of 15 and 20 years (Paxton, Neumark-Sztainer, Hannan, & Eisenberg, 2006). Other well-designed studies confirm that body dissatisfaction can lead to low self-esteem, depression, suicidal thoughts, and self-harm (Holsen et al., 2001; Kim & Kim, 2009; Muehlenkamp & Brausch, 2012; Stice & Bearman, 2001; van den Berg et al., 2010). A study of 1238 8- to 18-year-old school children in Norway further showed that body image had the strongest impact on health-related quality of life, more than age, BMI, pain, and being bullied (Haraldstad, Christophersen, Eide, Nativq, & Helseth, 2011).

In addition to mental health, appearance concerns affect academic domains. In one study students with lower grades were more likely to report that body image concerns interfered with their academic performance (Yanover & Thompson, 2008). In another study adolescents who perceived themselves as overweight, irrespective of their weight, were more likely to perform poorly on academic achievement (Florin, Shults, & Stettler, 2011). Moreover, 20% of teenagers in the U.K. report absenting themselves from school when they lacked confidence about their appearance (Lovegrove & Rumsey, 2005).

Body dissatisfaction has also been implicated in the development of health-risk behaviours among adolescents. This includes substance use (e.g., Kanayama, Barry, Hudson, & Pope, 2006; Marti, Stice, & Springer, 2010; Page, Scanlan, & Allen, 1995) and unsafe sexual practices (e.g., Muehlenkamp & Brausch, 2012; Schooler, 2013; Stice & Shaw, 2003). Given that adolescence is a time of increased experimentation and risk taking, adolescents with higher body dissatisfaction may be especially vulnerable to health-risk behaviours.

In one study the use of alcohol and other substances was found to be higher among both adolescent girls and boys who considered themselves unattractive and who reported body dissatisfaction (Page et al., 1995). Other studies have found a relationship between overall body image concerns and alcohol use among adolescent girls and boys (Palmqvist & Santavira, 2006; Wild, Flisher, Bhana, & Lombard, 2004). In addition, specific dissatisfaction with body weight has been found to be associated with higher levels of alcohol consumption and binge drinking among adolescent girls (Xie et al., 2006); while high concerns about muscularity have been found to be associated with binge drinking among adolescent and young adult males (Field et al., 2014). It has been suggested that alcohol and other substances may be used in the same way as binge eating to cope with negative affect and low self-esteem (Page et al., 1995; Ricciardelli & Williams, 2011; Wild et al., 2004). However, some drugs such as amphetamines and other stimulants may be specifically used to suppress appetite and increase weight loss behaviours, in the way that smoking is used as a weight loss strategy (Warren, Lindsay, White, Claudat, & Velasquez, 2013).

Lastly, body dissatisfaction is an important factor to consider in the development and maintenance of obesity, as the relationship between body dissatisfaction and a high BMI is one of the most consistent findings throughout the literature (see Chapter 4). A high level of body dissatisfaction among individuals who are overweight and obese is to be expected, given the widespread sociocultural pressures for females to be thin (Schwartz & Brownell, 2004) and the increasingly similar sociocultural pressures for males (Ricciardelli, 2012). This body dissatisfaction has at times been considered adaptive (Schwartz & Brownell, 2004), and it is generally assumed that this may motivate individuals to lose weight; however, this is not the case. For example, an 11-year follow-up of overweight and obese adolescent girls showed that girls with higher levels of body dissatisfaction gained more weight and were more likely to start binge eating than girls who were more satisfied with their bodies (Sonneville et al., 2012).

Conclusion

This chapter has highlighted a range of body change strategies associated with body image and appearance concerns. These included extreme weight loss methods, which are often associated with disordered eating and are more frequently found among girls. Also reviewed were body change strategies associated with the pursuit of muscularity, which are more frequently found among boys. Body modification practices including body depilation, tanning, tattooing and body piercing, and cosmetic surgery were also reviewed. On the whole, these were found to be more prevalent among girls than boys but they are also accepted and widely used by many boys. In addition, although these behaviours may be primarily used by adolescents to improve their appearance, in some cases they highlight how adolescents with higher body dissatisfaction may be more vulnerable to other health-risk behaviours. Finally, body dissatisfaction was shown to affect adolescents' quality of life in terms of mental health, academic performance, health-risk behaviours, and the maintenance of obesity.

References

American Society of Plastic Surgeons (2013). 2013 Plastic surgery statistics report: Cosmetic surgery age distribution. http://www.plasticsurgery.org/Documents/news-resources/statistics/2013-statistics/cosmetic-procedures-teens.pdf. Retrieved Nov 9, 2014.

Asvat, Y., Cafri, G., Thompson, J.K., & Jacobsen, P.B. (2010). Appearance-based tanning motives, sunbathing intentions, and sun protection intentions in adolescents. *Archives of Dermatology, 146,* 445–46.

Bercaw-Pratt, J.L., Santos, X.M., Sanchez, J., Auensu-Coker, L., Nebgen. D.R., & Dietrich, J.E. (2012). The incidence, attitudes and practices of the removal of pubic hair as a body modification. *Journal of Pediatric and Adolescent Gynaecology, 25,* 12–14.

Blashill, A.J. (2013). Psychosocial correlates of frequent indoor tanning among adolescent boys. *Body Image, 10,* 259–62.

Boroughs, M.S. (2012). Hair: Body and facial. In T.F. Cash, (Ed.), *Encyclopedia of body image and human appearance, Volume 2* (pp. 475–81). London: Elsevier.

Boroughs, M.S., & Thompson, J.K. (2014). Correlates of body depilation: An exploratory study into the health implications of body hair reduction and removal among college-aged men. *American Journal of Men's Health, 8,* 217–25.

Brownell, K.D. (1991). Dieting and the search for the perfect body: Where physiology and culture collide. *Behavior Therapy, 22,* 1–12.

Cafri, G., Thompson, J.K., Roehrig, M., Rojas, A., Sperry, S., Jacobsen, P.B., & Hillhouse, J. (2008). Appearance motives to tan and not tan: Evidence for validity and reliability of a new scale. *Annals of Behavioral Medicine, 35,* 209–20.

Carroll, S.T., Riffenburgh, R.H., Roberts, T.A., & Myhre, E.B. (2002). Tattoos and body piercings as indicators of adolescents' risk-taking behaviors. *Pediatrics, 109,* 1021–27.

Connan, F. (1998). Machismo nervosa: An ominous variant of bulimia nervosa? *European Eating Disorders Review, 6,* 154–59.

Crowther, J.H., & Williams, N.M. (2011). Body image and bulimia nervosa. In T.F. Cash and Smolak, L. (Eds.), *Body image: A handbook of science, practice and prevention* (2nd ed. pp. 288–95). New York, NY: Guilford Press.

Darcy, A. M. (2011). Eating disorders in adolescent males: A critical examination of five common assumptions. *Adolescent Psychiatry, 1,* 307–12.

De Vries, D.A., Peter, J., Nikken, P., & de Graaf, H. (2014). The effect of social network site use on appearance investment and desire for cosmetic surgery among adolescent boys and girls. *Sex Roles, 71,* 283–95.

Drewnowski, A., Kurth, C.L., & Krahn, D.D. (1995). Effects of body image on dieting, exercise and steroid use in adolescent males. *International Journal of Eating Disorders, 17,* 381–86.

Dunn, M., & White, V. (2011). The epidemiology of anabolic-androgenic steroid use among Australian secondary school students. *Journal of Science and Medicine in Sport, 14,* 10–14.

Eisenberg, M.E., Wall, M. & Neumark-Sztainer, D. (2012). Muscle-enhancing behaviors among adolescent girls and boys. *Pediatrics, 130,* 1019–26.

Field, A.E., Camargo, C.A., Taylor, C.B., Berkey, C.S., Frazier, A.L., Gillman, M.W., & Colditz, G.A. (1999). Overweight, weight concerns, and bulimic behaviors among girls and boys. *Journal of the Academy of Child and Adolescent Psychiatry, 38,* 754–60.

Field, A.E., Sonneville, K.R., Crosby, R.D., Swanson, S.A, Eddy, K.T., Camargo, C.A., Horton, N.J., & Micali, N. (2014). Prospective associations of concerns about physique and the development of obesity, binge drinking, and drug use among adolescent boys and young adult men. *Journal of American Medical Association. Pediatrics, 168,* 34–39.

Florin, T.A., Shults, J., & Stettler, N. (2011). Perception of overweight is associated with poor academic performance in U.S. adolescents. *Journal of School Health, 81,* 663–70.

Gillen, M.M. & Markey, C.N. (2012). The role of body image and depression in tanning behaviors and attitudes. *Behavioral Medicine, 38,* 74–82.

Goldschmidt, A.B., Wall, M.M., Loth, K.A., Bucchianeri, M.M., & Neumark-Sztainer, D. (2014). The course of binge eating from adolescence to young adulthood. *Health Psychology, 33,* 457–60.

Graber, J.A., Brooks-Gunn, J., Paikoff, R.L., & Warren, M.P. (1994). Prediction of eating problems: An 8-year study of adolescent girls. *Developmental Psychology, 30,* 823–34.

Grogan, S. (2008). *Body image: Understanding body dissatisfaction in men, women, and children* (2nd ed.). London: Routledge.

Guy, G.P. Jr. Tai, E. & Richardson, L.C. (2011). Use of indoor tanning devices by high school students in the United States. http://www.cdc.gov/pcd/issues/2011/sep/10_0261.htm. Retrieved 3rd Jan, 2014.

Haedt-Matt, A.A., & Keel, P.K. (2011). Revisiting the affect regulation model of binge eating: A meta-analysis of studies using ecological momentary assessment. *Psychological Bulletin, 137,* 660–81.

Haraldstad, K., Christophersen, K.A., Eide, H., Nativq, G.K., & Helseth, S. (2011). Predictors of health-related quality of life in a sample of children and adolescents: A school survey. *Journal of Clinical Nursing, 20,* 3048–56.

Harmer, P.A. (2010). Anabolic-androgenic steroid use among young male and female athletes: Is the game to blame? *British Journal of Sports Medicine, 44,* 26–31.

Hay, P. (1998). The epidemiology of eating disorder behaviour: An Australian community-based study. *International Journal of Eating Disorders, 23,* 371–82.

Holman, D.M., & Watson, M.C. (2013). Correlates of intentional tanning among adolescents in the United States: A systematic review of the literature. *Journal of Adolescent Health, 52*, S52–S59.

Holsen, I., Kraft, P., & Roysamb, E. (2001). The relationship between body image and depressed mood in adolescence: A five-year longitudinal panel study. *Journal of Health Psychology, 6*, 613–27.

Hudson, J.I., Hiripi, E., Pope, H.G., & Kessler, R.C. (2007). The prevalence and correlates of eating disorders in the National Comorbidity Survey Replication. *Biological Psychiatry, 61*, 348–58.

Jones, W.R., & Morgan, J.F. (2010). Eating disorders in men: A review of the literature. *Journal of Public Mental Health, 9*, 23–31.

Kanayama, G., Barry, S., Hudson, J. I., & Pope, H. D. (2006). Body image and attitudes toward male roles in anabolic-androgenic steroid users. *American Journal of Psychiatry, 163*, 697–703.

Kent, L. (2011). Body art and body image. In T.F. Cash & L. Smolak (Eds.), (2nd ed., pp. 387–93). *Body image: A Handbook of science, practice, and prevention*. New York, NY: Guilford Press.

Kim, D., & Kim, H. (2009). Body-image dissatisfaction as a predictor of suicidal ideation among Korean boys and girls in different stages of adolescence: A two-year longitudinal study. *Journal of Adolescent Health, 45*, 47–54.

Krowchuck, D.P., Kreiter, S.R., Woods, C.R., Sinal, S.H., & DuRant, R.H. (1998). Problem dieting behaviors among young adolescents. *Archives of Pediatrics & Adolescent Medicine, 152*, 884–89.

López-Guimeró, G., Neumark-Sztainer, D., Hannan, P., Fauquet, J., Loth, K., & Sánchez-Carracedo, D. (2013). Unhealthy weight-control behaviours, dieting and weight status: A cross-cultural comparison between North American and Spanish adolescents. *European Eating Disorders Review, 21*, 276–83.

Lovegrove, E., & Rumsey, N. (2005). Ignoring it doesn't make it stop: Adolescents, appearance, and bullying. *Cleft Palate Craniofacial Journal, 42*, 33–44.

Lunde, C. (2013). Acceptance of cosmetic surgery, body appreciation, body ideal internalization, and fashion blog reading among late adolescents in Sweden. *Body Image, 10*, 632–35.

Madden, S., Morris, A., Zurynski, Y.A., Kohn, M., & Elliot, E.J. (2009). Burden of eating disorders in 5–13-year-old children in Australia. *Medical Journal of Australia, 190*, 410–14.

Marcoux, D. (2000). Appearance, cosmetics, and body art in adolescents. *Dermatologic Clinics, 18*, 667–73.

Marti, C.N., Stice, E., & Springer, D.W. (2010). Substance use and abuse trajectories across adolescence: A latent trajectory analysis of a community-recruited sample of girls. *Journal of Adolescence, 33*, 449–61.

Martins, Y., Tiggemann, M., & Churchett, L. (2008). Hair today, gone tomorrow: A comparisons of body hair removal practices in gay and heterosexual men. *Body Image, 5*, 312–16.

McCabe, M.P., & Ricciardelli, L.A. (2001). Body image and body change techniques among young adolescent boys. *European Eating Disorders Review, 9*, 335–47.

Metzl, J.D., Small, E., Levine, S.R., Gershel, J.C. (2001). Creatine use among young athletes. *Pediatrics, 108*, 421–24.

Middleman, A.B., Vazquez, I., & DuRant, R.H. (1998). Eating patterns, physical activity, and attempts to change weight among adolescents. *Journal of Adolescent Health, 22*, 37–42.

Muehlenkamp, J.J., & Brausch, A.M. (2012). Body image as a mediator of non-suicidal self-injury in adolescents. *Journal of Adolescence, 35*, 1–9.

Murray, S.B., Rieger, E., Hildebrandt, T., Karlov, L., Russell, J., Boon, E., & … Touyz, S.W. (2012). A comparison of eating, exercise, shape, and weight related symptomatology in males with muscle dysmorphia and anorexia nervosa. *Body Image, 9*, 193–200.

Neumark-Sztainer, D., Story, M., Falkner, N.H., Beuhring, T., & Resnick, M.D. (1999). Sociodemographic and personal characteristics of adolescents engaged in weight loss and weight/muscle gain behaviors: Who is doing what? *Preventative Medicine, 28*, 40–50.

Neumark-Sztainer, D., Paxton, S.J., Hannan, P.J., Haines, M., & Story, M. (2006). Does body satisfaction matter? Five-year longitudinal association between body satisfaction and health behaviours in adolescent females and males. *Journal of Adolescent Health, 39*, 244–51.

Page, R.M., Scanlan, A., & Allen, O. (1995). Adolescent perceptions of body weight and attractiveness: Important issues in alcohol and illicit drug use? *Journal of Child and Adolescent Substance Abuse, 4*, 43–55.

Palmqvist, R., & Santavirta, N. (2006). What friends are for: The relationships between body image, substance use, and peer influence among Finnish adolescents. *Journal of Youth and Adolescence, 35*, 203–17.

Patton, G.C., Johnson-Sabine, Wood, E., Mann, A.H., & Wakeling, A. (1990). Abnormal eating attitudes in London school girls—A prospective epidemiological study: Outcome at twelve month follow-up. *Psychological Medicine, 20*, 383–94.

Paxton, S.J., Neumark-Sztainer, D., Hannan, P.J., & Eisenberg, M.E. (2006). Body dissatisfaction prospectively predicts depressive mood and low self-esteem in adolescent girls and boys. *Journal of Clinical Child and Adolescent Psychology, 35*, 539–49.

Pope, H.G., Phillips, K.A., & Olivardia, R. (2000). *The Adonis complex: The secret crisis of male body obsession.* New York, NY: The Free Press.

Prior, S.M., Fenwick, K.D., & Peterson, J.C. (2014). Adolescents' reasons for tanning and appearance motives: A preliminary study. *Body Image, 11*, 93–96.

Ray, T.R., Eck, J.C., Covington, L.A., Murphy, R.B., Williams, R., & Knudtson, J. (2001). Use of oral creatine as an ergogenic aid for increased sports performance. *Southern Medical Journal, 94*, 608–12.

Ricciardelli L.A. (2012). Body image development: Adolescent boys. In T.F. Cash, (Ed.), *Encyclopedia of body image and human appearance, Volume 1* (pp.180–86). London: Elsevier.

Ricciardelli, L.A., & McCabe, M.P. (2003). A longitudinal analysis of the role of psychosocial factors in predicting body change strategies among adolescent boys. *Sex Roles, 45*, 349–60.

Ricciardelli, L.A., & McCabe, M.P. (2004). A biopsychosocial model of disordered eating and the pursuit of muscularity in adolescent boys. *Psychological Bulletin, 130*, 179–205.

Ricciardelli, L.A., & Williams, R.J. (2011). The role of masculinity and femininity in the development and maintenance of health risk behaviors. In C. Blazina & D.S.S. Miller (Eds.), *An international psychology of men: Theoretical advances, case studies, and clinical innovation* (pp. 57–98). New York, NY: Routledge.

Ricciardelli, L. A., & McCabe, M. (2015). Eating disorders in boys and men. In L. Smolak and M.P. Levine (Eds.), *The Wiley Handbook of Eating Disorders*. John Wiley & Sons.

Rierdan, J.,Koff, E., & Stubbs, M.L. (1989). A longitudinal analysis of body image as a predictor of the onset and persistence of adolescent girls' depression. *The Journal of Early Adolescence, 9,* 454–66.

Robinson, J.K., Rademaker, A.W., Sylvester, J.A., & Cook, B. (1997). Summer sun exposure: Knowledge, attitudes and behaviors of Midwest adolescents. *Preventive Medicine, 26,* 364–72.

Rodgers, R.F., Ganchou, C., Franko, D.L., & Chabrol, H. (2012). Drive for muscularity and disordered eating among French adolescent males: A sociocultural model. *Body Image, 9,* 318–23.

Ross, H.E., & Ivis, F. (1999). Binge eating and substance use among male and female adolescents. *International Journal of Eating Disorders, 26,* 245–60.

Schooler, D. (2013). Early adolescent body image predicts subsequent condom use behaviour among girls. *Sexuality Research and Policy, 10,* 52–61.

Schwartz, M.B., & Brownell, K.D. (2004). Obesity and body image. *Body Image, 1,* 43–56.

Serdula, M.K., Collins, M.E., Williamson, D.F., Anda, R.F., Pamuk, E., & Byers, T.E. (1993). Weight control practices of U.S. adolescents and adults. *Annals of Internal Medicine, 119,* 667–71.

Smith, J., & Dahm, D.L. (2000). Creatine use among a select population of high school athletes. *Mayo Clinic Proceedings, 75,* 1275–1263. Available at: http://www.may.edu/proceedings/2000/dec/7512a2.pdf. Accessed September 20, 2002.

Sonneville, K.R., Calzo, J.P., Horton, N.J., Haines, J., Austin, S.B., & Field, A.E. (2012). Body satisfaction, weight gain and binge eating among overweight adolescent girls. *International Journal of Obesity, 36,* 944–49.

Stanford, S., & Lemberg, R. (2012). A clinical comparison of men and women on the Eating Disorder Inventory-3 (EDI-3) and the Eating Disorder Assessment for Men (EDAM). *Eating Disorders: The Journal of Treatment and Prevention, 20,* 379–94.

Stephen, E.M., Rose, J.S., Kenney, L., Rosselli-Navarra, F., & Weissman, R.S. (2014). Prevalence and correlates of unhealthy weight control behaviors; Findings from the national longitudinal study of adolescent health. *Journal of Eating Disorders, 2,* 16.

Stice, E. (2001). A prospective test of the dual-pathway model of bulimic pathology: Mediating effects of dieting and negative affect. *Journal of Abnormal Psychology, 110,* 129–35.

Stice, E. (2002). Risk and maintenance of factors for eating pathology: A meta-analytic review. *Psychological Bulletin, 128,* 825–48

Stice, E., & Bearman, S.K. (2001). Body image and eating disturbance prospectively predicted increases in depressive symptoms in adolescent girls: A growth curve analysis. *Developmental Psychology, 37,* 597–607.

Stice, E., Hayward, C., Cameron, R.P., Killen, J.D., & Taylor, C.B. (2000). Body image and eating disturbances predict onset of depression among female adolescents: A longitudinal study. *Journal of Abnormal Psychology, 109,* 438–44.

Stice, E., & Shaw, H. (2003). Prospective relations of body image, eating, and affective disturbances to smoking onset in adolescent girls: How Virginia slims. *Journal of Consulting and Clinical Psychology, 79,* 129–35.

Stice, E., Marti, C.N., & Durant, S. (2011). Risk factors for onset of eating disorders: Evidence of multiple risk pathways from an 8-year old prospective study. *Behaviour Therapy Research, 49*, 622–27.

Terry, G., & Braun, V. (2013). To let hair be, or not to let hair be? Gender and body hair removal practices in Aotearoa/New Zealand. *Body Image, 10*, 599–606.

Utter, J., Denny, S., Percival, T., Crengle, S., Ameraunga, S., Dixon R., Teevale, T., & Hall, A. (2012). Prevalence of weight-related concerns and behaviours among New Zealand young people. *Journal of Paediatrics and Child Health, 48*, 1021–28.

van den Berg, P.A., Mond, J., Eisenberg, M., Ackard, D., & Neumark-Sztaniner, D. (2010). The link between body dissatisfaction and self-esteem in adolescents: Similarities across gender, age, weigh status, react/ethnicity, and socioeconomic status. *Journal of Adolescent Health, 47*, 290–96.

Vander Wal, J. S. (2011). Unhealthy weight control behaviors among adolescents. *Journal of Health Psychology, 17*, 110–20.

Von Soest, T., Kvalem, I.L., & Wichstrom, L. (2012). Predictors of cosmetic surgery and its effects on psychological factors and mental health: A population-based follow-up study among Norwegian females. *Psychological Medicine, 42*, 617–26.

Warren, C.S., Lindsay, A.R., White, E.R., Claudat, K., & Velasquez, M.P.H. (2013). Weight-related concerns related to drug use for women in substance abuse treatment: Prevalence and relationships with eating pathology. *Journal of Substance Abuse Treatment, 44*, 494–501.

Watson, D., Clark, L.A., & Tellegen, A. (1988). Development and validation of brief measures of positive and negative affect: The PANAS scales. *Journal of Personality and Social Psychology, 54*, 1063–70.

Whitaker, A., Davies, M., Shaffer, D., Johnson, J., Abramam, S., Walsh, B.T., Kalikow, K. (1989). The struggle to be thin: A survey of anorexic and bulimic symptoms in a non-referred adolescent population. *Psychological Medicine, 19*, 143–63.

Wild, L.G., Flisher, A.J., Bhana, A., & Lombard, C. (2004). Associations among adolescent risk behaviors and self-esteem in six domains. *The Journal of Child Psychology and Psychiatry, 45*, 1454–67.

Williams, M., Jones, S.C., Caputi, P., & Iverson, D. (2011). Do Australian adolescent female fake tan (sunless tan) users practice better sun-protection behaviour than non-users? *Health Education Journal, 71*, 654–61.

Woodside, D.B., Garfinkel, P.E., Kin, E., Goering, P., Kaplan, A.S., Goldbloom, D.S., & Kennedy, S.H. (2001). Comparisons of men with full or partial eating disorders, men without eating disorders, and women with eating disorders in the community. *American Journal of Psychiatry, 158*, 570–74.

Xie, B., Chou, C., Svipruijt-Metz, D., Reynolds, K., Clark, F., Palmer, P.H., Gallaher, P., Sun, P., Guo, Q., & Johnson, C.A. (2006). Weight perception and weight-related sociocultural and behavioral factors in Chinese adolescents. *Preventive Medicine, 42*, 229–34.

Yager, Z., & O'Dea, J.A. (2104). Relationships between body image, nutritional supplement use, and attitudes towards doping in sport among adolescent boys: Implications for prevention programs. *Journal of International Society of Sports Nutrition, 11*, 13.

Yanover, T., & Thompson, J.K. (2008). Eating problems, body image disturbances, and academic achievement: Preliminary evaluations of the eating and body image disturbances academic interference scale. *International Journal of Eating Disorders, 41*, 184–87.

Yoo, J. (2009). Peer influence on adolescent boys' appearance management behaviors. *Adolescence, 44*, 1017–31.

Zuckerman, D., & Abraham, A. (2008). Teenagers and cosmetic surgery: Focus on breast augmentation and liposuction. *Journal of Adolescent Health, 43*, 318–24.

4

PHYSICAL AND BIOLOGICAL FACTORS THAT INFLUENCE BODY IMAGE

Adolescence is associated with important developmental changes in physical appearance, self-image, mood, and interactions with others. Many of the changes are associated with puberty, and many are physical, with an impact on body weight and shape. Research indicates that pubertal development is usually a positive experience for boys, as the majority of them move closer to the societal ideal shape for a man. During this time, boys add muscle, and their shoulder width increases, both physical characteristics that fit with the 'ideal' cultural messages for men's body shape and size. In contrast, puberty is often a less positive experience for girls. With pubertal growth, girls experience normative increases in body fat, and their hips widen, moving them further away from society's ideal body shape for a woman. After the onset of puberty, many girls report heightened levels of body dissatisfaction and poorer self-image that may lead to disordered eating, depression, and other mental health issues (Klump, 2013).

Body weight, and Body Mass Index [BMI] are some of the most consistent predictors of body dissatisfaction. Girls and boys who have increased body fat are more likely to deviate from societal ideals and are therefore theoretically more likely to be dissatisfied with their bodies. While BMI and weight are not perfect indicators of weight and shape, they are the most straightforward means of determining weight status we have. Cross-sectional and longitudinal research, with all age groups around the world, has demonstrated a clear relationship between increased body weight or higher BMI and body dissatisfaction (e.g., Holsen, Jones, & Birkeland, 2012; McCabe & Ricciardelli, 2005).

Genetic factors are also likely to contribute to body dissatisfaction. Most of the work in this area uses twin studies to determine the extent that genetics contribute to the development of eating disorders. There are a limited number of studies that investigate genetic influences on body image and body dissatisfaction. Klump and colleagues investigated the degree of influence of genetic factors on Weight and Shape Concerns (subscales of the EDE-Q) using a twin study in the United States. They found a greater degree of influence of genetics among adolescent participants, as opposed to pre-adolescents and adults (Klump et al., 2010). A study of Swedish male and female twins (15 to 17 years of age) also found that genetic factors accounted for 27% of the variance in the Body Dissatisfaction subscale scores of the EDI in girls, and 21% of the variance in boys (Baker et al., 2009). Very little research focuses on the genetic influences of body dissatisfaction, and this is therefore not a focus of this chapter. This chapter focuses on the relationship among body weight, puberty, and body image and how this differs for boys and girls.

Pubertal Development

Puberty is characterised by accelerated growth and a range of physical changes in both boys and girls that transform the body of a child into that of a sexually mature adult. This complex interplay of hormonal, physical, psychological, and emotional changes offers multiple pathways through which the status and experience of pubertal development has an influence on body image (Harden, Kretsch, Moore, & Mendle, 2014). Much of the research has focussed on three main issues: The effect of pubertal status or the psychological experience of pubertal development; the hormonal effects of androgens and ovarian hormones, in particular estradiol for girls; and the impact of the timing of pubertal development in terms of whether these changes occur earlier, later, or at the same time in the subject as in peers (Graber, 2013). Although puberty is experienced by all adolescents, the timing of pubertal development may differ considerably, and this can have a substantial impact on body image. A German study indicated that approximately 20% of 11- to 17-year-old adolescent boys and girls consider themselves to have developed early, 60% are on-time, and 20% develop later than their peers (Finne, Bucksch, Lampert, & Kolip, 2011). We will discuss the evidence of the relationship between these factors and body image in boys and girls separately.

Puberty and Girls

Puberty is recognised as a vulnerable time for girls. Pubertal development in girls leads to increased adiposity and therefore takes them further away from the highly valued thin ideal. In addition to the physical changes associated with puberty, girls experience increased desire for peer acceptance, which could have an additional impact on body image (see Chapter 6) (Smolak, Levine, & Striegel-Moore, 1996). Therefore, research that investigates the impact of puberty on body image has generally found that post-pubertal girls have higher levels of body dissatisfaction (e.g., O'Dea & Abraham, 1999). A U.S.-based study of middle-school girls (mean age of 12.32 years) also showed that body dissatisfaction was associated with pubertal development, such that those girls who were further along in terms of development had increased body dissatisfaction (Mitchell, Petrie, Greenleaf, & Martin, 2012). Furthermore, in a review of the literature, Klump and colleagues (2013) found that advanced pubertal status was associated with body dissatisfaction and weight/shape concerns among girls in 22 out of the 37 studies (59%) that met the inclusion criteria of the review.

One of the most consistent findings in the area of puberty and body image among girls is that early pubertal timing is correlated with, and predicts body dissatisfaction, dieting and disordered eating (Brooks-Gunn & Warren, 1985; Calzo et al., 2012; Hayward et al., 1997; Klump, 2013; Rierdan & Koff, 1991). Maturing earlier than peers also predicts a range of effects on psychological wellbeing, including depression, weight-related maturity fears, and low self-worth (Davison, Werder, Trost, B.L, & Birch, 2007). Girls who perceived their pubertal development to be 'on time' have been found to feel significantly better about their bodies than those who developed 'early' or 'late' (Siegal, Yancey, Aneshensel, & Schuler, 1999). Any evidence that contradicts this association between pubertal timing and body image tends to indicate that this may be due to the positive association between the development of breasts, and positive body image in adolescent girls (Brooks-Gunn & Warren, 1988; Slap, Khalid, Paikoff, Brooks-Gunn, & Warren, 1994).

Pubertal development involves a complex change in the secretion of both adrenal and gonadal hormones (Harden et al., 2014). Release of androgens (including testosterone) in girls results in skin changes, increased height, and the growth of pubic hair (Harden et al., 2014). Release of ovarian hormones, including progesterone and oestrogen, in girls is necessary for ovulation and menstruation (Harden et al., 2014). The most important hormone in relation to body image and eating disorders appears to be estradiol; however, relatively few studies have directly measured the levels of this hormone in studies about body image. A study in the U.S. found that there was a significant negative correlation between estradiol levels and body esteem, among 11- and 13-year-old girls (Davison, Werder, Trost, Baker, & Birch, 2007)—the only relationship between this pubertal hormone and the psychological variables. There was no relationship between estradiol levels and depression or self-esteem. In their twin study, Klump et al., (2013) found no absolute difference in eating disorder symptoms of girls aged 10 to 15 years with high and low estradiol levels, but there was some evidence that those girls with high estradiol levels had increased genetic heritability of eating disorders.

In summary, the impact of puberty in girls is relatively consistent. It is generally accepted that post-pubertal adolescent girls have higher levels of body dissatisfaction, and that early pubertal timing predicts, and is correlated with higher levels of body dissatisfaction.

Theoretical Explanations for the Impact of Pubertal Timing

There are different explanations for why pubertal timing may have such a strong impact on body image for girls. From a developmental perspective, experiencing pubertal development prior to one's peers is said to be associated with feelings of alienation and depression, as expressed in the 'deviancy hypothesis' (Petersen & Taylor, 1980). This has been more fully elaborated as "the off-time hypothesis" which predicts that both early and late maturing adolescents will manifest more social, emotional and behavioural problems than those who develop at the same time as their peers (Ge, Conger, & Elder, 1996; Williams & Currie, 2000). According to Graber, Lewinsohn, Seeley and Brooks-Gunn (1997, p. 1773) 'off-time' pubertal development "was associated with serious mental health outcomes during adolescence". In these studies, findings differ according to whether cross-sectional or longitudinal study designs are used, and often depend on the measurement of pubertal timing (self-report, parent-report or by physical examination) (Dorn, Susman, & Ponirakis, 2003).

RICCIARDELLI AND McCABE (2009): STUDY OF ADOLESCENT BOYS' HEALTH RISK BEHAVIOURS

This study was designed to examine the focus on sport, peer relationships, pubertal development and timing, BMI, and negative affect in the development of adolescent boys' body image and body change strategies over a period of 8 months. In addition, to the direct effects of focus on sport, peer relationships and negative affect, how each of these factors was moderated by pubertal development, pubertal timing and BMI, was examined.

Method

Participants: The participants were 330 boys aged between 12 and 14 years who were tested twice, eight months apart (T1 and T2). The mean age of the boys at T1 was 12.04 years, (SD = 1.07).
Materials: We used the following measures:

- Body image and body change strategies were assessed using the Body Image and Body Change Strategy [BI&BCS] scales: Body Dissatisfaction (4 items), Body Importance (4 items), Strategies to Decrease Weight (6 items), Strategies to Increase Muscles (6 items), Strategies to Increase Weight (6 items), and Food Supplements (6 items) (Ricciardelli & McCabe, 2000, 2002).

- Focus on sport. Three questions developed by the authors were used to assess the importance of sport to adolescent boys in terms of the appearance of their bodies and their relationship with friends (McCabe & Ricciardelli, 2004).
- Two scales from the Self-Description Questionnaire II (Marsh, 1990) were used to assess same and opposite-gender peer relations (10 items each).
- The Pubertal Development Scale (5 items; Petersen, Crockett, Richards, & Boxer, 1988) was used to assess pubertal maturation. In addition, boys were asked to rate pubertal timing in comparison to their peers according to established protocols (Dubas, Graber, & Petersen, 1991; Graber et al., 1997; Siegel et al., 1999).
- Students were asked to report their height and weight to calculate BMI

Procedure: The Deakin University Ethics Committee and the State and Catholic Education departments in Victoria approved this study. The boys were recruited from 10 secondary schools in the metropolitan area of Melbourne. These schools included adolescents from a broad range of socioeconomic and cultural backgrounds. All boys from grade 7 and grade 9 classes in these schools were invited to take part and were provided with information packs. Seventy percent of parents provided written consent for their sons to take part in the study, and boys provided verbal consent to complete the questionnaire. The survey described above was completed during one class period (40 minutes) on two occasions (T1 and T2) eight months apart.

Data analyses: Multiple regression was used to examine the direct effects of focus on sport, same gender and opposite gender peer relations, negative affect, BMI, pubertal development, and pubertal timing on each of the six dependent variables (body dissatisfaction, body image importance, strategies to decrease weight, strategies to increase muscles, strategies to increase weight, and the use of food supplements) at T1 and T2. In addition, the interactive effects of focus on sport, peer relations, and negative affect with pubertal development, pubertal timing, and BMI were examined. To reduce multicollinearity among the interaction terms and their constitute variables, all variables were centred (Aiken & West, 1991). Significant interaction terms were probed using the procedures described by Aiken and West (1991). Specifically, predicted values were estimated using the mean, one standard deviation above the mean, and one standard deviation below the mean of both the variables in the interaction term. This was then followed by examining whether the slopes of the resulting simple regression lines were significantly different from zero.

The results of this study are discussed in this chapter (Chapter 4), Chapter 9, and Chapter 10. More detailed results and tables of interactions are available in Appendix 2 at the end of this chapter.

Puberty and Boys

In contrast to the experience of girls, it is often suggested that puberty is a positive experience for boys, as it moves them closer to the societal ideal shape for a man (Petersen & Taylor, 1980). Pubertal changes include increased muscularity and shoulder width, which fit the 'ideal' cultural messages for men's body shape and size (Mishkind, Rodin, Silberstein, & Striegel-Moore, 1996). A review of the impact of pubertal status supports this, and five studies found that advanced pubertal status was related to *reduced* body dissatisfaction or weight and shape concerns among adolescent boys (Klump, 2013). However, other studies found that post-pubertal adolescent boys are significantly more likely to engage in body change strategies, including trying to 'build up their body', and lose weight (O'Dea & Abraham, 1999), as well as using food supplements and strategies to increase muscles (McCabe et al., 2001)—all strategies we tend to associate with increased body dissatisfaction.

In one of our own studies (Ricciardelli & McCabe, summarised in the Research Box on p. 58 and Appendix 2 at the end of this chapter) with adolescent boys aged between 12 and 14 years, we found that boys who reported that their pubertal development was less advanced were also more likely to report higher levels of body dissatisfaction. We found that pubertal timing directly predicted body dissatisfaction and strategies to increase muscles among adolescent boys. Those who matured later than their peers were more likely to report higher levels of body dissatisfaction; while boys who matured much earlier than peers were more likely to use strategies to increase muscles. In addition to these direct effects, pubertal timing was found to moderate the effects of other variables for body image importance, such as strategies to decrease weight and increase muscles food supplements, and body dissatisfaction.

Pubertal timing was also found to moderate the effects of negative affect in predicting body dissatisfaction, strategies to increase muscles, and strategies to increase muscles at the second testing. If pubertal timing was perceived to be earlier than their peers, higher levels of negative affect predicted higher levels of body dissatisfaction. On the other hand, if pubertal timing was perceived to be later than their peers, higher levels of negative affect predicted more strategies to increases muscles (and more strategies to increase weight).

Other research confirms that early pubertal timing is associated with higher body image for boys. Boys who mature early are viewed as more attractive and self-confident, have a more positive body image, are popular with peers, and are more successful athletes (Freedman, 1990). In Norwegian and American research (respectively) Alsaker (1992) and Siegel et al. (1999)

demonstrated that boys who perceived themselves to have developed earlier had more positive body image when compared to those who developed later. Both studies assessed pubertal timing using self-reports that required participants to compare themselves to same-age peers and rate whether they felt they were earlier, on-time or later in terms of physical development (Alsaker, 1992; Siegal et al., 1999). Boys who developed at the same time as or earlier than their peers had higher functional and aesthetic body satisfaction in another study of Australian adolescent boys (Abbott & Barber, 2010). Finally, the review by Klump (2013) reported that three out of the 10 studies conducted with boys demonstrated an association between pubertal timing and body dissatisfaction in adolescent boys.

Several studies have shown that late maturation in boys is associated with less social competence, low peer popularity, more conflict with parents, more internalising tendencies, more drinking problems, and lower school achievement (Ricciardelli & McCabe, 2004). Late-maturing boys have been found to be more likely to use food supplements to build up their body than early maturing boys, and this predicted an increased use of strategies to increase their muscle size (McCabe & Ricciardelli, 2004). The only study to contradict the association between pubertal timing and high body satisfaction is a large American longitudinal study that showed that pubertal timing did not predict body dissatisfaction or weight and shape concern for boys aged 9 to 18 years old (Calzo et al., 2012); however, in that study the measure of weight and shape concerns was focused on adiposity, not muscularity, and the measure of body dissatisfaction was one overall evaluative item.

In summary, adolescent boys who enter puberty earlier than their peers are more likely to have lower levels of body dissatisfaction. Post-pubertal adolescent boys are more likely to have lower levels of body dissatisfaction but may engage in more strategies to build muscle. While this research is relatively consistent, more could be conducted to confirm these findings. The relationship between body image and pubertal timing is made more complex by the fact that puberty generally results in increased BMI, which is related to increased body dissatisfaction.

Body Size and Weight

The relationship between body weight and body dissatisfaction is one of the strongest, and most consistent findings of body image and eating disorder research over the past 20 years. Both male and female adolescents with higher BMIs have been found to demonstrate significantly higher levels of body dissatisfaction (Holsen et al., 2012; Jones & Crawford, 2005; Jones, Vigfusdottir, & Lee, 2004; Lawlor & Nixon, 2011; McCabe & Ricciardelli, 2005). In one study, 100% of girls, and 79% of boys who were classified as overweight, expressed a desire to lose weight (Lawlor & Nixon, 2011).

In a number of longitudinal studies with adolescents, high BMI has emerged as the strongest predictor of increased body dissatisfaction among adolescent boys and girls (Field et al., 2001; Halpern, Udry, Campbell, & Suchindran, 1999; Ohring, Graber, & Brooks-Gunn, 2002; Paxton, Eisenberg, & Neumark-Sztainer, 2006; Quick, Eisenberg, Buccianeri, & Neumark-Sztainer, 2013). A large longitudinal study of early and mid-adolescents (Project EAT) in the U.S. also showed that high BMI predicted increases in body dissatisfaction at both 5- and 10- year follow-ups among males and females (Paxton et al., 2006; Quick et al., 2013). Data from the Growing Up Today Study [GUTS] in the U.S. indicated that BMI was a significant predictor of body dissatisfaction. Both overweight/obese (above the 75th percentile) and underweight (below the 25th percentile) boys were at risk for body dissatisfaction (Calzo et al., 2012). Interestingly, even girls in the healthy-weight range were more likely to develop weight and shape concerns as they approached late adolescence, as girls were more likely to be dissatisfied with their body as soon as they exceeded the 50th percentile (Calzo et al., 2012).

Some research has indicated that BMI is more strongly related to body image in boys and young men. Retrospective studies in males have shown a higher prevalence of eating disorders and disordered eating behaviours in those who were previously overweight (Carlat, Carmargo, & Herzog, 1997; Touyz, Kopec-Schrader, & Beumont, 1993). Field and colleagues (2001) found that the relationship among BMI, 'becoming highly concerned with weight', and dieting was stronger among boys than girls in the United States. One explanation for this might be that adolescent girls have high levels of body dissatisfaction and are engaged in body change strategies regardless of their weight (McCabe, Ricciardelli, & Banfield, 2001). However, in this Australian study among young boys, BMI was related to body dissatisfaction, and also directly predicted the use of body change strategies (McCabe et al., 2001). These researchers suggested that BMI was a stronger influence on young men's body image and decision to adopt body change strategies, whereas young girls were more likely to be influenced by other social pressures (McCabe et al., 2001).

The association between BMI and the pursuit of muscularity is less consistent. Lower BMI has been associated with steroid use (Ricciardelli & McCabe, 2004) but not other body change strategies that may be used by adolescents to gain weight and muscles (Ricciardelli & McCabe, 2003). In the work described in the Research Box on page 58, T1 BMI was not a significant predictor of strategies to increase muscles or increase weight. This may be because many adolescent males who have average BMIs are dissatisfied with their body build and use weightlifting, bodybuilding, and other strategies to increase their body mass, body frame, and/or muscles (Raudenbush & Zellner, 1997). Other studies report findings that are the opposite of what is expected—that those who are larger are more likely to be engaging in activities to increase muscle size and bulk. A large study of adolescent boys in the U.S. found that adolescent boys who were classified as overweight or obese were significantly more likely to report changing their eating, consuming protein powder, and using steroids than those of average BMI (Eisenberg, Wall, & Neumark-Sztainer, 2012). Furthermore, it is known that overweight adolescents are significantly more likely to engage in diet / muscle talk, which may exacerbate body dissatisfaction and attempts at weight change strategies (Jones & Crawford, 2006). Of course, there is the potential for increased muscularity to be mistaken for adiposity in BMI calculations, and it could be that these 'overweight' males are in fact very muscular, which interferes with the interpretation of many of these results.

The other important factor contributing to BMI, and to body image, is height. A Korean study of adolescents found that the average desired adult height was 8–9 cm taller than the actual Korean average adult height; and that 4.4–7.3% of 11–18 year old children had tried to promote their growth, mostly through the use of herbal supplements (Park, Kang, & Kim, 2011). A study of 3898 Icelandic adolescents also indicated that adolescents who were shorter were more likely to report more negative body image, and this was particularly the case for boys (Vilhjalmsson, Kristjansdottir, & Ward, 2012). Interestingly, being tall was related to more positive body image among both male and female adolescents in that study. The researchers explained the findings as being due to the existence of very strong social norms about 'ideal' height, particularly for men (Vilhjalmsson et al., 2012).

Explanations for the Relationship between BMI and Body Image

Explanations for the relationship between high BMI and body dissatisfaction have generally focused on the discrepancy between an individual's perception of his/her own body, and the socially accepted, thin ideal body. Theoretically, people with a higher BMI are more likely to have a body size and shape that is quite different to the sociocultural 'ideals', and are therefore more likely to experience increased pressure to be thin (Stice & Whitendon, 2002). This is thought to intensify the pressure to commence dieting and exercise in an attempt to reduce body fat levels.

The relationship between BMI and body dissatisfaction is further intensified by the fact that those who have a higher BMI tend to be the target of appearance-based teasing by peers (Eisenberg, Neumark-Sztainer, & Paxton, 2006; Helfert & Warschburger, 2013; Thompson et al., 2007). This relationship is discussed fully in Chapter 6. The high levels of stigmatisation and discrimination against individuals with a high BMI in every facet of daily life is well documented (Puhl & Brownell, 2001). These broader external pressures might then contribute to body dissatisfaction due to the impact of a perceived social consensus that being overweight is not desirable (Farrow & Tarrant, 2009). In fact, some argue that the link between increased body weight and increased body dissatisfaction might be due to this stigma and discrimination (Crandall, 1994; Latner, Stunkard, & Wilson, 2005; Puhl & Brownell, 2001; Puhl & Latner, 2007). However, in an American study, Stice and Whitendon (2002) found that even adolescent girls with higher BMIs who perceived less pressure to conform to the societal thin ideal were eight times more likely to develop high levels of body dissatisfaction than those with an average weight, which suggests that the weight itself might be contributing to the dissatisfaction more than the societal messages about the weight.

In addition, research has demonstrated a protective effect of body satisfaction for overweight girls. Two well-designed, U.S.-based longitudinal studies showed that overweight girls with less body dissatisfaction, or some degree of body satisfaction, were less likely to gain additional weight over the 5 or 11 year study periods (Sonneville et al., 2012; van den Berg & Neumark-Sztainer, 2007). Furthermore, girls who reported that they were 'somewhat satisfied' with their weight had a 6% less chance of developing binge eating (Sonneville et al., 2012). This is explained by other work from Project EAT that indicated that those girls with higher body satisfaction were more likely to engage in physical activity and less likely to engage in unhealthy eating behaviours (Neumark-Sztainer, Paxton, Hannan, Haines, & Story, 2006). This would indicate that those with high body satisfaction are more likely to look after their bodies, regardless of weight status.

Although there is a clear association between BMI and body dissatisfaction, decreasing body weight will not necessarily result in reduced body dissatisfaction. We now have good evidence to suggest that improving body dissatisfaction (by addressing psychological and sociocultural factors) is a more direct route to improving emotional wellbeing than attempting to modify BMI (Mond, van den Berg, Boutelle, Hannan, & Neumark-Sztainer, 2011). Body weight is very difficult to change and maintain for the vast majority (e.g., Brownell & Wadden, 1992), and the significant genetic contribution to weight cannot be ignored (e.g., Stunkard, Harris, Pedersen, & McClearn, 1990). Other studies indicate that dieting predicts weight gain over time and an increased use of disordered eating behaviours (Neumark-Sztainer, Wall, Haines, Story, & Eisenberg, 2007). For these reasons, biological factors have not generally been targeted in programs to improve body image.

Conclusion

Biological influences on body image are heightened during puberty. Two decades of research have revealed that puberty has the opposite impact on body dissatisfaction by gender. After going through puberty, girls are more likely and boys are less likely to be dissatisfied with their bodies. Early maturation is predictive of increased body dissatisfaction in girls and increased body satisfaction in boys. Research investigating the relationship between body image and BMI is more consistent by gender. Cross-sectional studies indicate increased body dissatisfaction among boys and girls with high BMIs. Longitudinal work also reveals that high BMI is predictive of poor body image and strategies to lose weight. Research in this area continues to investigate the influence of these risk factors and the relationship between them. Understanding the biological influences that contribute to the development of poor body image will ensure that prevention and intervention programs can be better targeted towards groups of girls or boys who are most at risk of body dissatisfaction, due to their pubertal status and timing or their BMI. Tailoring specific messages in this way might potentially be more effective in reducing shape and weight concerns and improving body image among adolescents.

References

Abbott, B.D., & Barber, B.L. (2010). Embodied image: Gender differences in functional and aesthetic body image among Australian adolescents. *Body Image, 7*, 22–31.

Alsaker, F.D. (1992). Pubertal timing, overweight, and psychological adjustment. *The Journal of Early Adolescence, 12*(4), 396–419.

Baker, J.H., Maes, H.H., Lissner, L., Aggen, S.H., Lichtenstein, P., & Kendler, K.S. (2009). Genetic risk factors for disordered eating in adolescent males and females. *Journal of Abnormal Psychology, 118*(3), 576–86.

Brooks-Gunn, J., & Warren, M.P. (1985). Effects of delayed menarche in different contexts: Dance and non-dance students. *Journal of Youth and Adolescence, 14*, 285–300.

Brooks-Gunn, J., & Warren, M.P. (1988). The psychological significance of secondary sexual characteristics in nine-to eleven-year-old girls. *Child Development, 59*(4), 1061–69.

Brownell, K.D., & Wadden, T.A. (1992). Etiology and treatment of obesity: Understanding a serious, prevalent and refractory disorder. *Journal of Consulting and Clinical Psychology, 60*(4), 505–17.

Calzo, J., Sonneville, K., Haines, J., Blood, E.A., Field, A.E., & Austin, B. (2012). The development of associations among body mass index, body dissatisfaction, and weight and shape concern in adolescent boys and girls. *Journal of Adolescent Health, 51*(5), 517–23. doi: doi:10.1016/j.jadohealth.2012.02.021.

Carlat, D.J., Carmargo, C.A., & Herzog, D.B. (1997). Eating disorders in males: A report on 135 patients. *American Journal of Psychiatry, 154*, 1127–32.

Crandall, C.S. (1994). Prejudice against fat people: Ideology and self-interest. *Journal of Personality and Social Psychology, 66*(5), 882–94.

Davison, K.K., Werder, J.L., Trost, S.G., Baker, B.L., & Birch, L.L. (2007). Why are early maturing girls less active? Links between pubertal development, psychological well-being, and physical activity among girls at ages 11 and 13. *Social Science and Medicine, 64*(12), 2391–2404.

Dorn, L.D., Susman, E.J., & Ponirakis, A. (2003). Pubertal timing and adolescent adjustment and behavior: Conclusions vary by rater. *Journal of Youth and Adolescence, 32*(3), 157–67.

Eisenberg, M.E., Neumark-Sztainer, D., & Paxton, S. (2006). Five-year change in body satisfaction among adolescents. *Journal of Psychosomatic Research, 61*, 521–27.

Eisenberg, M.E., Wall, M., & Neumark-Sztainer, D. (2012). Muscle-enhancing behaviors among adolescent girls and boys. *Pediatrics, 130*, 1019–29.

Farrow, C.V., & Tarrant, M. (2009). Weight-based discrimination, body dissatisfaction and emotional eating: The role of perceived social consensus. *Psychology and Health, 24*(9), 1021–34.

Field, A.E., Camargo, C.A., Taylor, C.B., Berkey, C.S., Roberts, S.B., & Colditz, G.A. (2001). Peer, parent and media influences on the development of weight concerns and frequent dieting among preadolescent and adolescent girls and boys. *Pediatrics, 107*, 54–60.

Finne, E., Bucksch, J., Lampert, T., & Kolip, P. (2011). Age, puberty, body dissatisfaction, and physical activity decline in adolescents. Results of the German Health Interview and Examination Survey (KiGGS). *International Journal of Behavioral Nutrition and Physical Activity, 8*, 119–33.

Freedman, R. (1990). Cognitive–behavioral perspectives on body image change. In T.F. Cash & T. Pruzinsky (Eds.), *Body image: development, deviance, and change* (pp. 272–95). New York, NY: The Guilford Press.

Ge, X., Conger, R.D., & Elder, G.H. (1996). Coming of age too early: Pubertal influences on girls' vulnerability to psychological distress. *Child Development, 67*, 3386–3400.

Graber, J. (2013). Pubertal timing and the development of psychopathology in adolescence and beyond. *Hormones and Behavior, 64*, 262–69.

Halpern, C.T., Udry, J.R., Campbell, B., & Suchindran, C. (1999). Effects of body fat on weight concerns, dating, and sexual activity: A longitudinal analysis of Black and White adolescent girls. *Developmental Psychology, 35*, 721–36.

Harden, K.P., Kretsch, N., Moore, S.R., & Mendle, J. (2014). Descriptive review: Hormonal influences on risk for eating disorder symptoms during puberty and adolescence. *International Journal of Eating Disorders, 47*(7), 718–26.

Hayward, C., Killen, J., Wilson, D., Hammer, L., Litt, I., & Kraemer, H. (1997). Psychiatric risk associated with early puberty in adolescent girls. *Journal of the American Academy of Child and Adolescent Psychiatry, 36*, 255–62.

Helfert, S., & Warschburger, P. (2013). The face of appearance-related social pressure: Gender, age and body mass variations in peer and parental pressure during adolescence. *Child and Adolescent Psychiatry and Mental Health, 7*, 16–27.

Holsen, I., Jones, D.C., & Birkeland, M.S. (2012). Body image satisfaction among Norwegian adolescents and young adults: A longitudinal study of influence of interpersonal relationships and BMI. *Body Image, 9*, 201–208.

Jones, D.C., & Crawford, J. (2005). Adolescent boys and body image: Weight and muscularity concerns as dual pathways to body dissatisfaction. *Journal of Youth and Adolescence, 34*(6), 629–36.

Jones, D.C., & Crawford, J.K. (2006). The peer appearance culture during adolescence: Gender and body mass variations. *Journal of Youth and Adolescence, 35*(2), 257–69.

Jones, D.C., Vigfusdottir, T.H., & Lee, Y. (2004). Body image and the appearance culture among adolescent girls and boys: An examination of friend conversations, peer criticism, appearance magazines, and the internalization of appearance ideals. *Journal of Adolescent Research, 19*, 323–39.

Klump, K.L. (2013). Puberty as a critical risk factor for eating disorders: A review of human and animal studies. *Hormones and Behavior, 64*, 399–410.

Klump, K.L., Burt, A., Spanos, A., McGue, M., Iacono, W.G., & Wade, T. (2010). Age differences in genetic and environmental influences on weight and shape concerns. *International Journal of Eating Disorders, 43*(8), 679–88.

Latner, J.D., Stunkard, A., & Wilson, G.T. (2005). Stigmatized students: Age, sex and ethnicity effects in the stigmatization of obesity. *Obesity Research, 13*(7), 1226–31.

Lawlor, M., & Nixon, E. (2011). Body dissatisfaction among adolescent boys and girls: The effects of body mass, peer appearance culture and internalization of appearance ideals. *Journal of Youth and Adolescence, 40*(1), 59–71.

McCabe, M.P., & Ricciardelli, L.A. (2004). A longitudinal study of pubertal timing and extreme body change behaviors among adolescent boys and girls. *Adolescence, 39*, 145–66.

McCabe, M.P., & Ricciardelli, L.A. (2005). A longitudinal study of body image and strategies to lose weight and increase muscles among children. *Applied Developmental Psychology, 26*, 559–77.

McCabe, M.P., Ricciardelli, L.A., & Banfield, S. (2001). Body image, strategies to change muscles and weight, and puberty. Do they impact on positive and negative affect among adolescent boys and girls? *Eating Behaviors, 2*, 129–49.

Mishkind, M., Rodin, J., Silberstein, L., & Striegel-Moore, R. (1996). The embodiment of masculinity: Cultural, psychological and behavioural dimensions. *American Behavioural Scientist, 29*, 545–62.

Mitchell, S.E., Petrie, T.A., Greenleaf, C.A., & Martin, S. B. (2012). Moderators of the internalization-body dissatisfaction relationship in middle school girls. *Body Image, 9*(4), 431–40.

Mond, J.M., van den Berg, P., Boutelle, K., Hannan, P.J., & Neumark-Sztainer, D. (2011). Obesity, body dissatisfaction and emotional well-being in early and late adolescence: Findings from the project EAT study. *Journal of Adolescent Health, 48*(4), 373–78.

Neumark-Sztainer, D., Paxton, S., Hannan, P.J., Haines, J., & Story, M. (2006). Does body satisfaction matter? Five-year longitudinal associations between body satisfaction and health behaviors in adolescent females and males. *Journal of Adolescent Health, 39*, 244–51.

Neumark-Sztainer, D., Wall, M., Haines, J., Story, M., & Eisenberg, M.E. (2007). Why does dieting predict weight gain in adolescents? Findings from Project EAT-II: A 5-year longitudinal study. *Journal of the American Dietetic Association, 107*(3), 448–56.

O'Dea, J., & Abraham, S. (1999). Onset of disordered eating attitudes and behaviors in early adolescence: Interplay of pubertal status, gender, weight and age. *Adolescence, 34*(136), 671–79.

Ohring, R., Graber, J.A., & Brooks-Gunn, J. (2002). Girls' recurrent and concurrent body dissatisfaction: Correlates and consequences over 8 years. *International Journal of Eating Disorders, 31*, 404–15.

Park, M.J., Kang, Y.J., & Kim, D.H. (2011). Dissatisfaction with height and weight, and attempts at height gain and weight control in Korean school-children. *Journal of Pediatric Endocrinology and Metabolism, 16*(4), 545–54.

Paxton, S., Eisenberg, M.E., & Neumark-Sztainer, D. (2006). Prospective predictors of body dissatisfaction in adolescent girls and boys: A five-year longitudinal study. *Developmental Psychology, 42*, 888–99.

Petersen, A.C., & Taylor, B. (1980). The biological approach to adolescence: Biological change and psychological adaptation. In J. Adelson (Ed.), *Handbook of Psychology* (pp. 117–58). New York, NY: Wiley.

Puhl, R.M., & Brownell, K.D. (2001). Bias, discrimination and obesity. *Obesity Research, 9*(12), 788–805.

Puhl, R.M., & Latner, J.D. (2007). Stigma, obesity, and the health of the nation's children. *Psychological Bulletin, 133*(4), 557.

Quick, V., Eisenberg, M.E., Buccianeri, M.M., & Neumark-Sztainer, D. (2013). Prospective predictors of body dissatisfaction in young adults: 10-year longitudinal findings. *Emerging Adulthood.* doi: 10.1177/2167696813485738.

Raudenbush, B., & Zellner, D.A. (1997). Nobody's satisfied: Effects of abnormal eating behaviors and actual and percieved weight status on body image satisfaction in males and females. *Journal of Social and Clinical Psychology, 16*(1), 95–110.

Ricciardelli, L.A., & McCabe, M.P. (2000). *Psychometric evaluation of the Body Image and Body Change Inventory: An assessment Instrument for adolescent boys and girls.* Unpublished manuscript, Deakin University, Melbourne, Australia.

Ricciardelli, L.A., & McCabe, M.P. (2002). Psychometric evaluation of the Body Change Inventory: An assessment instrument for adolescent boys and girls. *Eating Behaviors, 3*, 45–59.

Ricciardelli, L.A., & McCabe, M.P. (2003). A longitudinal analysis of the role of biopsychosocial factors in predicting body change strategies among adolescent boys. *Sex Roles, 48*, 349–59.

Ricciardelli, L.A., & McCabe, M.P. (2004). A biopsychosocial model of disordered eating and the pursuit of muscularity in adolescent boys. *Psychological Bulletin, 130*, 179–205.

Rierdan, J., & Koff, E. (1991). Depressive symptomatology among very early maturing girls. *Journal of Youth and Adolescence, 20*, 219–25.

Siegal, J.M., Yancey, A.K., Aneshensel, C.S., & Schuler, R. (1999). Body image, perceived pubertal timing, and adolescent mental health. *Journal of Adolescent Health, 25*(2), 155–65.

Slap, G.B., Khalid, N., Paikoff, R.L., Brooks-Gunn, J., & Warren, M.P. (1994). Evolving self-image, pubertal manifestations, and pubertal hormones: Preliminary findings in young adolescent girls. *Journal of Adolescent Health, 15*(4), 327–35.

Smolak, L., Levine, M.P., & Striegel-Moore, R. (1996). *The developmental psychopathology of eating disorders: Implications for research, prevention, and treatment.* Mahwah, NJ: L. Erlbaum Associates.

Sonneville, K.R., Calzo, J.P., Horton, N.J., Haines, J., Austin, S.B., & Field, A.E. (2012). Body satisfaction, weight gain and binge eating among overweight adolescent girls. *International Journal of Obesity, 36*(7), 944–49.

Stice, E., & Whitendon, K. (2002). Risk factors for body dissatisfaction in adolescent girls: A longitudinal investigation. *Developmental Psychology, 38*(5), 669–78.

Stunkard, A., Harris, J.R., Pedersen, N.L., & McClearn, G.E. (1990). A separated twin study of the body mass index. *New England Journal of Medicine, 322*, 1483–87.

Thompson, J.K., Shroff, H., Herbozo, S., Cafri, G., Rodriguez, J., & Rodriguez, M. (2007). Relations among multiple peer influences, body dissatisfaction, eating disturbance, and self-esteem: A comparison of average weight, at risk of overweight, and overweight adolescent girls. *Journal of Pediatric Psychology, 32*(1), 24–29.

Touyz, S.W., Kopec-Schrader, E.M., & Beumont, P.J.V. (1993). Anorexia Nervosa in males: A report of 12 cases. *Australian and New Zealand Journal of Psychiatry, 27*, 512–17.

van den Berg, P., & Neumark-Sztainer, D. (2007). Fat 'n happy 5 years later: Is it bad for overweight girls to like their bodies? *Journal of Adolescent Health, 41*(4), 415–17.

Vilhjalmsson, R., Kristjansdottir, G., & Ward, D.S. (2012). Bodily deviations and body image in adolescence. *Youth & Society, 44*(3), 366–84.

Williams, J. M., & Currie, C. (2000). Self-esteem and physical development in early adolescence. *Journal of Early Adolescence, 20*, 129–49.

APPENDIX 2

RICCIARDELLI AND McCABE (2009)

Study of Adolescent Health Risk Behaviours Detailed Findings

This study was designed to examine the focus on sport, peer relationships, pubertal development and timing, BMI, and negative affect in the development of adolescent boys' body image and body change strategies over a period of 8 months. In addition, to the direct effects of focus on sport, peer relationships and negative affect, we examined how each of these factors was moderated by pubertal development, pubertal timing, and BMI. Methods for this study are presented in brief in the Research Box on page 58, and further details can be obtained by contacting the first author.

A summary of the predictors of body image and body change strategies at T1 and T2 is provided in Tables 1 and 2. Only the effects that are significant at the .05 level are provided.

Predictors of Body Image and Body Change Strategies at T2

T1 Criterion Scores

T1 criterion scores were found to significantly predict each of the respective dependent variables at T2. The stability of the measures from T1 to T2, as indicated by the regression weights, β, ranged from .21 to .68. The most stable measures over the 8-month period were body dissatisfaction and strategies to decrease weight. The least stable were use of food supplements and both strategies to increase muscles and strategies to increase weight.

Pubertal Development and Pubertal Timing

Pubertal development was only found to directly predict body dissatisfaction at T2. Boys whose pubertal development was less advanced were more likely to report higher levels of body dissatisfaction. In addition, pubertal development was found to moderate the focus on sport in predicting strategies to decrease weight at T2. A probing of this interaction effect revealed that if boys had reached higher levels of pubertal maturation, a greater focus on sport was more likely to predict strategies to decrease weight ($B = .44, p < .05$). On the other hand, if pubertal development was less advanced, there was no relationship between focus on sport and strategies to decrease weight ($B = .04, n.s.$).

Pubertal timing was found to directly predict body dissatisfaction and strategies to increase muscles at T1. Boys who matured later than their peers were more likely to report higher levels of body dissatisfaction. However, boys who matured much earlier than the peers were more likely to use strategies to increase muscles. In addition to these direct effects, pubertal timing was found to play an indirect role in predicting body image importance, strategies to decrease weight, strategies to increase muscles and food supplements at T1, and body dissatisfaction, strategies to increase muscles, and strategies to increase weight at T2.

More specifically, pubertal timing was found to moderate the effects of same-gender peer relations in predicting body image importance, strategies to decrease weight, and strategies to increase muscles at T1. Probing of these three moderating effects revealed that if pubertal timing was earlier than peers, more positive same-gender peer relations predicted higher body image importance ($B = .39, p < .05$), greater strategies to decrease weight ($B = .23, p < .05$), and greater strategies to increase muscles ($B = .15, p < .05$). On the other hand, if pubertal timing was later than peers, more negative same-gender peer predicted strategies in decrease weight ($B = -.09, p < .05$). There was no relationship between same-gender peers and body image importance ($B = -.03, n.s$) or between same-gender peers and strategies to increase muscles ($B = .04, n.s.$).

Pubertal timing also moderated the effects of opposite-gender peer relations in predicting body image importance, strategies to decrease weight, and increase muscles and food supplements at T1. Probing of these interaction terms revealed that if pubertal timing was earlier than peers, more negative opposite-gender peer relations predicted greater body image importance ($B = -.27, p < .05$), greater strategies to decrease weight ($B = -.12, p < .05$), more strategies to increase muscles ($B = -.20, p < .05$), and higher levels of food supplements ($B = -.08, p < .05$). In contrast if pubertal timing was later than peers, more positive opposite-gender peer relations predicted greater strategies to decrease weight ($B = .10, p < .05$). There was no relationship between opposite-gender relation and body image importance ($B = .05$, *n.s.*), opposite-gender peer relations and strategies to increase muscles ($B = -.03$, *n.s.*), or opposite-gender peer relations and food supplements ($B = .04$, *n.s.*).

In addition, pubertal timing moderated the effects of focus on sport in predicting strategies to decrease weight at T1. If pubertal timing was perceived to be earlier than peers, a higher focus on sport was associated with more strategies to decrease weight ($B = .28$, $p < .05$). If pubertal timing was perceived to be later, there was no relationship between focus on sport and strategies to decrease weight ($B = -.05$, *n.s.*).

Pubertal timing was also found to moderate the effects of negative affect in predicting body dissatisfaction, strategies to increase muscles, and strategies to increase muscles at T2. If pubertal timing was perceived to be earlier than peers, higher levels of negative affect predicted higher levels of body dissatisfaction ($B = .18$, $p < .05$). If pubertal timing was perceived to be later than peers, there was no relationship between negative affect and body dissatisfaction ($B = -.04$, *n.s.*). On the other hand, if pubertal timing was perceived to be later than their peers, higher levels of negative affect predicted more strategies to increases muscles ($B = .23$, $p < .05$) and more strategies to increase weight ($B = .19$, $p < .05$). If pubertal timing was perceived to be earlier than peers, there was no relationship between negative affect and strategies to increase muscles ($B = -.07$, *n.s.*) or between negative affect and strategies to increase weight ($B = -.01$, *n.s.*).

BMI

BMI was found to directly predict body dissatisfaction, strategies to decrease weight, and strategies to increase weight at T1 and body image importance at T2. As would be expected a higher BMI predicted higher scores on body dissatisfaction, body image importance, and strategies to decrease weight. On the other hand, a lower BMI predicted higher scores on strategies to increase weight. In addition, BMI was found to moderate the effects of negative affect in predicting strategies to increase weight at T1. Negative affect predicted strategies to increase weight, but only when BMI was low ($B = -.18$, $p < .05$). There was no relationship between negative affect and strategies to increase weight when BMI was high ($B = .01$, *n.s.*). BMI was not found to directly predict or moderate any of the dependent measures at T2.

Other Factors

Focus on Sport

In addition to the indirect effects described above, focus on sport was found to predict body importance, strategies to increase muscles, and strategies to increase weight at T1 and body importance, strategies to decrease weight, strategies to increase muscles, and strategies to increase weight at T2. In each case, a higher focus sport predicted a greater importance placed on the body and body change strategies.

Peer relations

Same-gender peer relations only directly predicted body importance at T1. In contrast, opposite-gender peer relations predicted body dissatisfaction and strategies to increase muscles at T1 and food supplements at T2. More positive peer relations predicted body image concerns, but poorer peer relations predicted body change strategies.

Negative affect

Negative affect was found to predict strategies to decrease weight, increase muscles, and increase weight at T1 and body importance at T2. In each, higher levels of negative affect predicted body change strategies and the importance placed on the body.

TABLE 1 Summary of regression analyses for boys at T1

Dependent Variables	R^2	Unique Predictors	β	sr^2
T1 Body dissatisfaction	.14***			
		T1 Age	.13*	.01
		T1 BMI	.16*	.03
		T1 Pubertal timing	.11*	.01
		T1 Opposite-gender peer relations	−.20**	.02
T1 Body importance	.15**			
		T1 Focus on sport	.27***	.05
		T1 Same-gender peers	.16*	.01
		T1 Same-gender peer relations x pubertal timing	−.20**	.01
		T1 Opposite-gender peer relations x pubertal timing	.16*	.01
T1 Strategies to decrease weight	.18***			
		T1 BMI	.32***	.08
		T1 Negative affect	.11*	.01
		T1 Focus on sport x pubertal timing	−.11*	.01
		T1 Same-gender peer relations x pubertal timing	−.27***	.03
		T1 Opposite-gender peer relations x pubertal timing	.20**	.02

(Continued)

Dependent Variables	R^2	Unique Predictors	β	sr^2
T1 Strategies to increase muscles	.18★★★			
		T1 Pubertal timing	−.16★★	.02
		T1 Focus on sport	.22★★	.03
		T1 Negative affect	.12★	.01
		T1 Opposite-gender peer relations	−.17★	.01
		T1 Same-gender peer relations x pubertal timing	−.15★	.01
		T1 Opposite-gender peer relations x pubertal timing	.14★	.01
T1 Strategies to increase weight	.13★★★			
		T1 BMI	−.18★★	.02
		T1 Focus on sport	.11★	.01
		T1 negative affect	.12★	.01
		T1 negative affect x BMI	−.10★	.01
T1 Food supplements	.07★			
		T1 Opposite-gender relations x pubertal timing	.18★	.01

Note. ★ $p < .05$; ★★ $p < .01$; ★★★ $p < .001$.

TABLE 2 Summary of regression analyses for boys at T2

Dependent Variables	R^2	Unique Predictors	β	sr^2
T2 Body dissatisfaction	.44★★★			
		T1 Body dissatisfaction	.59★★★	.31
		T1 Pubertal development	−.12★	.01
		T1 Negative affect x pubertal timing	−.13★	.01
T2 Body importance	.39★★★			
		T1 Body importance	.47★★★	.22
		TI BMI	.12★	.01
		T1 Focus on sport	.25★★★	.02
		T1 Negative affect	.14★	.01
T2 Strategies to decrease weight	.52★★★			
		T1 Strategies to decrease weight	.68★★★	.35
		T1 Focus on sport	.12★	.01
		T1 Focus on sport x pubertal development	.11★	.01

(Continued)

Dependent Variables	R^2	Unique Predictors	β	sr^2
T2 Strategies to increase muscles	.25***			
		T1 Strategies to increase muscles	.35***	.10
		T1 Focus on sport	.20**	.03
		T1 Negative affect x pubertal timing	.23	.03
T2 Strategies to increase weight	.24***			
		T1 Strategies to increase weight	.35***	.10
		T1 Focus on sport	.19**	.02
		T1 Negative affect x pubertal timing	.16*	.01
T2 Food supplements	.13**	T1 Food supplements	.21**	.04
		T1 Opposite-gender relations	−.21*	.02

Note. * $p < .05$; ** $p < .01$; *** $p < .001$.

5
THE MEDIA AND BODY IMAGE

The mass media provide a constant reminder of what is considered to be attractive, how important it is to look that way, and how to achieve that look. In the last two centuries, young people have been subjected to socio-cultural pressures from an ever-increasing range of media that promote a profoundly image-conscious society and culture defined by consumerism. Media includes traditional forms such as print media, broadcast media such as television, film and music videos, and new media such as the Internet and social networking sites such as Facebook.

Accurate estimates of the amount of time adolescents spend using media sources are made more difficult by the fact that young people rarely use one form of media at a time. The Kaiser Family Foundation reported that, in the U.S., 8–18 year olds spent an average of 4.29 hours in a typical day watching television, and 7.5 hours using media, 4.29 hours of which was spent watching television, but multitasking meant that total exposure was 10 hours and 45 minutes a day (Rideout, Foehr, & Roberts, 2010). Media use is also gendered. A study conducted in 2007 showed that girls were more likely to talk on mobile phones, use text and instant messaging, send messages on social networking sites, and e-mail, while boys spent more time playing computer games (Lenhart et al., 2008). A study of British adolescent girls found that they spent a comparatively short amount of time engaging with magazines in comparison to the proportion of time spent watching television, with reality TV and soap operas being the most common TV programs consumed (Bell & Dittmar, 2011).

For some time, researchers have been aware of the potential for the media to cause harm (Levine & Murnen, 2009). Television, movies, and magazines have long been criticised for contributing to increased risky behaviours, including violence, use of alcohol, and initiation of sexual activity (Villani, 2001), and new media such as the Internet and mobile phones have a similar effect (Brown & Bobkowski, 2011). Both old and new media are also blamed for the development of body dissatisfaction and eating disorders among adolescents (Levine & Murnen, 2009). A thorough review by Levine and Murnen (2009) showed that there is some evidence to support a causal relationship among exposure to mass media (predominantly television and magazines), body dissatisfaction, and eating disorders as indicated by exposure studies, mostly conducted among young women in college (Levine & Murnen, 2009).

The media has both a direct and indirect effect on body image, through the content of the articles and the images that accompany them. The aspirational manner in which the images of bodies are presented has led to researchers calling these the 'thin ideal' for women and the 'muscular ideal' for men. However, the impact of the media goes beyond the presentation of thinness or muscularity as the images that are presented also depict utter perfection in terms of beauty, appearance, and attractiveness. Faces are symmetrically balanced, skin is unblemished, and no hair is out of place thanks to digital airbrushing and enhancement programs. The pervasive presence of these sociocultural 'ideals' and standards of attractiveness means that adolescents are often surrounded by unrealistic portrayals of beauty and success. New forms of media, including the Internet and in particular social networking sites are largely image focused and add to the impact of the traditional array of media such as newspapers, magazines, television, films, and advertising. To add complexity to the array of sociocultural influences at work, adolescents are likely to use multiple forms of traditional and new media at once, and new media use is heavily networked and shared with peers (Brown & Bobkowski, 2011). Today's adolescents' consumption of and attitudes about media forms are typically shared with peers through social networking sites, particularly music and music videos. Young people are therefore likely to be under greater pressure from these multiple sociocultural forces in their quest to fit in with their peers and develop their own identities (Brown & Bobkowski, 2011).

The sorts of images depicted in the media do not happen in a vacuum. They exist due to much larger societal and industry forces, and the fashion and advertising industries often receive the bulk of the blame. Advertisers carefully select and then digitally alter the thin or muscular models and images they use in order to increase sales and revenue and might be afraid of the financial impact of using diverse models. Similarly, the fashion industry seems to have a long-standing culture of using thin models. However, there is now good evidence that thin and muscular images are not necessary to drive sales and that there may be benefits from embracing size diversity. Consumer research has shown that consumers support the use of diverse images in the media (D'Alessandro & Chitty, 2011). Numerous exposure studies in Australia using more realistic-sized male and female models also show that these advertisements are just as effective, and still appeal to consumers (Diedrichs & Lee, 2010, 2011; Dittmar & Howard, 2004). In another Australian study, D'Alessandro and Chitty (2011) found that there was no difference in source credibility and attractiveness of two advertisements, one that used a thin model, and one using a more realistic model (D'Alessandro & Chitty, 2011). There is even some evidence that young people might be more likely to purchase products that are advertised by more realistic and diverse models. The long-term commercial success of the Dove 'real beauty' campaign demonstrates the demand for change in advertising. Their billboard advertisements featuring 'real women' were said to be responsible for an initial sales boom that is reported to be anywhere between 6 and 20 percent in just one year (Spitznagal, 2013). The company also experienced unprecedented exposure when their 'Real Beauty Sketches' advertisements went viral and were viewed over 26 million times (Spitznagal, 2013).

The demand from the market is clear. Focus groups with young men and women in Australia indicate a frustration with the limited nature of current images and a desire for the use of more diverse models in advertising and the media (Diedrichs, Lee, & Kelly, 2011). The benefits of using diverse models have also been confirmed. Multiple exposure studies have found that the use of more realistic images improves the body image of young people (Diedrichs & Lee, 2010, 2011). All available evidence indicates that media outlets and advertisers have the opportunity to be more socially responsible by using realistically sized models in their marketing without damaging their brand or their bottom line. It will be interesting to observe whether there are any changes over the next 5 to 10 years and whether these are driven internally or need to be externally regulated or motivated through government action and public policy initiatives.

In this chapter we explore the research that has investigated the impact of the media as risk factors for the development of negative body image in adolescents. This includes an examination of the nature of the images that have been used over time and a review of the research on the impact of viewing traditional and new forms of media on adolescent body image. Finally, we investigate the moderators of the impact of the media on young boys and girls.

Trends in Presentation of Media Images over Time

The mass media have long been blamed for the perpetuation of the thin ideal and the development of body image problems and eating disorders (Thompson & Heinberg, 1999). Editorial and advertising content in television, movies, magazines, and newspapers are said to be responsible, due to both the images used and the nature of the editorial content that focuses heavily on appearance and judging celebrities based on changes in their appearance. Images of men and women who represent the muscular and thin ideals are ubiquitous in print and electronic media.

Images of thin, attractive women have always featured in the media, yet some historical trends can be observed. The appearance of female models and celebrities has been observed as becoming less curvaceous and more androgynous over the past 30 years, and to represent a pre-pubescent female (Silberstein, Striegel-Moore, Timko, & Rodin, 1988; Thomsen, McCoy, & Williams, 2001). Studies of the appearance of models and celebrities on the cover of popular women's magazines in the U.S. from 1959 to 1999 indicated a general trend towards extreme thinness in cover models in the 1980s and 1990s (Sypeck, Gray, & Ahrens, 2004). In addition, there appeared to be a trend towards showing full body shots of the model in the 1990s, thus reinforcing the importance of both an attractive face and the thin ideal body (Sypeck et al., 2004).

In contrast to this research, there seems to have been an overt discourse about a movement towards a more positive approach, incorporating 'real women' and average or larger body sizes that originates from the media sources themselves. For example, the Australian Cosmopolitan magazine implemented a 'body love' policy in 1997 and has launched a 'Size Hero' campaign that asks readers to sign a petition demanding that the fashion industry provide a broader range of sizes (Campbell, 2013). While this represents a positive step, 'body love' type movements of this nature could also be seen as tokenistic and could end up emphasizing a focus on the body. In addition, the messages that are sent are often contradicted by the advertising content that features very thin or muscular models.

As with the female body, the male body has been depicted, evaluated, and scrutinised as an aesthetic product since ancient times. However, the history of male beauty has been less frequently documented and subjected to analysis (Ricciardelli & Williams, 2012). The past 10 years have seen an increased research focus on the media as risk factors for body dissatisfaction among young men (Ricciardelli & McCabe, 2004). During the last 30 years, there has been a growing trend for muscular male bodies to be featured in popular magazines, television, and films (Labre, 2005; Law & Labre, 2002). The average

U.S. *Playgirl* centrefold man has been observed as becoming increasingly lean and muscular between 1973 and 1997, shedding 12 pounds of fat and gaining 27 pounds of muscle (Leit, Pope Jr. & Gray, 1999). The size of males in both the population and the media has been reported to have increased from the 1950s (Spitzer, Henderson, & Zivian, 1999); however, this study made no distinction between fat-free mass and adipose tissue. In addition, it has been found that action figures such as G.I. Joe and Star Wars characters have increased in muscularity over time, with major increases in the chest and shoulder measurements (Pope, Olivardia, Gruber, & Borowiecki, 1999). Current models of these toys far exceed levels of muscularity that are achievable by adult human beings, let alone pre-pubescent boys. Content analyses of movies have found that the average size of male characters has become more lean and muscular over time and that those characters that represented the muscular 'ideal' were more likely to be depicted as being romantically successful but also more violent (Morrison & Halton, 2009). Finally, research that mapped the body dimensions of male characters in the top 150 video games showed that they were significantly and disproportionally larger than the average American male (Martins, Williams, Ratan, & Harrison, 2010).

The content of magazine articles is also concerning. Magazines that feature images of muscular men, such as *Men's Health* and *Men's Fitness* are commonly dominated by articles that focus on leanness and muscularity. One content analysis found that 25% of the articles in these magazines focused on 'burning fat and building muscle', followed by articles that focused on other aspects of mental or physical health (18%). Advertisements focused on media and communications (18%), clothing and accessories (17%), and performance enhancing supplements (16%); and leanness or muscularity was the most frequently purported benefit of using the products that were advertised (Labre, 2005).

Impact of the Media on Adolescent Body Image

The constant barrage of images of muscular men and slim women in the media is often considered to be responsible for young people internalising these unrealistic standards as the norm (Thomsen et al., 2001). After a thorough review of the literature, Levine and Murnen (2009) concluded that there was evidence that exposure to the media has a causal effect on body dissatisfaction and eating disorders and that adolescent girls are more likely to be affected than adult women. This phenomenon was demonstrated quite clearly in a study that investigated disordered eating attitudes among adolescent schoolgirls (mean age 17 years) in Fiji. A cross-section of young girls was surveyed in 1995, when television was first introduced, and a similar cohort was studied three years later. Scores on the Eating Attitudes Test [EAT-26] were significantly higher after girls had been exposed to Western television programming, and 83% of girls indicated that television had influenced their friends or themselves to feel differently about the way that they look (Becker, Burwell, Gilman, Herzog, & Hamburg, 2002). A follow-up examination of adolescent girls' media exposure and disordered eating pathology in Fiji confirmed the effect of the media in this setting, and indicated that the extent of exposure to media among girls' social network predicted the impact on eating pathology, independent of the amount of direct exposure to media (Becker et al., 2011). Additional studies, reviewed in this chapter, show that globalisation and acculturation to Western ideals are promoting the same thin ideal for girls across all cultures.

Meta-analyses of the effect of the media on body image have shown that there is a small to medium negative effect for women (Grabe, Ward, & Hyde, 2008; Groesz, Levine, & Murnen, 2002; Holmstrom, 2004) and men (Barlett, Vowels, & Saucier, 2008) in correlational and experimental studies. These meta-analyses showed that the overall effects of exposure studies, and the impact of the images seemed to vary according to the type of media used, with photographs of thin women eliciting the strongest effect, but with the greatest variance (Holmstrom, 2004). The impact of the media also varied according to the control condition that was utilised. Studies comparing exposure to images of thin and large women found that those viewing the images of larger women were significantly more likely to feel better about their bodies (Holmstrom, 2004). Groesz et al. (2002) also found that effect sizes were larger for female participants aged less than 19 years, indicating that adolescent girls were more likely to be negatively affected by exposure to images of thin models (Groesz et al., 2002). The two meta-analyses that have investigated correlational studies also showed that there was a relationship between the amount of media consumed, and the extent of body dissatisfaction in both boys (Barlett et al., 2008) and girls (Grabe et al., 2008).

Correlational Studies

Concern about the possibility of the presentation of popular media articles about eating disorders initiating disordered eating behaviour has been present since these articles began to appear in the 1970s (Schulze & Gray, 1990). Researchers have used correlational studies to determine whether there is a relationship between media consumption and body dissatisfaction in natural settings. Studies using this method typically require adolescents to complete a series of questions about their media use, what and how much they consume. This is correlated with standardised measures on related variables such as self-esteem, body image, eating attitudes, and so on. In one large study of adolescents in the U.S., girls who reported being occasional or frequent readers of dieting and weight loss articles were twice as likely to report engaging in healthy, unhealthy and extremely unhealthy dieting behaviours five years later (van den Berg, Paxton, et al., 2007).

Correlational studies conducted among adolescents have shown that media consumption is related to increased body dissatisfaction, weight concerns, depression, and anxiety (Martin & Gentry, 1997; Shaw, 1995; Stice, Spangler, & Agras, 2001). More detailed correlational work has revealed the importance of media type and TV genre as well as the motivations for media consumption. In an Australian study, total time reading magazines was related to drive for thinness, drive for muscularity and bulimic pathology among girls but not boys (Tiggemann, 2005). The total amount of time spent watching television was not related to body image variables among girls or boys, but the time spent watching soap operas was related to high levels of drive for thinness among adolescent girls and boys, and time spent watching both soap operas and music videos predicted high levels of drive for muscularity among the boys (Tiggemann, 2005). Finally, among those adolescents who indicated that they watched TV for social learning and escape from negative affect, there was a greater negative impact of television exposure on body image than among those who reported watching television for entertainment (Tiggemann, 2005). The relationship between media exposure and body dissatisfaction seems to be more complex for males, and one U.S. study found that media body comparison was not a significant predictor of body dissatisfaction among adolescent boys (van den Berg, Paxton, et al., 2007). One of the limitations of many of the studies conducted with adolescent boys is that they often do not assess the body image concerns that are more salient and pertinent to males, such as levels of muscularity.

Longitudinal Studies

Another method used to determine the impact of the media is to conduct questionnaires over time, similar to the ones used in correlational research. A large U.S. study of 6770 boys and 5287 girls aged 9 to 14 years found that those who reported that they made an effort to look like same-sex peers in the media were more likely to indicate that they had become concerned about their weight in a follow up survey one year later (Field et al., 2001). Another large, five-year longitudinal study of adolescents in the U.S. showed that the frequency of reading magazines was related to weight control behaviours in adolescent girls. Those girls who indicated that they read magazine articles about diet and weight loss at time 1 were twice as likely to be using unhealthy weight control behaviours such as fasting, skipping meals, and smoking and three times as likely to be engaging in disordered behaviours such as vomiting and laxative use. However, reading these articles was not related to measures of body dissatisfaction, self-esteem, and depression (van den Berg, Neumark-Sztainer, Hannan, & Haines, 2007).

Experimental Research

Investigations of the effect of the mass media are frequently conducted in the form of controlled experimental studies where participants are shown magazine and television advertisements or media images depicting ideal male or female or neutral images. In these experimental studies, the researchers purposely manipulate the images that are shown to the participants, and their body image is measured before and after to evaluate the impact of exposure to ideal images on *state* body image, i.e., how participants feel about their bodies at that particular point in time. Studies of this type using all forms of media have shown that there is a negative impact of viewing idealised images in the media in the short term (Bell & Dittmar, 2011). For example, in Australia, Durkin and Paxton (2002) measured adolescent girls' body image, and then, one week later, randomly allocated individual girls to view either images of models that represent the thin ideal (experimental condition) or images of fashion accessories (control condition) on a computer. The girls that saw the thin models were significantly more likely to have higher levels of body dissatisfaction when was measured again immediately after they saw the images (Durkin & Paxton, 2002). Just under half of the girls that saw the thin images had an increase in body dissatisfaction after exposure (42% of grade 7 girls and 49% of grade 10 girls), and those that had a higher BMI and higher levels of thin ideal internalisation and body comparison were more likely to be affected (Durkin & Paxton, 2002).

Stice and Colleagues (2001) have also confirmed the impact of long-term exposure to ideal media images in a U.S. study. They randomly assigned adolescent girls to receive a 15-month subscription to a fashion magazine or not (control condition). While there was no long-term effect of magazine exposure on body dissatisfaction and dieting on the sample as a whole, there was a significant increase in the levels of body dissatisfaction and dieting among those girls who initially had low levels of social support (Stice, Spangler, & Agras, 2001).

Media exposure studies among adolescent boys have had mixed results. Some studies have reported that adolescent male participants report heightened muscle dissatisfaction and depression after viewing ideal male images. An Australian experimental study where 12, 14, and 16 year olds were shown a five-minute clip of music videos featuring either average or muscular male singers found that the boys who viewed the muscular clip had significant increases in body dissatisfaction, and they also reported increased depressive feelings and lower levels of happiness. Boys viewing the muscular music videos also reported higher levels of social comparison to the singers (Mulgrew, Volcevski-Kostas, & Rendell, 2014). Farquhar and Wasylkiw (2007) also found that when early adolescent boys (mean age 12.5 years) were shown images of idealised images where the male models were presented as objects (highly posed with a focus on appearance), rather than being presented as engaging in high levels of activity, there was a more negative effect on the appearance self-esteem. These authors indicated that music video clips may be a particularly potent media source but that there were no significant differences in the impact of viewing the media clips among the three age groups that represented early mid, and late adolescence. However, other studies have found that exposure to idealised media images had a negative impact on the body image of adolescent girls but not boys (Hargreaves & Tiggemann, 2004). Hargreaves and Tiggeman (2004) examined the impact of television commercials among adolescent boys (mean age 14 years) in Australia. They found no impact of viewing these advertisements featuring idealised male bodies. Humphreys & Paxton (2004) also reported that late adolescent Australian boys (15 to 16 years) did not experience any significant decrease in body dissatisfaction following exposure to idealised male images in print advertisements; however, those who had higher levels of internalisation of the muscular ideal were more likely to be affected by viewing the ideal muscular images (Humphreys & Paxton, 2004).

With some exceptions, it seems that young adolescent men are not as prone to the negative effects of the media. This reduced vulnerability to media images has been explained by theories that boys are less likely to be influenced by sociocultural pressures (Anderson & Holman, 1997) and that the media is a less powerful transmitter of these pressures for boys (Vincent & McCabe, 2000). Hargreaves and Tiggemann (2004) found that adolescent boys were less likely to engage in social comparison processes than the girls. However this knowledge is contrasted with the research among college men that shows that they are affected by experimental exposure to idealised male figures. This has led researchers to propose that the social comparison processes and appearance schemas that are necessary for the negative impact of viewing ideal media images are developed later in boys than in girls (Hargreaves & Tiggemann, 2004). Hargreaves and Tiggemann (2004) suggest that males may not become susceptible to the impact of the media until late adolescence at which point being muscular becomes more important. Humphreys and Paxton (2004) further propose that adolescent boys may not see these images as unrealistic, as they believe that their body might develop to look like the images that they are seeing. Work with a large sample of adolescent boys in Belgium (mean age 15 years) found that there was a significant relationship between exposure to sexualised male images, self-objectification, and internalisation of media ideals (Vandenbosch & Eggermont, 2013). More research on the impact of different types of media on the body dissatisfaction of young boys is clearly required.

Impact of New Media on Body Image

The impact of traditional media (such as newspapers, magazines, and television) on body image has been the predominant focus of body image research over the past 20 years or so. However, the evolving media environment means that there is now a range of means by which adolescents interact with the media, and this may impact on them in different ways.

Reality Television

Reality television is a relatively new phenomenon that depicts 'real people' in a range of different situations (Egbert & Belcher, 2012). Several reality television programs focus on changing appearance, such as modelling competitions that reinforce the thin-ideal for women (e.g., *America's Next Top Model*), cosmetic surgery shows (e.g., *The Swan*), and weight loss programs (e.g., *The Biggest Loser*). The key focus of these programs is a dramatic change and modification to one's body and appearance that is associated with increased happiness, wealth, and success. These programs claim to educate viewers about the adoption of a healthier lifestyle, promote weight management, and increase self-esteem but they may in fact be detrimental to public health (Egbert & Belcher, 2012). One study conducted with adolescent girls in the U.S. found that watching reality television was associated with increased self-esteem and expectations of respect in romantic relationships, two very positive outcomes (Ferguson, Salmond, & Modi, 2013). However, reality TV consumption was associated with an increased focus on the importance of appearance and desire for fame at the expense of other things (Ferguson et al., 2013). More research is needed in order to determine the impact of reality television on adolescent audiences, and with adolescent boys.

Internet and Social Media

Research that investigates the impact of the media on body image has largely neglected the Internet. This is a far messier source of the media, given that adolescents can potentially access a range of information that is often accompanied by advertisements and editorial images on a range of topics at any one time. One study found that Internet use was associated with body weight dissatisfaction, internalisation of the thin ideal, and drive for thinness among adolescent girls (Tiggemann & Miller, 2010).

Prevalence research has found that teenagers spend more time on the Internet than with any other media source. A large proportion (87.8%) of American adolescents has access to the Internet at home, and in 2007 it was found that they spent about 10 hours per week using the Internet (Subrahmanyam & Lin, 2007). An Australian study conducted in 2010 reported a mode of 2 to 3 hours of Internet use per day (Tiggemann & Miller, 2010), while another U.S. study reported a mode of 1 to 2 hours per day (35.9% of participants), with almost 20% of adolescents using the Internet for 30 to 60 minutes, and 20% using for 2 to 3 hours per day (Meier & Gray, 2013).

Advertisers recognise this exposure, and direct substantial marketing budgets towards this group. A content analysis of the advertisements on popular teen websites found that cosmetics and beauty products were the most common products featured (Slater, Tiggemann, Hawkins, & Werchon, 2011). Further analysis of this category found that 46.5% of the fashion, cosmetics, and beauty advertisements analysed were classified as having 'a lot' of focus on appearance (Slater et al., 2011). The interactive, moving, and 'pop up' nature of these advertisements might mean that Internet–based advertising has a stronger impact on young consumers than advertisements in traditional media.

Social networking sites are some of the most common websites used by adolescents. In addition to being popular, these sites may have a huge impact on body image. There are many potential reasons for this impact, from the social comparison arising from viewing friends' photos, to the comments and feedback they receive on the photos they post. Tiggemann and Miller (2010) were some of the first to investigate this phenomenon and revealed that time spent on Facebook was significantly correlated with internalisation, weight satisfaction, and drive for thinness, but not appearance comparisons in Australian adolescent girls. Tiggemann and Slater (2013) then found that time spent on the Internet was related to increased thin–ideal internalisation, body surveillance, and drive for thinness. More specifically, those who spent more time on Facebook, and those who had a greater number of Facebook friends, were more likely to have significantly higher levels of body image concerns (Tiggemann & Slater, 2013). Another study of U.S. adolescents found that appearance-related photo activity on Facebook was correlated with poor body esteem, internalisation, drive for thinness, and self-objectification, but the total amount of time using Facebook was not (Meier & Gray, 2013). A study of Korean and American adolescent girls found that there was a significant relationship between the use of social media for information and negative body image; however, the use of social media for self-status seeking only had an impact on the body image of Korean girls (Lee, Lee, Choi, Hyun, & Han, 2014). The unique feature of social networking sites such as Facebook is the potential to give and receive immediate written feedback on the images posted. A study of adolescents using the Dutch friend networking site 'CU2' found that the tone of the feedback adolescents received on their profiles had a significant effect on their self-esteem. Those who received positive feedback had higher levels of self-esteem (Valkenburg, Peter, & Schouten, 2006). Another Dutch study revealed that adolescent girls who viewed YouTube videos featuring very underweight models that were accompanied by peer 'comments' that underrepresented the level of thinness of that model experienced a significant increase in body dissatisfaction, particularly among girls who scored highly on measures of appearance schematicity (Veldhuis, Konijn, & Seidell, 2014).

As this is a new and emerging area of interest in the body image field, much of the new and exciting research in this area has been conducted with college women, presumably due to the increased ethical complexity of conducting this work among adolescents. However the impact of this work is likely to be similar for a younger age group. A study with U.S. college women aged 18 to 19 years found that those young women who reported spending more time on social media sites such as Facebook had higher levels of disordered eating (Mabe, Forney, & Keel, in press), but other similar work with Hispanic women did not replicate these results (Ferguson, Munoz, Garza, & Galindo, In Press). Experimental research with 18-year-old female college students found a significant increase in weight and shape preoccupation and state anxiety after 20 minutes of using Facebook, compared to a control group (Mabe et al., In Press). Haferkamp and Kramer (2011) also replicated the traditional media exposure studies with Facebook profile pictures and found that young women experienced increased body dissatisfaction after viewing profile pictures of attractive people as opposed to profiles of unattractive people (Haferkamp & Krämer, 2011). Further, one study of users of social networking sites found that women were significantly more likely to select their profile picture because it made them appear attractive or digitally manipulate images to emphasise attractiveness (Strano, 2008). This research highlights the potential impact of social media, but also suggests that prevention and intervention programs should include materials to counter the strong impact of this new media format.

Unlike the traditional media, who have been very slow to act to improve body image among consumers, social networking sites have introduced policies designed to improve the wellbeing of users. Social networking sites Pinterest and Tumblr (predominantly visual forms of social media) have banned the creation of 'thinspiration' boards through an update to their acceptable use policy to discourage the pinning of images that promote self-abuse or self-harm (Gibson, 2012). Although difficult to regulate, this step represents positive action that may be used to create a more positive social media environment.

Variations in the Impact of Media Images

Media images exist everywhere and are virtually impossible to avoid, and yet some adolescents seem to be more vulnerable to the impact of the media than others. A number of researchers have investigated *moderating* factors that may make adolescents more or less likely to be negatively influenced by exposure to the media. The main moderators for the impact of media exposure relate to the type and dose of the media consumed or individual factors, such as the existing level of body dissatisfaction, internalisation of the thin or muscular ideals (see Chapter 9), and the extent to which adolescents make appearance comparisons (see Chapter 6).

Dose, or Extent of Exposure

One study involving 2516 male and female middle and high school students in the U.S. showed that females were significantly more likely to read articles about dieting and weight loss compared to males (44% and 14% respectively) and that females read articles about dieting and weight loss regardless of their weight status (van den Berg, Paxton, et al., 2007). Some studies have further shown that the overall amount of media consumed is not related to body dissatisfaction, but that other factors such as the type of TV genre (Tiggemann, 2005) or the extent of identification with the models presented in the media (Bell & Dittmar, 2011) were more influential. This was further replicated in a study of adolescent social media use—where the overall amount of time spent on Facebook did not impact any of the measures of wellbeing, but the appearance-related interactions, such as posting, viewing, and commenting on photos and profile pictures was associated with greater weight dissatisfaction, drive for thinness, thin-ideal internalisation, and self-objectification (Meier & Gray, 2013).

Media Type

Research has also revealed that the type of media used in experimental studies may moderate the effects. In an Australian study, total amount of time spent reading fashion magazines was linked more strongly to body dissatisfaction, internalisation and drive for thinness among adolescent girls and young women; whereas the total amount of time viewing TV was not (Tiggemann, 2003, 2005). Other research has found a stronger impact of particular TV genres, such as soap operas, on internalisation and body dissatisfaction among children aged 6 to 9 years in the Netherlands (Anschutz, Engels, van Leeuwe, & van Strien, 2009), and adolescent boys and girls in Australia (Tiggemann, 2005). Music videos have also been found to be particularly potent (Mulgrew et al., 2014; Tiggemann & Slater, 2004). However, in experiments in the U.K. where researchers tested the impact of exposure to either a music video or still images from that music video, it was found there was no difference on the impact on body dissatisfaction (Bell & Dittmar, 2011). It is assumed that video games are an influential media type for adolescent boys; however, the research to date has only tested the impact of these among college-aged men (Barlett & Harris, 2008).

Individual Levels of Body Dissatisfaction

Adolescent girls with higher initial levels of body dissatisfaction are known to be the most vulnerable to exposure to ideal media images (Posavac, Posavac, & Posavac, 1998; Stice et al., 2001). Those adolescent girls who have higher trait body dissatisfaction experience the greatest increases in state body satisfaction during experimental exposure to media images (Bell & Dittmar, 2011). Research has also shown that young girls with high levels of body dissatisfaction are more likely to consume thin-focused media and to make upward social comparisons that compound the negative impact of the media (Lopez-Guimera, Levine, Sanchez-Carracedo, & Fauquet, 2010).

Researchers in Sweden have investigated this from a different angle and asked young boys and girls with positive body image about their media ideals. In this interview study, young people with high body satisfaction were able to articulate the nature of the idealised images that are used, and the reasons marketers might use them, demonstrating media literacy. They were critical of the narrow definition of beauty that is portrayed in the media and emphasised the importance of 'looking like oneself'. This study demonstrates the potential for young people to have increased resistance against the impact of media images if they have a higher body image, which provides a strong rationale for programs to improve this construct (Holmqvist & Frisén, 2012).

Conclusion

The nature of the media and opportunities for interaction with the media is changing constantly. Research investigating the impact of the media on body image and body dissatisfaction of adolescents has had some varied results over the past 20 years, and it is not clear whether male adolescents are affected to the same extent as females. However, overall media seem to have a negative impact. Given that we now have good evidence of the negative impact of the media on this aspect of psychological wellbeing and the near impossibility of avoiding exposure to all forms of the media, it makes sense that we target the media itself and the way that young people consume and critique the media, to ensure that we can reduce harm to young people.

Reference

All Party Parliamentary Group [APPG]. (2012). Reflections on body image. Report of the All Party Parliamentary Group. Retrieved from http://www.ymca.co.uk/bodyimage/report.

American Medical Association [AMA]. (2011). AMA adopts new policies at annual meeting. Retrieved from http://www.ama-assn.org/ama/pub/news/news/a11-new-policies.page.

British Broadcasting Corporation [BBC]. (2012). Israel passes law banning use of underweight models. Retrieved from http://www.bbc.co.uk/news/world-middle-east-17450275.

Anderson, A.E., & Holman, J.E. (1997). Males with eating disorders: Challenges for treatment and research. *Psychopharmacology Bulletin, 33*(3), 391–97.

Anschutz, D.J., Engels, R.C., van Leeuwe, J., & van Strien, T. (2009). Watching your weight? The relations between watching soaps and music television and body dissatisfaction and restrained eating in young girls. *Psychology and Health, 24*(9), 1035–50.

Barlett, C.P., & Harris, R.J. (2008). The impact of body emphasizing video games on body image concerns in men and women. *Sex Roles, 59*, 586–601.

Barlett, C.P., Vowels, C.L., & Saucier, D.A. (2008). Meta-analyses of the effects of media images on men's body-image concerns. *Journal of Social and Clinical Psychology, 27*(3), 279–310.

Becker, A.E., Burwell, R.A., Gilman, S.E., Herzog, D., & Hamburg, P. (2002). Eating behaviours and attitudes following prolonged exposure to television among ethnic Fijian adolescent girls. *British Journal of Psychiatry, 180*, 509–14.

Becker, A.E., Fay, K.E., Agnew-Blais, J., Khan, A.N., Striegel-Moore, R.H., & Gilman, S.E. (2011). Social network media exposure and adolescent eating pathology in Fiji. *The British Journal of Psychiatry, 198*, 43–50.

Bell, B.T., & Dittmar, H. (2011). Does media type matter? The role of identification in adolescent girls' media consumption and the impact of different thin-ideal media on body image. *Sex Roles, 65*, 478–90.

Brown, J.D., & Bobkowski, P.S. (2011). Older and newer media: Patterns of use and effects on adolescents' health and well-being. *Journal of Research on Adolescence, 21*(1), 95–113.

Campbell, M. (2013). Cosmopolitan magazine's 'size hero' campaign makes zero sense. *The Guardian.*

D'Alessandro, S., & Chitty, B. (2011). Real or relevant beauty? Body shape and endorser effects on brand attitude and body image. *Psychology and Marketing, 28*(8), 843–78.

Diedrichs, P.C., & Lee, C. (2010). GI Joe or Average Joe? The impact of average-size and muscular male fashion models on men's and women's body image and advertising effectiveness. *Body Image, 7*(3), 218–26.

Diedrichs, P.C., & Lee, C. (2011). Waif goodbye! Average-size female models promote positive body image and appeal to consumers. *Psychology and Health, 26*(10), 127–391.

Diedrichs, P., Lee, C., & Kelly, M. (2011). Seeing the beauty in everyday people: A qualitative study of young Australians opinions on body image, the mass media and models. *Body Image, 8*, 259–66.

Dittmar, H., & Howard, S. (2004). Professional hazards? The impact of models' body size on advertising effectiveness and women's body-focused anxiety in professions that do and do not emphasise the cultural ideal of thinness. *British Journal of Social Psychology, 43*, 477–97.

Durkin, S., & Paxton, S. (2002). Predictors of vulnerability to reduced body image satisfaction and psychological wellbeing in response to exposure to idealized female media images in adolescent girls. *Journal of Psychiatric Research, 53*, 995–1005.

Egbert, N., & Belcher, J.D. (2012). Reality Bites: An investigation of the genre of reality television and its relationship to viewers' body image. *Mass Communication and Society, 15*, 407–31.

Farquhar, J.C., & Wasylkiw, L. (2007). Media images of men: Trends and consequences of body conceptualization. *Psychology of Men and Masculinity, 8*, 145–160.

Ferguson, C.J., Munoz, M.E., Garza, A., & Galindo, M. (In Press). Concurrent and prospective analyses of peer, television, and social media influences on body dissatisfaction, eating disorder symptoms and life satisfaction. *Journal of Youth and Adolescence.*

Ferguson, C.J., Salmond, K., & Modi, K. (2013). Reality television predicts both positive and negative outcomes for adolescent girls. *The Journal of Pediatrics, 162*(6), 1175–80.

Field, A.E., Camargo, C.A., Taylor, C.B., Berkey, C.S., Roberts, S.B., & Colditz, G.A. (2001). Peer, parent and media influences on the development of weight concerns and frequent dieting among preadolescent and adolescent girls and boys. *Pediatrics, 107*, 54–60.

Gibson, M. (2012). Thinterest? When social networks and body image collide. *Time Magazine.*

Grabe, S., Ward, M.L., & Hyde, J.S. (2008). The role of the media in body image concerns among women: A meta-analysis of experimental and correlational studies. *Psychological Bulletin, 134*(3), 460–76.

Groesz, L., Levine, M., & Murnen, S.K. (2002). The effect of experimental presentation of thin media images on body satisfaction: a meta-analytic review. *International Journal of Eating Disorders, 31*, 1–16.

Haferkamp, N., & Krämer, N.C. (2011). Social comparison 2.0: Examining the effects of online profiles on social-networking sites. *Cyberpsychology, Behavior, and Social Networking, 14*(5), 309–14.

Hargreaves, D.A., & Tiggemann, M. (2004). Idealized media images and adolescent body image: "comparing" boys and girls. *Body Image, 1*(4), 351–61.

Holmqvist, K., & Frisén, A. (2012). "I bet they aren't perfect in reality" Appearance ideals viewed from the perspective of adolescents with a positive body image. *Body Image, 9*, 388–95.

Holmstrom, A. (2004). The effects of the media on body image: A meta-analysis. *Journal of Broadcasting & Electronic Media, 48*(2), 196–217.

Humphreys, P., & Paxton, S. (2004). Impact of exposure to idealised male images on adolescent boys' body image. *Body Image, 1*, 253–66.

Labre, M.P. (2005). Burn fat, build muscle: A content analysis of men's health and men's fitness. *International Journal of Men's Health, 4*(2), 187–200.

Law, C., & Labre, M.P. (2002). Cultural standards of attractiveness: A thirty-year look at changes in male images in magazines. *Journalism and Mass Communication Quarterly, 90*(2), 697–711.

Lee, H.-R., Lee, H.E., Choi, J., Hyun, K., & Han, L. (2014). Social media use, body image, and psychological wellbeing: A cross-cultural comparison of Korea and the United States. *Journal of Health Communication*. doi: 10.1080/10810730.2014.904022.

Leit, R.A., Pope Jr., H.G., & Gray, J.J. (1999). Cultural expectations of muscularity in the evolution of playgirl centrefolds. *International Journal of Eating Disorders, 29*, 90–93.

Lenhart, A., Kahne, J., Middaugh, E., Macgill, A.R., Evans, C., & Vitak, J. (2008). Teens, video games, and civics. Washington, DC: Pew Internet & American Life Project.

Levine, M., & Murnen, S. K. (2009). "Everybody knows that mass media are/are not [pick one] a cause of eating disorders": A critical review of evidence for a causal link between media, negative body image, and disordered eating in females. *Journal of Social and Clinical Psychology, 28*, 9–42.

Lopez-Guimera, G., Levine, M.P., Sanchez-Carracedo, D., & Fauquet, J. (2010). Influence of mass media on body image and eating disordered attitudes and behaviors in females: A review of effects and processes. *Media Psychology, 13*(4), 387–416.

Mabe, A.G., Forney, K.J., & Keel, P.K. (In Press). Do you "like" my photo? Facebook use maintains eating disorder risk. *International Journal of Eating Disorders*.

Martin, M.C., & Gentry, J.W. (1997). Stuck in the model trap: The effects of beautiful models in ads on female pre-adolescents and adolescents. *Journal of Advertising, 26*, 19-33.

Martins, N., Williams, D.C., Ratan, R.A., & Harrison, K. (2010). Virtual muscularity: A content analysis of male video game characters. *Body Image, 8*, 43–51.

Meier, E.P., & Gray, J. (2013). Facebook photo activity associated with body image disturbance in adolescent girls. *Cyberpsychology, Behavior, and Social Networking, 17*(4), 199–206.

Morrison, T.G., & Halton, M. (2009). Buff, tough, and rough: Representations of muscularity in action motion pictures. *The Journal of Men's Studies, 17*, 57–74.

Mulgrew, K.E., Volcevski-Kostas, D., & Rendell, P.G. (2014). The effect of music video clips on adolescent boys' body image, mood, and schema activation. *Journal of Youth and Adolescence, 43*, 92–103.

Pope, H.G.J., Olivardia, R., Gruber, A.J., & Borowiecki, J.J. (1999). Evolving ideals of male body image as seen through action toys. *International Journal of Eating Disorders, 26*, 65–72.

Posavac, H.D., Posavac, S.S., & Posavac, E.J. (1998). Exposure to media images of female attractiveness and concern with body weight among young women. *Sex Roles, 38*, 187–201.

Ricciardelli, L.A., & Williams, R.J. (2012). Beauty over the centuries-Male. In T. Cash (Ed), *Encyclopedia of body image and human appearance (Vol 1., pp. 50–57). London: Elsevier.*

Ricciardelli, L.A., & McCabe, M.P. (2004). A biopsychosocial model of disordered eating and the pursuit of muscularity in adolescent boys. *Psychological Bulletin, 130*, 179–205.

Rideout, V., Foehr, U. G., & Roberts, D. F. (2010). *Generation M2: Media in the lives of 8–18 year-olds.* Menlo Park, CA: The Henry J. Kaiser Family Foundation.

Schulze, E., & Gray, J. (1990). The effects of popular and textbook presentations of bulimia nervosa on attitudes toward bulimia nervosa and individuals with bulimia nervosa. *British Review of Bulimia & Anorexia Nervosa, 4*, 83–91.

Silberstein, L.R., Striegel-Moore, R., Timko, C., & Rodin, J. (1988). Behavioural and psychological implications of body dissatisfaction: Do men and women differ? *Sex Roles: A Journal of Research, 19*(3/4), 219–32.

Slater, A., Tiggemann, M., Hawkins, K., & Werchon, D. (2011). Just one click: A content analysis of advertisements on teen web sites. *Journal of Adolescent Health, 50*(4), 399–45.

Spitzer, B.L., Henderson, K.A., & Zivian, M.T. (1999). Gender differences in population versus media body sizes: A comparison over four decades. *Sex Roles, 40*(7–8), 545–55.

Spitznagal, E. (2013). How those Dove 'Real Beauty Sketches' went viral. *Bloomberg Businessweek.* Retrieved from http://www.businessweek.com/articles/2013-04-26/ how-those-dove-real-beauty-sketch-ads-went-viral.

Stice, E., Spangler, D., & Agras, W.S. (2001). Exposure to media-portrayed thin-ideal images adversely affects vulnerable girls: A longitudinal experiment. *Journal of Social and Clinical Psychology, 20*(3), 270–88.

Strano, M. (2008). User descriptions and interpretations of self-presentation through Facebook profile images. *Cyber Psychology: Journal of Psychology in Cyberspace, 2*(2).

Subrahmanyam, K., & Lin, G. (2007). Adolescents on the net: Internet use and well-being. *Adolescence, 42,* 659–77.

Sypeck, M., Gray, J.J., & Ahrens, A.H. (2004). No longer just a pretty face: Fashion magazines' depictions of ideal female beauty from 1959 to 1999. *International Journal of Eating Disorders, 36,* 342–47.

Thomsen, S.R., McCoy, J.K., & Williams, M. (2001). Internalizing the impossible: Anorexic outpatients' experiences with women's beauty and fashion magazines. *Eating Disorders: The Journal of Treatment & Prevention, 9*(1), 49–64.

Thompson, J.K., & Heinberg, L.J. (1999). The media's influence on body image disturbance and eating disorders: We've reviled them, now can we rehabilitate them? *Journal of Social Issues, 55*(2), 339–53.

Tiggemann, M. (2003). Media exposure, body dissatisfaction and disordered eating: Television and magazines are not the same! *European Eating Disorder Review, 11,* 418–30.

Tiggemann, M. (2005). Television and adolescent body image: The role of program content and viewing motivation. *Journal of Social and Clinical Psychology, 24*(3), 361–81.

Tiggemann, M., & Miller, J. (2010). The Internet and adolescent girls' weight satisfaction and drive for thinness. *Sex Roles, 63*(1–2), 79–90.

Tiggemann, M., & Slater, A. (2004). Thin ideals in music television: A source of social comparison and body dissatisfaction. *International Journal of Eating Disorders, 35*, 48–58.

Tiggemann, M., & Slater, A. (2013). NetGirls: The Internet, Facebook, and body image concern in adolescent girls. *International Journal of Eating Disorders, 46*, 630–33.

Valkenburg, P.M., Peter, J., & Schouten, A. (2006). Friend networking sites and their relationship to adolescents' well-being and social self-esteem. *Cyberpsychology & Behavior, 9*(5), 584–90.

van den Berg, P., Neumark-Sztainer, D., Hannan, P. J., & Haines, J. (2007). Is dieting advice from magazines helpful or harmful? Five-year associations with weight-control behaviors and psychological outcomes in adolescents. *Pediatrics, 119*, 30–37.

van den Berg, P., Paxton, S., Keery, H., Wall, M.M., HGuo, J., & Neumark-Sztainer, D. (2007). Body dissatisfaction and body comparison with media images in males and females. *Body Image, 4*, 257–68.

Vandenbosch, L., & Eggermont, S. (2013). Sexualization of adolescent boys: Media exposure and boys' internalization of appearance ideals, self-objectification, and body-surveillance. *Men and Masculinities*.

Veldhuis, J., Konijin, E.A., & Seidell, J.C. (2014). Negotiated media effects. Peer feedback modifies effects of media's thin-body ideal on adolescent girls. *Appetite, 73*, 172–82.

Villani, S. (2001). Impact of media on children and adolescents: A 10-year review of the research. *Journal of the American Academy of Child and Adolescent Psychiatry, 40*(4), 392–401.

Vincent, M.A., & McCabe, M.P. (2000). Gender differences among adolescents in family, and peer influences on body dissatisfaction, weight loss, and binge eating behaviors. *Journal of Youth and Adolescence, 29*, 205–21.

6

PEER INFLUENCES ON BODY IMAGE

Peers play an influential role in adolescent body image and appearance concerns. Early research established that the influence of peers overtakes that of parents during adolescence (Coleman, 1980), and a meta-analysis found that the influence of peers was stronger than the influence of family on body dissatisfaction (Quiles Marcos, Quiles Sebastian, Pamies Aubalat, Botella Ausina, & Treasure, 2013). Peers are children or adolescents at the same age or maturity level, and they play a range of roles, such as to provide direct and indirect guidance as to what is 'acceptable and appropriate' (Rayner, Schniering, Rapee, & Hutchinson, 2013). In terms of body image, peer groups exert their influence through the establishment of norms and reinforcement of societal ideals through pressure, social comparisons, appearance-based conversations, and teasing.

Peer influence in adolescence has been found to vary according to age and gender. A large U.S. study revealed that resistance to peer influences is at its lowest in early adolescence (ages 10 to 14) but undergoes a peak period of development in mid-adolescence (14 to 18 years), meaning that younger adolescents are more likely to conform to the overt influence of peers and friends (Steinberg & Monahan, 2007). A German study found that the transition from seventh to eighth grade was a peak time for the indirect influences of appearance-related pressure such as peer norms and modelling (Helfert & Warschburger, 2013). A meta-analysis of peer and family effects on body dissatisfaction and eating disorders reported that although only 25% of the studies reviewed included boys, gender did not moderate the influence of peers on body dissatisfaction, but there was a gender difference in the impact on dieting behaviour (Quiles-Marcos et al., 2013). However, some other work suggests that the appearance-related influence of peers is stronger for girls than for boys (Helfert & Warschburger, 2013). In one study, girls reported significantly higher levels of peer teasing about appearance, exclusion on the basis of appearance, modelling of appearance standards by friends, and perceptions of appearance-related school and class norms (Helfert & Warschburger, 2013). Gender differences in the influence of peers may relate to differences in the nature of peer interactions for girls and boys. For example, girls' friendships compared with boys' are likely to be more emotionally supportive, more intense, and more intimate, with girls spending more time in quiet, small group activities and boys spending more time in structured, competitive games and sports (Rose & Rudolph, 2006).

In this chapter, we provide an overview of the research that has examined the direct and indirect influence of peers and friends. Direct influences include peer pressure and appearance-based teasing, and indirect influences include peer group norms and social comparisons.

Peer Pressure

Peer pressure refers to the influence young people have on each other's attitudes and behaviours, mostly through a desire to conform. At times, peer pressure has been defined as the direct or overt pressure to do something. In constructing their Peer Pressure Inventory, Brown and colleagues (1986) defined peer pressure as "when people your own age encourage you to do something or to keep from doing something else, no matter if you personally want to or not" (p. 522). For example, young people might directly encourage their peers to go on diets to see who can lose the most weight or to start using protein powder. Peer pressure is also sometimes referred to as the subjective feeling that we should or should not do certain things due to the influence of others (Brown, Clasen, & Elcher, 1986; Santor, Messervey, & Kusumaker, 2000). For example, young people might feel the need to engage in fat-talk and express body dissatisfaction because their peers are doing so and due to the perception that individuals need to behave in certain ways in order to 'fit in' with the group (Reed & Wilcox Rountree, 1997). Peer pressure to be thin or muscular may therefore be derived indirectly from peer comments that perpetuate societal beauty ideals or more direct encouragement to engage in weight change behaviours (Blowers, Loxton, Grady-Flesser, Occhipinti, & Dawe, 2003). These overt and covert mechanisms are important in communicating group norms (Lieberman, Gauvin, Bukowski, & White, 2001).

Adolescent Socialisation Theory (Kandel, 1980), based on Social Learning Theory (Bandura, 1989) describes two processes by which peer pressure influences adolescent behaviour. The first is by modelling, where peers observe direct demonstration of attitudes and behaviours and then imitate them (Kandel, 1980). In relation to body image, these attitudes might include communication of negative attitudes towards certain body shapes and weights and overt demonstrations of body dissatisfaction. 'Fat talk', social comparisons, and weight change behaviours such as dietary restraint, binging, vomiting, and exercise might also be observed and replicated by adolescents (Stice, 1998). The second process, social reinforcement, relates to the provision of rewards to those who conform to group norms and pressure and undesirable consequences to those who don't (Kandel, 1980; Lieberman et al., 2001) and is discussed in the next section.

Several studies have shown a positive correlation between perceived peer pressure and body image concerns among adolescents. Lieberman and colleagues (2001) found that perception of peer pressure was correlated with measures of body esteem and eating behaviours. Girls who endorsed the belief that they would be more popular with their peers if they were thinner and more attractive had lower body esteem (Lieberman et al., 2001). Similarly, higher perceived pressure from peers, parents, and the media correlated with higher levels of body dissatisfaction among 16-year-old girls and boys (Peterson, Paulson, & Williams, 2007) and higher levels of body dissatisfaction and dietary restraint amongst adolescent girls (Dunkley, Wertheim, & Paxton, 2001). The latter study also found that peers made the greatest contribution towards girls' perceived pressure to be thin when their actual size was accounted for. In relation to gender, a recent study of young adolescents found that girls compared with boys perceived greater levels of peer pressure to be thin and were more likely to be influenced by modelling of peer behaviours to change weight (Helfert & Warschburger, 2013). However, some other studies comparing the strength of the different sociocultural influences have failed to find a relationship between peer pressure and body image concerns. For example, Blowers et al. (2003) found that perceived pressure from the media was the only sociocultural factor to correlate with internalisation of the thin ideal.

Peer Group Norms

Peer group norms refer to the "informal norms that groups adopt to regulate and regularise group members' behaviour" (Feldman, 1984, p. 47). Ideas about the 'ideal body' are generated, communicated, and reinforced through group norms in the peer context (Lawlor & Nixon, 2011; Lieberman et al., 2001; Thompson et al., 2007). For example, a group of girls might leave one of their peer group members out of the preparations for a dance performance, as she is not deemed to be thin enough to fit into the costumes that they have planned. This communicates the group norm that thinness is preferred, exerting indirect pressure on all group members to conform to a certain weight and shape, and to discriminate against people at larger weights. These norms are reinforced through the demonstration of a negative outcome for those who are larger, by ostracising them from the group.

In one of the first comprehensive studies to demonstrate adherence to peer group norms, Paxton et al. (1999) found that friendship cliques of 15-year-old girls shared similar levels of body image concerns, dietary restraint, and use of extreme weight-loss behaviours. Furthermore, perceived group attitudes and behaviours toward weight-related concerns predicted the behaviour of individual members. Another interesting finding to emerge was that girls within friendship groups were very similar to one another with respect to body mass index, depression and self-esteem, suggesting that "friendship-group similarities go deeper than shared behaviours to similar beliefs of self-worth and mood" (Paxton et al., 1999, p. 263).

Peer Social Comparisons

Another indirect way that peers may exert an indirect influence is through social comparisons. Social comparisons are likely to begin in preadolescence, and contribute to both global self-evaluations and specific self-evaluations, such as academic performance (Blowers et al., 2003; Fraser, Sproal, & Ricciardelli, 2010; Holt & Ricciardelli, 2002). Social comparisons involve the assessment of one's own characteristics in relation to the characteristics of others, and can explain how individuals evaluate their own attributes and behaviours (Buunk & Gibbons, 2007). The main purpose of social comparisons is to evaluate or to enhance some aspect of the self (Suls, Martin, & Wheeler, 2002). In particular, individuals utilise social comparisons when they need to reduce uncertainty about their abilities, performance, and other attributes, and when they need to rely on external standards against which to judge themselves (White, Langer, Yariv, & Welch, 2006). Some researchers argue that social comparisons are integral to 'fat-talk' and appearance conversations (Corning & Gondoli, 2012).

A recent meta-analysis has found a moderate effect for the impact of social comparisons with peers on body image (Myers & Crowther, 2009). The impact of social comparisons was stronger for women than for men (Cohen's $d = .83$; and $d = .54$, respectively), and was moderated by age, such that effect sizes were stronger in studies reporting a younger participant mean age. The mean age of participants in studies included in the analysis ranged from 11.12-32.70, suggesting that impacts are greater for adolescents. The meta-analysis also showed that social comparisons with familiar peers had the largest impact on body image (d = .87), followed by unfamiliar peers (d = .79), and thin images in the media (d = .75).

In relation to adolescent girls in particular, other studies have shown a strong association between appearance-related social comparisons and body image (Halliwell & Harvey, 2006; Jones, 2004) and the relative importance of peer comparisons compared with television and social media comparisons (Ferguson, Munoz, Garza, & Galindo, 2014). In the latter study, comprising predominantly Hispanic adolescent girls, peer competition, defined as feelings of insecurity compared to other girls, was reported to more strongly predict body dissatisfaction and disordered eating when compared with the influence of social media and television.

Interestingly, many studies have shown that appearance-related social comparisons are not associated with body image concerns among boys and young men (Humphreys & Paxton, 2004; Jones, 2004; Ricciardelli, McCabe, & Banfield, 2000). This reflects a general trend in the literature, in which many of the relationships found among girls and women are not reported among boys and men (Ricciardelli & McCabe, 2004). Two studies have shown that adolescent boys engage in fewer appearance-related social comparisons than adolescent girls (Jones, 2004; Ricciardelli et al., 2000) and in the latter study, almost half of the boys interviewed stated that they did not make social comparisons. Moreover, most of the boys who made social comparisons reported feeling more positive or neutral about their body. These studies suggest that the nature of boys' social comparisons with peers is likely to differ to that of girls.

Appearance-Related Peer Teasing

Teasing by peers increases dramatically during early adolescence, and is both a common and challenging aspect of peer relations (Jones, Newman & Bautista, 2005). Given the importance of peer acceptance, and the friendship and peer group changes during adolescence, peer teasing has been described as an especially salient and critical aspect of the adolescent experience (Jones, Newman, & Bautista, 2005). Some have defined teasing as a form of personal communication, directed by an agent toward a target, which combines elements of aggression, humour, and ambiguity (Hayden-Wade et al., 2005). In relation to body image and appearance concerns, appearance-related teasing has been considered a form of peer pressure; however, it has also been studied as a construct in its own right. Regarding gender, some studies report that adolescent girls are more likely to receive negative comments about weight and shape (Vincent & McCabe, 2000), while others have found that adolescent boys perceive appearance-related teasing at levels similar to or higher than females (Jones & Crawford, 2005; Jones & Crawford, 2006).

Considerable cross-sectional and longitudinal work has demonstrated a relationship between teasing and body image, but the extent and nature of this relationship in boys and girls continues to be debated. A meta-analysis examining teasing and body dissatisfaction in both boys and girls found a moderate correlation between teasing and body dissatisfaction in children and adolescents ($d = .41$) and a slightly weaker association in adults ($d = .32$) (Menzel et al., 2010). Some cross-sectional studies have found a positive correlation between appearance-related peer criticism or teasing and body dissatisfaction among adolescent boys (Barker & Galambos, 2003; Jones, 2004; Smolak & Stein, 2006) and girls (Paxton, Schutz, Wertheim, & Muir, 1999). For example, one study found that weight-related teasing was the only significant risk factor for boys, and was one of three risk factors for adolescent girls' body dissatisfaction (Barker & Galambos, 2003). The relationship between peer teasing and body dissatisfaction is considered to be well-established among preadolescent girls and boys in the cross-sectional literature (Gardner, Sorter, & Friedman, 1997).

Some longitudinal studies indicate that teasing is significant in the development of body dissatisfaction; however, others are in disagreement. An early study among adolescent girls reported that teasing predicted appearance dissatisfaction at three-year post-test (Cattarin & Thompson, 1994). Some prospective studies found that the amount of weight related teasing experienced by boys and girls predicted future body dissatisfaction (Barker & Galambos, 2003), and others reported that this relationship was only significant for girls (Cattarin & Thompson, 1994; Paxton et al., 1999). Other studies have found that teasing did not predict body dissatisfaction among girls (Helfert & Warschburger, 2011; Jones, 2004; Stice & Whitendon, 2002; Wojtowicz & von Ranson, 2012) or boys (Helfert & Warschburger, 2011; Jones, 2004). Those who are teased about their weight, body shape, and appearance tend to develop higher levels of body dissatisfaction, and are also more likely to diet (Lieberman et al., 2001).

In Project EAT, a large longitudinal study in the U.S., the cross-sectional and longitudinal findings were inconsistent. Weight-related teasing was correlated with concurrent lower self-esteem and body dissatisfaction, and higher depression amongst adolescent boys and girls in the cross sectional work (Eisenberg, Neumark-Sztainer, & Paxton, 2006). However weight-related teasing did not predict body dissatisfaction five years later (Paxton, Eisenberg, & Neumark-Sztainer, 2006). Interestingly, weight-related teasing did correlate with later body dissatisfaction amongst 12-year-old, but not 15-year-old boys. The authors argued that different influences may affect girls and boys, and that changes in the peer environment across middle and late adolescence may weaken peer influences on changes in body dissatisfaction (Paxton, Eisenberg, & Neumark-Sztainer, 2006). Studies that examine the nature of these differences are now needed.

Larger children are a particular concern as they are already vulnerable to high levels of body dissatisfaction, and are more likely to be targets of appearance-related peer teasing. In a U.S. study of 10- to 14-year-old children, Hayden-Wade et al. (2005) found that 78% of overweight children versus 37.2% of non-overweight children reported having been teased or criticised about some aspect of their appearance. Overweight children also experienced weight-related teasing more than non-overweight children (89.1% vs. 31.3%), found teasing to be more upsetting, and reported that teasing occurred for longer periods of time, than non-overweight children. Similarly, a Swedish study found that 10-year-old girls and boys who expressed beliefs about being 'too fat' reported greater frequencies of peer victimisation (Frisén & Anneheden, 2014). There is a clear consensus amongst cross-sectional studies from around the world regarding the relationship between weight and bullying: adolescents who have higher BMI's, or who are overweight, are significantly more likely to be the target of bullying (Brixval, Rayce, Rasmussen, Holstein, & Due, 2011; Helfert & Warschburger, 2013). In a large Danish study of 4781 adolescents aged 11–15 years, significantly more males and females who reported being the target of bullying were overweight or obese (Brixval et al., 2011). Furthermore, the relationship between weight status and bullying was mediated by body image and body dissatisfaction (Brixval et al., 2011; Fox & Farrow, 2009). Being teased about weight in particular has also been correlated with low self-esteem, depression, and suicide ideation (Eisenberg, Neumark-Sztainer, & Story, 2003).

Studies investigating the impact of teasing often neglect the potential influence of vicarious teasing. Jones and Crawford (2006) suggest that vicarious teasing is another means by which the norms and expectations regarding appearance ideals are shared among peers. Social Learning Theory suggests that the experiences of others can provide important information and learning for the self (Bandura, 1986). When adolescents witness others being teased about aspects of their appearance, they learn that their peers view and critique the appearance of others, and that some attributes are desirable while others are the subject of ridicule (Jones & Crawford, 2006).

In a qualitative study of girls attending Australian private schools, Carey and colleagues (2010) described the prevailing presence of 'weight gossip'. For example, one participant explained: "*I can't think of anyone that I know who's that nasty to go up to someone and say something ... but yeah, I think we do, we do definitely [gossip about weight behind people's backs] ... it's all about teenagers gossiping about each other*" (p.14) (Carey, Donaghue, & Broderick). Although the girls interviewed indicated that most comments were eventually reported to the person in question, the culture of weight gossip resulted in a strong awareness that weight and appearance is noticed and judged, which reinforced the understanding that one's weight is crucial in obtaining status within the school (Carey et al.). While the impact of vicarious teasing is likely to be different to that of the criticisms that adolescents might experience personally, it is still thought to contribute very strongly to the development and reinforcement of peer norms, expectations, and interpretations of the societal ideal. This is an area of peer influence on body image that warrants further attention.

Appearance-Based Conversations

The conversations that peers have about bodies, weight and appearance can have a significant influence on body image. Jones and Crawford (2006) define conversations about appearance as "verbal exchanges that focus attention on general appearance-related issues, reinforce the value and importance of appearance to close friends, and promote the construction of appearance ideals" (p. 258). This may take the form of direct comments and criticisms about one's own or others' bodies, discussions about body change strategies, such as dieting or muscle building strategies, and 'fat talk'. Appearance-based conversations establish the particular expectations and norms for peer group members, define the 'ideal image' and set the parameters for what is acceptable and what is unacceptable. In an U.S. study, Jones (2004) found that appearance conversations with friends predicted increases in girls' body dissatisfaction one year later (mediated by social comparisons), but the relationship was not significant for boys. An Irish study of adolescents (mean age of 16 years) also found a positive correlation between appearance conversations and body dissatisfaction for girls, but not boys (Lawlor & Nixon, 2011). This work supports the idea that girls, compared with boys, are more invested in the appearance culture and the formulation of peer-referenced appearance goals from an earlier age.

The concept of fat talk was first described in the early 1990s by Nichter and Vuchovic (1994) and refers to 'ritualised derogatory talk' focusing on body, weight, and shape. Fat talk is generally undertaken by girls and women about their own appearance. An example is provided by Corning and Gondoli (2012):

"FIRST FRIEND: My arms are so fat and flabby; no matter what I do, they are so embarrassing.

SECOND FRIEND: At least you can wear a regular bathing suit to the pool. I have to wear long shorts to cover my huge thighs" (Corning & Gondoli, 2012, p. 529).

Corning and Gondoli (2012) suggest that the subtext communicated is:

"FIRST FRIEND: I believe my arms are worse than other women's.

SECOND FRIEND: "I too am below an acceptable standard of attractiveness and, in my case, it is because of my thighs, which are a worse problem than your arms" (p. 529).

A meta-analysis of the impact of fat talk also found that fat talk predicted body dissatisfaction in longitudinal studies with children, adolescents, and adults (Sharpe, Naumann, Treasure, & Schmidt, 2013). This study also found a small positive association between fat talk and body dissatisfaction in adolescents and a large one for adults but no relationship in children (Sharpe et al., 2013). Fat talk and appearance-related conversations are influential as they remind adolescents of the importance of appearance and help to build and reinforce peer norms for body image and weight change attitudes and behaviours (Jones, 2004; Lawlor & Nixon, 2011). Corning and Gondoli (2012) have also argued that fat talk is a verbalisation of female social comparisons to peers.

The relatively greater influence of appearance-related conversations for girls compared with boys could be due to the fact that girls engage in such conversations more frequently. In a study of both adolescent boys and girls, those who reported increased appearance-related conversations were more likely to report increased body dissatisfaction (Jones, 2004). Some studies have shown that, amongst adolescents, girls engage in more appearance-related talk than boys (Jones, Vigfusdottir, & Lee, 2004; Vincent & McCabe, 2000). Vincent and McCabe (2000) found that girls were more likely than boys to discuss weight loss with peers; however, they did not measure the frequency of conversations about muscle building or other appearance-related activities relevant to boys. Others have found that males engage in more conversations about muscle-building, than females engage in conversations about dieting, which can be equally as negative (Jones & Crawford, 2006). Finally, Jones and Crawford (2006) found that conversations about dieting or muscle building were more common among adolescents with higher BMI and among adolescents in 10th grade (15 to 16 years old) compared with those in 7th grade (12 to 13 years old).

Appearance may be a natural focus of conversation among adolescents; however, the content and intent of appearance-related conversations appear to have negative impacts for body image, eating, and exercise behaviour, particularly among girls. Such conversations may overtly and covertly convey peer norms and encourage negative social comparisons. More research is needed to fully understand this phenomenon, and resources to reduce the negative impact of appearance related conversations are urgently required.

The Influence of Friends

Although much of the research has focused on the influence of peers, some research has specifically examined the influence of friends on body image. Friends differ from peers in that they have a closer association, including a higher degree of exclusivity and confidence, and the evidence for the influence of friends on body image concerns is inconclusive.

Cross-sectional studies show a relationship between body image and friend-related influences. For example, the perceived weight-related attitudes and behaviour of a best friend (e.g., "I think my best friend tries to lose weight") was related to body dissatisfaction in a study among girls in the U.K. aged 9 to 12 years (Sands & Wardle, 2003). Also, more frequent appearance-related conversations with friends was related to greater internalised appearance ideals and body dissatisfaction in a study among 12- and 14-year-old girls and boys in the U.S. (Jones, Vigfusdottir, & Lee, 2004). In another American study, a range of measures that assessed 'friend pressure' (i.e., perceived friend preoccupation with weight and dieting and appearance conversations with friends) was associated with body dissatisfaction among 14-year-old girls (Shroff & Thompson, 2006).

In contrast, longitudinal studies suggest that friends do not influence body dissatisfaction. van den Berg et al. (2007) found that dieting by friends did not predict later body dissatisfaction in either adolescent boys or girls in the U.S.-based Project EAT (van den Berg, Neumark-Sztainer, Hannan, & Haines, 2007). Similarly, in another study among 13-year-old girls in the Netherlands, initial levels of body dissatisfaction within the friendship group did not predict body image and dieting one year later (Woelders, Larsen, Scholte, Cillessen, & Engels, 2010). Furthermore, in a large longitudinal study among Australian girls aged 12 to 13 years, Rayner et al. (2013) found that friend-related influences did not predict dieting and bulimic behaviours or changes in body dissatisfaction over time. Only one study has found that friend dieting predicted body dissatisfaction five years later among 12-year-old girls (Eisenberg, Neumark-Sztainer, & Paxton, 2006). However, this relationship was not found among 12-year-old boys or among the 15-year-olds, thus highlighting the need to more closely examine differences according to gender and age (Paxton et al., 2006). More research is needed to differentially examine the effects of friends versus peers. Such research will require the development of alternatives to self-report and survey methods in order to accurately identify differences in peer and friend influences.

A number of studies has also used social network analysis to investigate body dissatisfaction and disordered eating in relation to friendship groups. In these studies, adolescent girls have been asked to identify their 'best friends' or the girls belonging to their friendship group. An early study utilising this method found that Australian girls aged 15 to 16 years in the same friendship group shared many similarities in terms of body image concern, dietary restraint, and disordered eating behaviours but not binge eating (Paxton et al., 1999). Other Australian researchers found that girls aged 12 to 13 years in the same friendship group shared similarities in terms of dieting and disordered eating behaviours including binge eating but not in terms of body image concern (Hutchinson & Rapee, 2007). The authors concluded that friendship group members are more likely to display similarities in observable behaviours than in hidden attitudes and psychological variables, as dieting behaviours can be more directly modelled (Hutchinson & Rapee, 2007). In other research using social network analysis, Carey and colleagues (2013) found that female friendship groups were similar in terms of body image and dieting behaviours in single-sex but not mixed sex schools in another Australian sample. No males were reported as members of friendship groups, so the difference was not due to the inclusion of boys. Those friendship groups that had higher levels of media influence and social comparisons had higher levels of body dissatisfaction, whereas the groups that had higher levels of peer influence and appearance conversations had higher levels of dieting behaviour (Carey, Donaghue, & Broderick, 2013). More research using this method is needed to fully understand the nature of body image among friendship groups and how this changes across the different stages of adolescence. Research using social network analysis among males and mixed-sex friendship groups is also required.

Friendship qualities and other individual factors, such as negative affect and self-esteem, may also moderate the influence of friends. For example, friends may provide emotional security and protect against the impact of stresses and life-strains (Schultz & Paxton, 2007), and several studies have shown that lower levels of peer support are associated with higher body image concerns among adolescent girls (Alta, Ludden, & Lally, 2007; Stice & Whitendon,

2002). Schultz and Paxton (2007) examined body image and eating concerns among 15-year-old girls in Australia, in terms of positive aspects of friendships (i.e., quality of friend communication, friend trust, and peer acceptance) and negative aspects of friendships (i.e., friend conflict, friend alienation, and social anxiety and insecurity). There was no relationship between positive aspects and body image concerns, but girls with greater body image and eating concerns reported more negative aspects including conflict and alienation and greater social anxiety and insecurity (Schultz & Paxton, 2007). Interestingly, these relationships were no longer significant when the researchers controlled for depressive symptoms. These findings are consistent with research suggesting that depressive symptoms contribute to a negative view of the quality of social relationships and social functioning. Another possible explanation for these findings is that conflicted friendships and poorer social functioning precede body concerns and disturbed eating (Schultz & Paxton, 2007). Having difficulties with friends may lead girls to engage in restrictive eating practices in an effort to bring increased social approval, acceptance, and belonging. Moreover, existing body image concerns and eating disturbances may interfere with the capacity to sustain healthy relationships with friends. Longitudinal studies are now needed to more fully understand the nature and development of these associations, and additional studies are needed to investigate how the role of friendships may differ for boys.

Conclusion

This chapter has highlighted the centrality of peers and friends in understanding adolescents' body image and appearance concerns. The focus in the majority of studies was on the negative aspects of peer pressure and related concepts such as peer weight-based teasing, and appearance-related conversations. However, research is now also examining the positive dimensions of peers and friends. More work is needed to fully understand how age, gender, culture, BMI, negative affect, self-esteem, and the importance placed on appearance may moderate the influence of peers on body image and appearance concerns. In addition, most of the researchers have employed self-reports and correlational designs, which means that it is difficult to separate peer influences from other sociocultural influences and/or separate causes from effects. For example, the majority of studies utilised retrospective self-report to assess messages communicated by friends and peers (i.e., perceived messages). Future studies could employ more objective methods to assess the impact of friendship and peer messages. Qualitative, longitudinal, and/or experimental studies are also needed to verify and explore findings further.

References

Alta, R.N., Ludden, A.B., & Lally, M.M. (2007). The effects of gender and family, friend, and media influences on eating behaviours and body image during adolescence. *Journal of Youth and Adolescence, 36*, 1024–37.

Bandura, A. (1986). *Social foundations of thought and action: A social-cognitive theory.* Englewood Cliffs, NJ: Prentice Hall.

Bandura, A. (1989). Human agency in social cognitive theory. *American Psychologist, 44*, 1175–84.

Barker, E., & Galambos, N.L. (2003). Body dissatisfaction of adolescent girls and boys: Risk and resource factors. *The Journal of Early Adolescence, 23* (141–65). doi: 10.1177/0272431603251081.

Blowers, L.C., Loxton, N.J., Grady-Flesser, M., Occhipinti, S., & Dawe, S. (2003). The relationship between sociocultural pressures to be thin and body dissatisfaction in preadolescent girls. *Eating Behaviors, 4*, 229–44.

Brixval, C.S., Rayce, S.L.B., Rasmussen, M., Holstein, B.E., & Due, P. (2011). Overweight, body image and bullying—an epidemiological study of 11- to 15-year olds. *European Journal of Public Health, 22*(1), 126–30.

Brown, B.B., Clasen, D.R., & Elcher, S.A. (1986). Perceptions of peer pressure, peer conformity dispositions, and self-reported behavior among adolescents. *Developmental Psychology, 22*(4), 521–30.

Buunk, A.P., & Gibbons, F.X. (2007). Social comparison: The end of a theory and emergence of a field. *Organizational Behavior and Human Decision Processes, 102*, 3–21.

Carey, R., Donaghue, N. & Broderick, P. (2010). What you look like is such a big factor: interviews with adolescent girls about the appearance culture in an all-girls' school. *Feminism & Psychology, 21*(3), 299–316.

Carey, R., Donaghue, N., & Broderick, P. (2013). Peer culture and body image concern among Australian adolescent girls: A hierarchical linear modelling analysis. *Sex Roles, 69*(5–6), 250–63.

Cattarin, J.A., & Thompson, J.K. (1994). A 3-year longitudinal study of body image, eating disturbance, and general psychological functioning in adolescent females. *Eating Disorders, 2*, 114–25.

Coleman, J.C. (1980). Friendship and the peer group in adolescence. In J. Adelson (Ed.), *Handbook of adolescent psychology* (pp. 408–31). New York, NY: Wiley.

Corning, A.F., & Gondoli, D.M. (2012). Who is most likely to fat talk? A social comparison perspective. *Body Image, 9*(4), 528–31.

Dunkley, T.J., Wertheim, E., & Paxton, S. (2001). Examination of a model of multiple sociocultural influences on adolescent girls' body dissatisfaction and dietary restraint. *Adolescence, 29*, 85–89.

Eisenberg, M.E., Neumark-Sztainer, D., & Paxton, S. (2006). Five-year change in body satisfaction among adolescents. *Journal of Psychosomatic Research, 61*, 521–27.

Eisenberg, M.E., Neumark-Sztainer, D., & Story, M. (2003). Associations of weight-based teasing and emotional well-being among adolescents. *Archives of Pediatric Adolescent Medicine, 157*, 733–38.

Feldman, D.C. (1984). The development and enforcement of group norms. *Academy of Management Review, 9*(1), 47–55.

Ferguson, C.J., Munoz, M.E., Garza, A., & Galindo, M. (*2014*). Concurrent and prospective analyses of peer, television, and social media influences on body dissatisfaction, eating disorder symptoms and life satisfaction. *Journal of Youth and Adolescence, 43*(1), 1–14.

Fox, C.L., & Farrow, C.V. (2009). Global and physical self-esteem and body dissatisfaction as mediators of the relationship between weight status and being a victim of bullying. *Journal of Adolescence, 32*, 1287–1301.

Fraser, J.K., Sproal, A.W., & Ricciardelli, L.A. (2010). *Social comparisons and perceived media pressure in relation to body image concerns among 8 to 11 year old girls*. Deakin University, Melbourne.

Frisén, A., & Anneheden, L. (2014). Changes in 10-year-old children's body esteem: A time-lag study between 2000 and 2010. *Scandinavian Journal of Psychology, 55*, 123–29.

Gardner, R.M., Sorter, R.G., & Friedman, B.N. (1997). Developmental changes in children's body images. *Journal of Social Behavior and Personality, 12*, 1019–36.

Halliwell, E., & Harvey, M. (2006). Examination of a sociocultural model of disordered eating among male and female adolescents. *British Journal of Health Psychology, 11*, 235–48.

Hayden-Wade, H.A., Stein, R.I., Ghaderi, A., Saelens, B.E., Zabinski, M.F., & Wilfley, D.E. (2005). Prevalence, characteristics, and correlates of teasing experiences among overweight children vs. non-overweight peers. *Obesity Research, 13*, 1381–92.

Helfert, S., & Warschburger, P. (2011). A prospective study on the impact of peer and parental pressure on body dissatisfaction in adolescent girls and boys. *Body Image, 8*, 101–109.

Helfert, S., & Warschburger, P. (2013). The face of appearance-related social pressure: Gender, age and body mass variations in peer and parental pressure during adolescence. *Child and Adolescent Psychiatry and Mental Health, 7*, 16–27.

Holt, K., & Ricciardelli, L.A. (2002). Social comparisons and negative affect as indicators of problem eating and muscle preoccupation among children. *Journal of Applied Developmental Psychology, 23*(3), 285–304.

Humphreys, P., & Paxton, S. (2004). Impact of exposure to idealised male images on adolescent boys' body image. *Body Image, 1*, 253–66.

Hutchinson, D.M., & Rapee, R.M. (2007). Do friends share similar body image and eating problems? The role of social networks and peer influences in early adolescence. *Behaviour Research and Therapy, 45*, 1557–77.

Jones, D.C. (2004). Body image among adolescent girls and boys: A longitudinal study. *Developmental Psychology, 40*(5), 823–35.

Jones, D., & Crawford, J. (2005). Adolescent boys and body image: Weight and muscularity concerns as dual pathways to body dissatisfaction. *Journal of Youth and Adolescence, 34*(6), 629–36.

Jones, D.C., & Crawford, J.K. (2006). The peer appearance culture during adolescence: Gender and body mass variations. *Journal of Youth and Adolescence, 35*(2), 257–69.

Jones, D.C., Newman, J.B., & Bautista, S. (2005). A three-factor model of teasing: The influence of friendship, gender, and topic on expected emotional reactions to teasing during early adolescence. *Social Development, 14*, 421–39.

Jones, D.C., Vigfusdottir, T.H., & Lee, Y. (2004). Body image and the appearance culture among adolescent girls and boys: An examination of friend conversations, peer criticism, appearance magazines, and the internalization of appearance ideals. *Journal of Adolescent Research, 19*, 323–39.

Kandel, D.B. (1980). Drug and drinking behavior among youth. *Annual Review of Sociology, 6*, 235–85.

Lawlor, M., & Nixon, E. (2011). Body dissatisfaction among adolescent boys and girls: The effects of body mass, peer appearance culture and internalization of appearance ideals. *Journal of Youth and Adolescence, 40*(1), 59–71.

Lieberman, M., Gauvin, L., Bukowski, W.M., & White, D.R. (2001). Interpersonal influence and disordered eating behaviors in adolescent girls the role of peer modeling, social reinforcement, and body-related teasing. *Eating Behaviors, 2*, 215–36.

Menzel, J.E., Schaefer, L.M., Burke, N.L., Mayhew, L.L., Brannick, M.T., & Thompson, J.K. (2010). Appearance-related teasing, body dissatisfaction, and disordered eating: A meta-analysis. *Body Image, 7*(4), 261–70.

Myers, T.A., & Crowther, J.H. (2009). Social comparison as a predictor of body dissatisfaction: A meta-analytic review. *Journal of Abnormal Psychology, 118*(4), 683–98.

Nichter, M. & Vuckovic, N. (1994). Fat Talk: Body image among adolescent girls. N. Sault (Ed.), *Many mirrors*. New Brunswick, NJ: Rutgers University Press.

Paxton, S., Eisenberg, M.E., & Neumark-Sztainer, D. (2006). Prospective predictors of body dissatisfaction in adolescent girls and boys: A five-year longitudinal study. *Developmental Psychology, 42*, 888–99.

Paxton, S., Schutz, H.K., Wertheim, E.H., & Muir, S.L. (1999). Friendship clique and peer influences on body image concerns, dietary restraint, extreme weight loss behaviors, and binge eating in adolescent girls. *Journal of Abnormal Psychology, 108*, 255–66.

Peterson, K.A., Paulson, S.E., & Williams, K.K. (2007). Relations of eating disorder symptomology with perceptions of pressures from mother, peers, and media in adolescent girls and boys. *Sex Roles, 57*, 629–39.

Quiles Marcos, Y., Quiles Sebastian, M.J., Pamies Aubalat, L., Botella Ausina, J., & Treasure, J. (2013). Peer and family influence in eating disorders: A meta-analysis. *European Psychiatry, 28*, 199–206.

Rayner, K.E., Schniering, C.A., Rapee, R.M., & Hutchinson, D.M. (2013). A longitudinal investigation of perceived friend influence on adolescent girls' body dissatisfaction and disordered eating. *Journal of Clinical Child and Adolescent Psychology, 42*(5), 643–56.

Reed, M.D., & Wilcox Rountree, P. (1997). Peer pressure and adolescent substance use. *Journal of Quantitative Criminology, 13*(2), 143–80.

Ricciardelli, L.A., & McCabe, M.P. (2004). A biopsychosocial model of disordered eating and the pursuit of muscularity in adolescent boys. *Psychological Bulletin, 130*, 179–205.

Ricciardelli, L.A., McCabe, M.P., & Banfield, S. (2000). Body image and body change methods in adolescent boys: Role of parents, friends, and the media. *Journal of Psychosomatic Research, 49*, 189–97.

Rose, A.J., & Rudolph, K.D. (2006). A review of sex differences in peer relationship processes: Potential trade-offs for the emotional and behavioral development of girls and boys. *Psychological Bulletin, 132*, 98–131.

Sands, E.R., & Wardle, J. (2003). Internalization of ideal body shapes in 9–12-year-old girls. *International Journal of Eating Disorders, 33*, 193–204.

Santor, D.A., Messervey, D., & Kusumaker, V. (2000). Measuring peer pressure, popularity, and conformity in adolescent boys and girls: Predicting school performance, sexual attitudes, and substance abuse. *Journal of Youth and Adolescence, 29*(2), 163–82.

Schultz, H.K., & Paxton, S.J. (2007). Friendship quality, body dissatisfaction, dieting and disordered eating in adolescent girls. *British Journal of Clinical Psychology, 46*, 67–83.

Sharpe, H., Naumann, U., Treasure, J., & Schmidt, U. (2013). Is fat talking a causal risk factor for body dissatisfaction? A systematic review and meta-analysis. *International Journal of Eating Disorders, 46*(7), 643–52.

Shroff, H., & Thompson, J.K. (2006). Peer influences, body-image dissatisfaction, eating dysfunction and self-esteem in adolescent girls. *Journal of Health Psychology, 11*, 533–51.

Smolak, L., & Stein, J.A. (2006). The relationship of drive for muscularity to sociocultural factors, self-esteem, physical attributes, gender role, and social comparison in middle school boys. *Body Image, 3*, 121–29.

Steinberg, L., & Monahan, K.M. (2007). Age differences in resistance to peer influence. *Developmental Psychology, 43*, 1531–43.

Stice, E. (1998). Modeling of eating pathology and social reinforcement of the thin-ideal predict onset of bulimic symptoms. *Behaviour Research and Therapy, 36*, 931–44.

Stice, E., & Whitendon, K. (2002). Risk factors for body dissatisfaction in adolescent girls: A longitudinal investigation. *Developmental Psychology, 38*(5), 669–78.

Suls, J., Martin, R., & Wheeler, L. (2002). Social comparison: Why, with whom, and with what effect? *Current Directions in Psychological Science, 11*, 159–63.

Thompson, J.K., Shroff, H., Herbozo, S., Cafri, G., Rodriguez, J., & Rodriguez, M. (2007). Relations among multiple peer influences, body dissatisfaction, eating disturbance, and self-esteem: A comparison of average weight, at risk of overweight, and overweight adolescent girls. *Journal of Pediatric Psychology, 32*(1), 24–29.

van den Berg, P., Neumark-Sztainer, D., Hannan, P.J., & Haines, J. (2007). Is dieting advice from magazines helpful or harmful? Five-year associations with weight-control behaviors and psychological outcomes in adolescents. *Pediatrics, 119*, 30–37.

Vincent, M.A., & McCabe, M.P. (2000). Gender differences among adolescents in family, and peer influences on body dissatisfaction, weight loss, and binge eating behaviors. *Journal of Youth and Adolescence, 29*, 205–21.

White, J.B., Langer, E.J., Yariv, L., & Welch, J.C. (2006). Frequent social comparisons and destructive emotions and behaviors: The dark side of social comparisons. *Journal of Adult Development, 13*, 36–44.

Woelders, L.C.S., Larsen, J.K., Scholte, R.H.J., Cillessen, A.H.N., & Engels, R.C.M.E. (2010). Friendship group influences on body dissatisfaction and dieting among adolescent girls: A prospective study. *Journal of Adolescent Health, 47*(5), 1–7.

Wojtowicz, A.E., & von Ranson, K.M. (2012). Weighing in on risk factors for body dissatisfaction: A one-year prospective study of middle-adolescent girls. *Body Image, 9*(1), 20–30.

7

THE FAMILY

In addition to the media and peers, the family is the other main transmitter of sociocultural messages about the ideal body to adolescents. Researchers have primarily focused on parents, and more research has been conducted with mothers than fathers. However, it is also important to acknowledge that the family includes siblings and extended family members, who are not often studied. Parents and other family members primarily exert their influence directly via the messages they give adolescents about their bodies. In addition, they exert their influence indirectly via their own attitudes and behaviours, and these may then be modelled by adolescents. The nature of the relationship adolescents have with their family members is also important. Although adolescence is the time to become more independent physically, cognitively, emotionally, and socially, adolescents continue to need a positive and secure family environment where they can receive support, reassurance, and guidance. In addition, while adolescents overall spend less time with the family during the teenage years, the one-to-one time adolescents spend with their mothers and fathers does not change (Coleman, 2011).

In a comprehensive review, Rodgers and Chabrol (2009) concluded that, overall, studies "show that parents do have an influence on body shape and weight concerns, but their relative importance with respect to other agents remains unclear" (p. 143). This is in part due to the fact that in some studies the messages transmitted by family members, peers, and even dating partners have been combined, so it is not possible to examine and evaluate the separate influences. More recently, Quiles-Marcos and colleagues (2013) concluded, based on their meta-analysis of 25 studies conducted between 1995 and 2010, with adolescents and young adults, that both family and peers influence body dissatis-faction. However, a stronger relationship was found between peer influences and body dissatisfaction (0.35) than family influences and body dissatisfaction (0.22).

In this chapter, we first review the studies that have focused on parents. These include studies that have examined direct messages from parents or indirect messages via parental modelling. We also review studies that have compared parental influences to those from peers and the media. In addition, we consider the nature of the relationships adolescents have with their family, and the role of siblings and other family members.

Parental Messages

Parents have been shown to influence adolescent body image through their direct messages, which include criticism of present body shape and weight and encouragement to diet (Rodgers & Chabrol, 2009). These direct mes-sages have been found to be associated with body dissatisfaction and body change strategies among girls (Benedikt, Wertheim, & Love, 1998; Huon & Walton, 2000; Keel et al., 1997; Neumark-Sztainer et al., 2010; Wertheim, Mee, & Paxton, 1999). However, girls' perceptions of parental messages, rather than the parental reports of the same messages, have been shown to be more strongly related to girls' body image concerns and weight loss strategies (Baker, Whisman, & Brownell, 2000; Rodgers & Chabrol, 2009; Wertheim et al., 1999). Wertheim et al. (1999) suggested that this finding may be due to girls perceiving more pressure from their parents than is actually commu-nicated. It may be that girls are distorting the messages from parents or that these messages are internalised more by girls because they are reinforced more strongly by both media and peer messages. It is also possible that ado-lescents with higher levels of concerns may be more sensitive to parental messages (Rodgers & Chabrol, 2009). Another possibility is that parents may be under-reporting because they may feel uncomfortable reporting their messages, or they may even be unaware of the messages they are transmitting.

It is interesting to note that adolescents aged 12 to 16 years consistently received the most negative evaluations of their eating and exercise behaviours from parents, in addition to the most criticism regarding their weight (Striegel-Moore & Kearney-Cooke, 1994). This fits with the view that there is more parental-adolescent conflict at this age, and the interactions between parents and offspring are by no means one directional. That is, as adolescents separate themselves from parents and other formative influences and make more and more of their own decisions, they are likely to clash on many domains. This then leads to more negative comments by parents, and both parents and adolescents may focus more on the negatives in their interactions.

Several studies have differentiated between the messages conveyed by mothers and those by fathers. Overall, this research has shown that although both mothers and fathers directly transmit messages regarding body size and shape, boys and girls perceive more body-related messages from mothers than their fathers (McCabe, Ricciardelli, & Ridge, 2006; Phares, Steinberg, & Thompson, 2004; Thelen & Cormier, 1995). In one study, Wertheim et al. (1999) found that mothers were more likely than fathers to assist girls with dieting, diet with their daughters, and criticise their daughters' weight. In another study, Benedikt et al. (1998) demonstrated that mothers directly communicated to their daughters that they would like them to be thinner and explicitly encouraged them to lose weight.

It is not clear whether mothers also pressure their sons to lose weight. Some studies show that mothers are as equally as likely to encourage their sons and daughters to diet (Striegel-Moore & Kearney-Cooke, 1994; Thelen & Cormier, 1995; Wertheim, Martin, Prior, Sanson, & Smart, 2002). Other studies have shown that daughters are more likely than sons to perceive that their mothers were encouraging them to lose weight (McCabe & Ricciardelli, 2001; McCabe et al., 2007; Phares et al., 2004). However, it may be that weight loss messages are less relevant for boys, as boys are more focused on strategies to increase muscles. The evidence from studies that have examined whether boys perceive messages that encourage them to gain more muscles has been more consistent. In one study, McCabe and Ricciardelli (2005) found that perceived pressure from mothers to increase muscles predicted their sons' use of strategies to increase muscles. Similarly, Smolak, Murnen, and Thompson, (2005) found that adolescent boys who thought that their parents teased them and commented about the inadequacy of their body size as being too small or large were more likely to utilise food supplements and/or steroids to increase muscle size.

Although fewer studies have focused specifically on fathers, the research does show that fathers play an important role in transmitting messages about weight and shape to their daughters (Dixon, Adair, & O'Connor, 1996; Keel, Heatherton, Harnden, & Hornig, 1997; Thelen & Cormier, 1995; Wertheim et al., 1999). As with mothers, fathers' perceived messages about losing weight have been found to predict girls' dieting behaviours (Dixon et al., 1996; Thelen & Cormier, 1995; Wertheim et al., 1999). Moreover, one study suggested that fathers were more likely to tease their daughters about their weight than their mothers (Keery, Boutelle, van den Berg, & Thompson, 2005).

Two studies have also shown that paternal messages are associated with more extreme weight loss behaviours and disordered eating among girls. For example, Vincent and McCabe (2000) found that perceived paternal negative comments about body weight or shape were related to girls' use of extreme weight loss behaviours. Similarly, Keery et al. (2005) found that perceived messages by fathers were significant predictors of dieting and bulimic behaviours in their girls. However, two studies showed no relationship (Kanakis & Thelen, 1995; Moreno & Thelen, 1993), therefore, more studies examining fathers are needed before conclusions can be drawn.

The research suggests that fathers are also influential for boys, although there has been less work done in this area. In one study, Smolak, Levine, and Schermer (1999) found that fathers' messages regarding their sons' weight were significantly related to boys' concerns about being overweight. Similarly, in another study, fathers were found to encourage their sons to lose weight but only if they were overweight (Thelen & Cormier, 1995). Moreover, Vincent and McCabe (2000) found that perceived paternal encouragement to lose weight was significantly associated with bulimic behaviour among adolescent boys.

All the studies that have been reviewed so far have examined parental influences on weight loss strategies and disordered eating. In an unpublished study that specifically examined both mothers' and fathers' encouragement to adolescents to lose weight and/or increase muscles, Same (2007) found that girls were more likely than boys to perceive that their mothers were encouraging them to lose weight, and the mothers themselves were also more likely to indicate that they transmitted these messages. On the other hand, mothers were more likely to encourage their sons to increase the size of their muscles than to encourage weight loss. Interestingly, girls and boys perceived similar levels of encouragement to lose weight from their fathers, and the paternal reports also indicated similar messages to both sons and daughters (Same, 2007). In addition, fathers were more likely to report that they encouraged their sons and daughters to lose weight rather than increase muscles. However, boys perceived more paternal encouragement to increase muscles than lose weight. Given this discrepancy it is difficult to conclude whether boys are being influenced more by the other pressures in their environment, such as their peers and the media, and thus may be misattributing these messages to their fathers. Alternatively, it may be that fathers are not fully aware of the messages they are communicating. A more in-depth study and observations of the interactions between adolescents and parents is needed to more fully examine parental messages and their influences on adolescents. Such studies will also help us better understand the bidirectional nature of these influences, as to date most researchers study parental messages as if they were static and unidirectional.

In line with many of the earlier and published studies, Same (2007) found that girls' and boys' body dissatisfaction and body change strategies were more strongly related to perceived maternal messages to lose weight than the messages reported by parents. In the case of girls, perceived maternal messages to increase muscles were associated with lower levels of body dissatisfaction. It is possible that messages that focus more on muscles than weight loss are protective; however, the findings need to be replicated, and more in-depth studies are needed. In the case of boys, maternal encouragement to lose weight, as reported by both boys and their mothers, was associated with boys' strategies to lose weight. In addition, in the case of boys, perceived maternal encouragement to increase muscles was associated with boys' strategies to both lose weight and increase muscles. This again highlights how boys may be engaging in strategies to both increase muscles and lose weight to achieve lean muscularity (see Chapter 2). It was also interesting to note, and in contrast for girls, that boys' use of body change strategies were related to boys' perceptions as well as mothers' reports. It may be that boys are more accurate at detecting parental messages than are girls. However, again the finding needs to be verified, and more in-depth studies are needed.

In Same's (2007) study, girls' perceptions of paternal encouragement to lose weight were also associated with their body dissatisfaction and weight loss strategies. In addition, paternal encouragement to increase muscles was associated with girls' muscle gain strategies. For boys, perceptions of paternal encouragement and messages as reported by fathers to lose weight and increase muscles were associated with boys' weight loss and muscle gain strategies. Again these findings highlight the importance of both kinds of strategies for boys.

Less attention has been placed on the specific communication of positive messages by parents. However, studies show that these are also important. For example, one study showed that girls who reported receiving affirming reactions to their bodies from parents throughout childhood developed higher levels of body satisfaction (Kearney-Cooke, 2002). Similarly, in another study, girls who believed that their mothers encouraged them to eat healthy food and be active, which de-emphasised the importance of dieting to lose weight, were found to be more likely to have high body satisfaction (Kelly, Wall, Eisenberg, Story, & Neumark-Sztainer, 2005).

The importance of positive messages has also been highlighted in studies with boys. In an interview study, Ricciardelli, McCabe, and Banfield (2000) found that boys thought that their mothers predominantly communicated body-related values though compliments and praise such as "You've got a good body"; "You've got pretty big muscles"; "You're tall and got pretty good legs". These positive messages may help protect many boys from developing a negative body image and may compensate for other competing messages that drive boys to eat less, engage in more exercise, or lose weight (Ricciardelli et al., 2000).

It has also been argued that a combination of messages from both mothers and fathers regarding body image and body change strategies may be more strongly associated with adolescents' body image concerns than if transmitted by either parent alone (Rodgers & Chabrol, 2009). However, studies that have examined this hypothesis have not found any evidence to support it (Neumark-Sztainer et al., 2010; Wertheim et al., 1999, 2002). These studies suggest that having both parents engage in dieting behaviors or in weight talk is not significantly worse than having only one parent diet or engage in weight talk (Neumark-Sztainer et al., 2010).

Parental Modelling

In addition to direct messages, parents may transmit messages and pressure to achieve the ideal body indirectly via their own attitudes and behaviours. This is often referred to as parental modelling, as adolescents' observations of their parents' attitudes and behaviours may lead them to take up the same eating and exercise patterns. In their 2009 review, Rodgers and Chabrol conclude that girls' levels of body dissatisfaction were associated with both mothers' and fathers' levels of body dissatisfaction. However, some studies have also demonstrated a discordance between mothers' and their adolescent daughters' weight loss strategies. For example, Benedikt et al. (1998) found that mothers' dieting, exercise, and body dissatisfaction did not predict girls' dieting behaviours and body dissatisfaction. Similarly, Keery, Eisenberg, Boutelle, Neumark-Sztainer, and Story (2006) found no relationship between mothers' dieting and daughters' weight concerns. The level of agreement between mothers' and their girls' attitudes and behaviours has been found to be more consistent when more extreme weight loss strategies have been examined. For example, Keery et al. (2006) found stronger associations between mothers' and daughters' behaviour in terms of skipping meals, fasting, or crash dieting. Similarly, Benedikt et al. (1998) found a correspondence between mothers' and daughters' use of fasting, crash dieting, and skipping meals. In another study, Wertheim et al. (1999) also showed that girls' use of fasting and skipping meals was associated with mothers' use of these strategies. Extreme weight loss methods are more likely to be more noted by adolescents and thus have a greater impact than less extreme methods.

There have been mixed findings in terms of the influence of mothers' attitudes and behaviours on boys. The studies that have examined actual maternal attitudes and behaviours have not found any correlation with boys' body image and dieting behaviour (Fulkerson et al., 2002; Ruther & Richman, 1993; Thelen & Cormier, 1995; Wertheim et al., 2002). On the other hand, two studies that have examined boys' perceptions of their mothers' behaviours (as opposed to their actual behaviours) have found some support for this relationship. In one study, Field et al. (2001) found that boys who thought that their mothers were frequently trying to lose weight were more likely to become highly concerned with their weight. Similarly, Keery et al. (2006) found that adolescent sons' perception of their mothers' behaviours were related to their weight concerns and dieting.

Even fewer studies have examined the influence of paternal modelling on either girls or boys, and these studies on the whole show that fathers' weight concerns and use of weight loss strategies are not related to girls or boys' attitudes and behaviours. These include pre-adolescent girls (Abramovitz & Birch, 2000), pre-adolescent boys (Thelen & Cormier, 1995), and adolescent girls (Attie & Brooks-Gunn, 1989; Ogden & Stewart, 2000; Steiger, Stotland, Trottier, & Ghadirian, 1996). However, in one study, Dixon et al. (1996) showed that fathers' dieting behaviour was associated with a range of extreme dieting behaviours in their girls. Similarly, Smolak et al. (1999) found that fathers' complaints about their own weight were related to their young daughters' weight loss attempts and body dissatisfaction.

In a more recent study that specifically focused on overweight adolescents, Cromley, Neumark-Sztainer, Story, and Boutelle (2010) found that parents' body dissatisfaction and both unhealthy and healthy weight control behaviours were associated with adolescents' higher body dissatisfaction. However, the separate influence of mothers versus fathers, and whether the findings differed for girls and boys were not examined.

Direct Parental Messages versus Modelling

Two studies that compared the relative effects of direct parental messages versus the modelling of parental body image attitudes and behaviours among girls showed that direct messages are more important. In an early study, Benedikt et al. (1998) found that girls' body dissatisfaction and weight loss attempts were associated with maternal encouragement to lose weight but were not associated with mothers' body dissatisfaction and weight loss strategies. Similar results were found in a more recent study by Rodgers, Faure, and Chabrol (2009). For girls, parental messages and not parental modelling predicted body dissatisfaction. These included more frequent maternal negative comments such as "You need to lose weight" and "You look like you've put on weight, you should watch what you eat"; and less frequent paternal positive comments such as "It's ok if you put on some weight, don't worry about it" and "You always look wonderful". In contrast, Same (2007) found that for girls, both direct and indirect parental influences were associated with girls' body dissatisfaction and strategies to lose weight. Specifically, girls who perceived pressure from their fathers to lose weight and who thought that their mothers were attempting to lose weight were more likely to report body dissatisfaction. In addition, daughters who perceived pressure from their mothers to lose weight and who were of the view that their mothers adopted strategies to lose weight were more likely to report strategies to decrease weight.

Two of the above studies also included adolescent boys. In contrast to what was found among the girls, Same (2007) found that direct encouragement from mothers was a more important influence than maternal attitudes and behaviours for boys. That is, only perceived maternal encouragement to increase muscles, and not mothers' perceived use of strategies to increase muscles, was associated with sons' use of strategies to increase muscles. Unfortunately, the relative direct and indirect influences from fathers could not be examined due to the low number of fathers that took part in that study (N = 19). In the study by Rodgers et al. (2009), greater negative paternal comments and modeling from fathers predicted body dissatisfaction for adolescent boys, thus showing that both direct and indirect influences are important for boys.

Given the limited number of studies that examined the relative effects of direct versus indirect influences and the inconsistent findings, no overall conclusions can yet be drawn. Moreover, it is important to consider how parental influences compare with other influences such as peers and the media.

Parental Influences versus Other Influences

The studies that compared parental and peer influences have shown that peers are more influential than parents. In a 9-month longitudinal study, Presnell, Bearman and Stice (2004) found that pressure from peers predicted increases in body dissatisfaction in a combined sample of girls and boys but pressure from family did not. The relative influence of parents and peers was also examined in a 4-year longitudinal study of adolescent girls and their mothers by Blodgett Salafia, and Gondoli (2011). These researchers examined a range of parental and peer influences, which included perceived parental encouragement to lose weight, parental discussion of dieting, perceived peer pressure to be thin, and peer discussion about becoming thin. Overall, peers were found to be more important than parents in predicting body dissatisfaction. In another longitudinal study, Paxton, Eisenberg, and Neumark-Sztainer (2006) found that parent dieting environment (combination of perceived parents' dieting behaviours and parents' encouragement to diet/control weight) was not predictive of body dissatisfaction among adolescent girls or boys over a 5-year period. The researchers argued that parents are a more distal influence and thus may be less relevant than other factors such as peers and individual factors over a longer period.

Studies that have compared parental and media influences have also shown that media influences are more highly related to body dissatisfaction than parental influences. In one study with adolescent girls, Keery, van den Berg, and Thompson (2004) found perceived media influences on weight and appearance were more highly correlated with body dissatisfaction than either perceived parental or peer influences. In another study with adolescent girls, Shroff and Thompson (2006) found that media influence was more highly correlated with body dissatisfaction than parental influence, but in this study media and peer influences were equally important. One study conducted by Smolak and Stein (2006) specifically targeted adolescent boys, and this showed that parental and peer influences were less important than the perceived influence of muscular media images in predicting the drive for muscularity.

Adolescents' Relationships with Parents

Several studies have shown that parent-adolescent conflict and negative parent-adolescent relationships are associated with body image concerns, dieting, and eating problems among adolescent girls (e.g., Archibald et al., 1999; Hanna & Bond, 2005; Leon, Fulkerson, Perry, & Dube, 1994). Some studies have shown that girls who display more eating disordered behaviour appear to feel less accepted and more criticised by their parents, while more positive family relationships have been shown to be associated with less problematic eating attitudes and behaviour (Graber, Brooks-Gunn, Paikoff, & Warren, 1994; Swarr & Richards, 1996). These latter findings suggest that positive family relationships may serve as a protective factor against developing more serious eating problems (Archibald et al., 1999). Indicators of parental attachment have also been found to be related to body image concerns and disordered eating among adolescent girls. In one study, secure-mother attachment, that is, easily being able to talk to their mother about problems, was found to be associated with a more positive body image and lower levels of disordered eating. On the other hand, fearful mother attachment, that is, feeling uncomfortable about talking to their mother, was related to more body image problems and disordered eating (Bäck, 2011).

The limited research with adolescent boys has shown that the quality of parent relations and indicators of attachment are not related to their body dissatisfaction, weight loss behaviours, and eating problems (Bäck, 2011; Vincent & McCabe, 2000). However, a frequent limitation of the studies conducted with adolescent boys is that the focus has been on body image concerns that are more salient for females. One of our studies, which examined body change strategies that are more relevant for adolescent boys, showed that a negative parent-adolescent relationships predicted increases in the use of food supplements (e.g., protein powders) to change body weight among adolescents boys over an 8-month period (Ricciardelli & McCabe, 2003). This measure of parent-adolescent relationships assessed how well adolescents thought they got along with their parents and the extent to which adolescents experienced parental acceptance and approval.

A more recent survey has examined the relationship between communication with parents and body weight dissatisfaction among adolescents in 24 countries/regions in Europe, Canada and the U.S. (Al Sabbah et al., 2009). As classified by the researchers, these included rich countries (Canada, Norway, Sweden, and the United States), poor countries (Lithuania, the Russian Federation, and Ukraine), and middle-income countries (Austria, Belgium, Croatia, the Czech Republic, Denmark, England, Estonia, Finland, France, Germany, Greece, Greenland, Hungary, Ireland, Israel, Latvia, Malta, the Netherlands, Poland, Portugal, Scotland, Slovenia, Spain, Switzerland, Macedonia, and Wales). In the majority of cases difficulties talking to mothers was associated with body weight dissatisfaction among girls, but among boys this relationship was supported in only two countries (Estonia and Netherlands). Difficulty talking to fathers was also associated with weight dissatisfaction among girls in the majority of cases, while for boys this relationship was supported in 58% of the countries/regions. As suggested by the researchers, problems in parent-adolescent communication may be an indicator of low parental involvement, but more comprehensive evaluations of the parent-adolescent relationship and how this may differentially influence adolescent girls' and boys' body image concerns are needed.

Siblings and Other Family Members

It is also important to acknowledge the body image influences that may come from other family members. In Western culture, these primarily include siblings, but in other cultures they also include members from the extended family such as cousins, aunts, and uncles.

Of the sparse research that has been conducted, the data suggest that adolescents perceive sisters to communicate similar pressure about body ideals to that of their parents (Bliss, 2005). In one study with adolescent girls, the influence of sister modelling was associated with body image concerns and weight loss strategies, and pressure from sisters was found to predict bulimic behaviour (Bliss, 2005). Similarly, in another study with young adult females, the influence of sister modelling and perceived pressure to be thin from sisters was found to be associated with body dissatisfaction and to be similar to the influence of mothers (Coomber & King, 2008). In our research, we have also found that both brothers and sisters were perceived by some adolescent boys as having an influence over the methods they used to change the body size and shape (Ricciardelli et al. 2000).

Our research with adolescents from Fiji and Tonga has more fully highlighted how siblings and the extended family can influence adolescents' body image concerns. In one study with Indigenous Fijian, Indo-Fijian, and Tongan adolescent boys, we found that boys identified other family members, particularly brothers and cousins, as important role models who encouraged them to do more training to attain the ideal body size (McCabe et al., 2011). Similarly, we found that although Indigenous Fijian girls were highly influenced by messages to attain thinner body size from mothers and their peers, other family members such as sisters, cousins, and aunts were also important (Williams, Ricciardelli, & McCabe, 2006). The roles of culture and other sociocultural influences are examined more fully in the next chapter.

Conclusion

In this chapter we have examined the different ways in which the family influences adolescents' body image concerns. These include direct messages from family members, which can be transmitted via teasing, criticism, encouragement, and compliments, but they also include indirect messages where adolescents observe and then model parental attitudes and behaviours. More studies have examined the influence of mothers than fathers; however, the overall findings suggest that both parents influence girls and boys. Moreover, although peer and media influences have been shown to be more important than parental influences, more in-depth studies of the adolescent–parent relationship and how it affects adolescents' body image concerns are needed. This will help us more fully understand how parental messages are perceived and experienced by adolescents, but it will also help us better understand the bidirectional nature of these influences, as adolescent attitudes and behaviours will also be affecting how parents react and respond.

References

Abramovitz, B.A., & Birch, L.L. (2000). Five-year-old girls' ideas about dieting are predicted by their mothers' dieting. *Journal of the American Dietetic Association, 100,* 1157–63.

Al Sabbah, H., Vereecken, C.A., Elgar, F.J., Nansek, T., Aasvee, K., Abdeen, Z., Ojala, K., Ahuwali, N., & Maes, L. (2009). Body weight dissatisfaction and communication with parents among adolescents in 24 countries: International cross-sectional survey. *BMC Public Health, 9,* 52.

Archibald, A.B., Graber, J.A., & Brooks-Gunn, J. (1999). Associations among parent-adolescent relationships, pubertal growth, dieting, and body image in young adolescent girls: A short-term longitudinal study. *Journal of Research on Adolescence, 9*, 395–415.

Attie, I., & Brooks-Gunn, J. (1989). Development of eating problems in adolescent girls: A longitudinal study. *Developmental Psychology, 25*, 70–79.

Bäck, E.A. (2011). Effects of parental relations and upbringing in troubled adolescent eating behaviors. *Eating Disorders: The Journal of Treatment and Prevention, 19*, 403–24.

Baker, C., Whisman, M.A., & Brownell, K.D. (2000). Studying intergenerational transmission of eating attitudes and behaviors: Methodological and conceptual questions. *Health Psychology, 19*, 376–81.

Benedikt, R., Wertheim, E.H., & Love. A. (1998). Eating attitudes and weight-loss attempts in female adolescents and their mothers. *Journal of Youth and Adolescence, 27*, 43–57.

Bliss, N.D. (2005). *Body image in adolescent girls: Evaluation of the Tripartite Influence Model.* Unpublished Doctor of Psychology thesis, Deakin University, Geelong, Victoria.

Blodgett Salafia, E.H., & Gondoli, D.M. (2011). A 4-year longitudinal investigation of the processes by which parents and peers influence the development of girls' bulimic symptoms. *Journal of Early Adolescence, 31*, 390–414.

Coleman, J.C. (2011). *The nature of adolescence* (4th ed.). London: Routledge.

Coomber, K., & King, R.M. (2008). The role of sisters in body image disturbance and disordered eating. *Sex Roles, 59*, 81–93.

Cromley, T., Neumark-Sztainer, D., Story, M., & Boutelle, K.N. (2010). Parent and family associations with weight-related behaviors and cognitions among overweight adolescents. *Journal of Adolescent Health, 47*, 263–69.

Dixon, R., Adair, V., & O'Connor, S. (1996). Parental influences on the dieting behaviors of adolescent girls. *Eating Disorders, 11*, 39–50.

Field, A.E., Camargo, C.A., Barr Taylor, C., Berkey, C.S., Roberts, S.B., & Colditz, G.A. (2001). Peer, parent, and media influences on the development of weight concerns and frequent dieting among preadolescent and adolescent girls and boys. *Pediatrics, 107*, 54–60.

Fulkerson, J.A., McGuire, M.T., Neumark-Sztainer, D., Story, M., French, S.A., & Perry, C.L. (2002). Weight-related attitudes and behaviors of adolescent boys and girls who are encouraged to diet by their mothers. *International Journal of Obesity, 26*, 1579–87.

Graber, J.A., Brooks-Gunn, J., Paikoff, R.L., & Warren, M.P. (1994). Prediction of eating problems: An 8-year study of adolescent girls. *Developmental Psychology, 30*, 823–34.

Hanna, A.C., & Bond, M.J., (2005). Relationships between family conflict, perceived maternal verbal messages, and daughter's disturbed eating symptomatology. *Appetite, 47*, 205–11.

Huon, G.F., & Walton, C.J. (2000). Initiation of dieting among adolescent females. *International Journal of Eating Disorders, 28*, 226–30.

Kanakis, D.M., & Thelen, M.H. (1995). Parental variables associated with bulimia nervosa. *Addictive Behaviors, 20*, 491–500.

Kearney-Cooke, A. (2002). Familial influences on body image development. In T.F. Cash & T. Pruzinsky (Eds.), *Body Image* (pp. 99–107). New York, NY: Guilford Press.

Keel, P.K., Heatherton, T.T., Harnden, J.L., & Hornig, C.D. (1997). Mothers, fathers, daughters: Dieting and disordered eating. *Eating Disorders, 5*, 216–28.

Keery, H., van den Berg, P., & Thompson, J.K. (2004). An evaluation of the tripartite influence model of body dissatisfaction and eating disturbance with adolescent girls. *Body Image, 1*, 237–51.

Keery, H., Boutelle, K., van den Berg, P., & Thompson, J.K. (2005). The impact of appearance-related teasing by family members. *Journal of Adolescent Health, 37*, 120–27.

Keery, H., Eisenberg, M.E., Boutelle, E., Neumark-Sztainer, D., & Story, M. (2006). Relationships between maternal and adolescent weight-related behaviors and concerns: The role of perception. *Journal of Psychosomatic Research, 61*, 105–11.

Kelly, A.M., Wall, M., Eisenberg, M.E., Story, M., & Neumark-Sztainer, D. (2005). Adolescent girls with high body satisfaction: Who are they and what can they teach us? *Journal of Adolescent Health, 37*, 391–96.

Leon, G.R., Fulkerson, J.A., Perry, C.L., & Dube, A. (1994). Family influences, school behaviors, and risk for later development of an eating disorder. *Journal of Youth and Adolescence, 23*, 499–515.

McCabe, M.P., Mavoa, H., Ricciardelli, L., Waqa, G., Fotu, K., & Goundar, R. (2011) Sociocultural influences on body image among adolescent boys from Fiji, Tonga, and Australia. *Journal of Applied Social Psychology, 41*, 2708–22.

McCabe, M.P., & Ricciardelli, L.A. (2001). Parent, peer, and media influences on body image and strategies to both increase and decrease body size among adolescent boys and girls. *Adolescence, 36*, 225–40.

McCabe, M.P., & Ricciardelli, L.A. (2005). A prospective study of pressures from parents, peers and the media on extreme weight change behavior among adolescent boys and girls. *Behaviour Research and Therapy, 43*, 653–68.

McCabe, M.P., Ricciardelli, L.A., & Ridge, D (2006). "Who thinks I need a perfect body?" Perceptions and internal dialogue among adolescents about their bodies. *Sex Roles, 409–19*.

Moreno, A., & Thelen, M.H. (1993). Parental factors related to bulimia nervosa. *Addictive Behaviors, 18*, 681–89.

Neumark-Sztainer, D., Bauer, K.W., Friend, S., Hannan, P.J., Story, M., & Berge, J.M. (2010). Family weight talk and dieting: How much do they matter for body dissatisfaction and disordered eating behaviors in adolescent girls? *Journal of Adolescent Health, 47*, 270–76.

Ogden, J., & Steward, J. (2000). The role of the mother-daughter relationship in explaining weight concern. *International Journal of Eating Disorders, 23*, 309–16.

Paxton, S.J., Eisenberg, M.E., & Neumark-Sztainer, D. (2006). Prospective predictors of body dissatisfaction in adolescent girls and boys: A five-year longitudinal study. *Developmental Psychology, 42*, 888–99.

Phares, V., Steinberg, A.R., & Thompson, J.K. (2004). Gender differences in peer and parental influences: Body image disturbance, self-worth, and psychological functioning in preadolescent children. *Journal of Youth and Adolescence, 33*, 421–29.

Presnell, K., Bearman, K.D., & Stice, E. (2004). Risk factors for the body dissatisfaction in adolescent boys and girls: A prospective study. *International Journal of Eating Disorders, 36*, 389–401.

Quiles Marcos, Y., Quiles Sebastián, M.J., Pamies Aubalat, L.P., Botella Ausina, J.B., & Treasure, J. (2013). Peer and family influences in eating disorders: A meta-analysis. *European Psychiatry, 28*, 199–206.

Ricciardelli, L.A., & McCabe, M.P. (2003). A longitudinal analysis of the role of biopsychosocial factors in predicting body change strategies among adolescent boys. *Sex Roles, 48*, 349–59.

Ricciardelli, L.A., McCabe, M.P., & Banfield, S. (2000). Body image and body change methods in adolescent boys: Role of parents, friends and the media. *Journal of Psychosomatic Research, 49*, 189–97.

Rodgers, R., & Chabrol, H. (2009). Parental attitudes, body image disturbance and disordered eating amongst adolescents and young adults. *European Eating Disorders Review, 17*, 137–51.

Rodgers, R.F., Faure, K., & Chabrol, H. (2009). Gender differences in parental influences on adolescent body dissatisfaction and disordered eating. *Sex Roles, 61*, 837–849.

Ruther, N.M., & Richman, C.L. (1993). The relationship between mothers' eating restraint and their children's attitudes and behaviors. *Bulletin of the Psychonomic Society, 31*, 217–20.

Same, R. (2007). *Parental influences upon their children's body image concerns and behaviours.* Unpublished doctoral thesis. Deakin University, Melbourne.

Shroff, H., & Thompson, J.K. (2006). The tripartite influence model of body image and eating disturbance: A replication with adolescent girls. *Body Image, 3*, 17–23.

Smolak, L., Levine, M.P., & Schermer, F., (1999). Parental input and weight concerns among elementary school children. *International Journal of Eating Disorders, 25*, 263–71.

Smolak, L., Murnen, S.K., & Thompson, J.K. (2005). Sociocultural influences and muscle building in adolescent boys. *Psychology of Men and Masculinity, 6*, 227–39.

Smolak, L., & Stein, J.A. (2006). The relationship of drive for muscularity to sociocultural factors, self-esteem, physical attributes, gender role, and social comparison in middle school boys. *Body Image, 2*, 121–29.

Steiger, H., Stotland, S., Trottier, J., & Ghadirian, A.M. (1996). Familial eating concerns and psychopathological traits: Causal implications of transgenerational effects. *International Journal of Eating Disorders, 19*, 147–57.

Striegel-Moore, R.H., & Kearney-Cooke, A. (1994). Exploring parents' attitudes and behaviors about their children's physical appearance. *International Journal of Eating Disorders, 15*, 377–85.

Swarr, A.E., & Richards, M.H. (1996). Longitudinal effects of adolescent girls' pubertal development, perceptions of pubertal timing, and parental relations on eating problems. *Developmental Psychology, 32*, 636–46.

Thelen, M.H., & Cormier, J.F., (1995). Desire to be thinner and weight control among children and their parents. *Behavior Therapy, 26*, 85–89.

Vincent, M., & McCabe, M.P. (2000). Gender differences among adolescents in family, and peer influences on body dissatisfaction, weight loss and binge eating behaviors. *Journal of Youth and Adolescence, 29*, 205–21.

Wertheim, E.H., Martin, G., Prior, M., Sanson, A., & Smart, D. (2002). Parent influences in the transmission of eating and weight-related values and behaviours. *Eating Disorders, 10*, 321–34.

Wertheim, E.H., Mee, V., & Paxton, S.J. (1999). Relationships among adolescent girls' eating behaviors and their parents' weight-related attitudes and behaviors. *Sex Roles, 41*, 169–87.

Williams, L., Ricciardelli, L.A., & McCabe, M.P. (2006). A comparison of the sources and nature of body image messages perceived by Indigenous Fijian and European Australian adolescent girls. *Sex Roles, 55*, 555–66.

8
CULTURE AND OTHER SOCIOCULTURAL FACTORS

'Culture' reflects a dynamic system of rules established by groups, concerning attitudes, values, beliefs, norms and behaviours, which can be explicit or implicit (Matsumoto & Juang, 2004). In addition, each culture has its own notions about which physical traits are considered beautiful or handsome (Jackson, 2002). Thus, we can learn more about body image and the extent to which societal ideals of beauty are culture bound by studying the nature of body image concerns in different cultures.

Early studies more consistently showed that that body type preferences differed according to culture, thus one's cultural background was viewed as a protective factor for some women against body dissatisfaction and disordered eating (Dounchis, Hayden, & Wilfley, 2001; Wildes, Emery, & Simons, 2001). This included Black and Hispanic American women who, in comparison to White women, displayed a greater preference for a heavier body type (Douchis et al., 2001). Pacific Islander culture has also traditionally placed a great deal of importance on a large body size, which represents high status, power, authority and wealth (Becker et al., 2002).

More recent studies show that the idealisation of the thin ideal for women and body dissatisfaction have become 'transnational phenomena', a development usually attributed to the globalisation of Western media (Tiggemann, 2012). Anderson-Frye (2011) has also concluded that "the global diffusion of sex-typed ultra-thin images of women seems to have left an imprint on other ethnic groups, as thinness ideals can be found around the world. For example, Latina, Argentine, Malaysian Chinese, and Fiji women have displayed considerable body dissatisfaction or Western-style desires for thinness" (p. 250).

Nevertheless, Anderson-Frye continues to maintain that "Western individualistic notions of body image are not universal" (p. 250), as there still exist communities such as those found in Belize, where women reject Western-style thinness ideals, and body shape is more highly valued than body size. In addition, Black American women are often found to display less body dissatisfaction than Whites (Roberts, Cash, Feingold, & Johnson, 2006). This has been attributed to Black women's less narrow and rigid notions of beauty and the more positive feedback about their appearance that they receive from friends and family (Parker et al., 1996).

The majority of studies prior to the 1990s focused on girls, who were primarily from Western countries. Boys and other cultures were largely excluded by researchers. Increasingly, more research is targeting boys and adolescents from other cultural groups. In this chapter we first review the nature of body image concerns among adolescents from non-Western countries such as China, Japan, and Malaysia. In addition, we consider differences across Western and non-Western countries and across minority cultural groups living in Western countries. Last, we consider other important cultural factors, which include acculturation, socioeconomic status (SES), and gender roles.

Non-Western Countries

Several studies have examined the body image of adolescents from non-Western countries. These include Botswana, China, Japan, Malaysia, the Pacific Islands, South Korea, and countries in South America. Overall, these studies show that body image concerns are widespread among non-Western countries. In addition, these studies reflect the main findings from Western countries, which highlight gender differences in body image concerns, and show that adolescents with higher BMIs report more body dissatisfaction. These studies also show that the media, peers, and/or family are important sociocultural influences for adolescents' body image concerns across different countries.

Botswana

In a recent study conducted in Botswana, boys were found to be more dissatisfied with muscle tone, chest size, and strength than girls (Malete et al., 2013). There were no gender differences on other aspects of appearance and body image that were examined, such as height, skin complexion, hair texture, facial features, body proportions, weight, coordination, and overall appearance. However, as frequently found in other studies, overweight adolescents were more dissatisfied with their body proportions and weight.

China

In a large survey of over 9,000 children and adolescents in China (Guangzhou, Shanghai, Jinan, and Haerbin), Li and collegues (2005) found that the levels of body dissatisfaction were similar to those found in developed countries. In a more recent study, Xu et al. (2010) examined body dissatisfaction, body change strategies, and sociocultural pressures among adolescent boys and girls aged between 12 and 16 years from the Chengdu region in China. In line with Western countries, girls reported greater body dissatisfaction than boys, and boys reported more frequent use of strategies to increase their muscles. In addition, boys reported receiving pressure to increase their muscles and weight from all three different sources, that is, the family, peers and media. On the other hand, girls primarily reported pressure to lose weight from the media.

Chen and Jackson (2009, 2012) also found that Chinese adolescent girls reported more body dissatisfaction than boys. In addition, body image concerns among Chinese adolescent girls were predicted by similar factors to those found among girls from the U.S. and other Western countries. For girls these included a thin ideal, sociocultural pressures, social comparisons, negative affect, and BMI. For Chinese adolescent boys the predictors of body image concerns were sociocultural pressures and social comparisons (Chen & Jackson, 2009). Interestingly, preference for a muscular body was not a predictor of Chinese boys' body image concerns. However, it has been noted that 'hyper-muscularity' is not viewed as an appearance ideal for males in Chinese culture (Chen & Jackson, 2009). Rather, Chinese males place more importance on traits that emphasise cerebral and scholarly qualities (Chen & Jackson, 2012).

Japan

In their review, Chisuwa and O'Dea (2010) found that two-thirds of adolescent Japanese girls were dissatisfied with their bodies and were primarily preoccupied with thinness. Fewer studies have been conducted with Japanese boys, but these mirror those from Western countries, which show that boys are more dissatisfied with their muscularity than girls. In addition, similar sociocultural factors to those found in Western countries have been found to influence Japanese girls' body image. These include the media (Chisuwa & O'Dea, 2010), peers (Mukai, Crago, & Shisslak, 1994), and mothers (Mukai, 1996). More recently, self-reported media pressure has also been found to be associated with higher levels of body dissatisfaction among Japanese adolescent boys (Brockhoff et al., 2014).

Malaysia

Khor et al. (2009) found that height was the main body image concern of Malaysian adolescent girls and boys, with close to 80% of males and 70% of females desiring to be taller. In addition, more males preferred a larger body size while more females preferred a smaller body size. However, as is often found in Western samples, the overweight boys and girls expressed greater preoccupation with their body weight and shape.

In another study, Mellor et al. (2010), who surveyed Malay, Indian and Chinese adolescents in Malaysia, found no gender differences in body dissatisfaction or strategies to decrease weight, but boys reported more strategies to increase muscles. There were also differences among the three cultural groups on body change strategies. Malay and Indian adolescents, who were on the whole heavier, reported engaging in more strategies to lose weight than the Chinese. On the other hand, Indian adolescents were found to engage in more strategies to increase muscles than the Chinese. The reason for this finding was not explored, but in other research, we found Indo-Fijian adolescent boys placed more focus on strategies to increase muscles because of their smaller body size (Ricciardelli et al., 2007).

Pacific Islands

Research that has compared Indigenous and Indo-Fijians living in Fiji, and Tongans living in Tonga, with European Australians living in Australia, has shown that girls in Fiji and Tonga report more dissatisfaction with their weight and shape, whereas boys are more dissatisfied with their muscles (McCabe, Ricciardelli, Waqa, Goundar, & Fotu, 2009). In addition, Indo-Fijian boys demonstrated the highest level of dissatisfaction with their body. This may be because Indo-Fijian boys tend to have, on average, a smaller build than Indigenous Fijians. Other studies have shown that boys who are below average weight for their height or view themselves as underweight tend to be more negative about their body image, achievement aspirations, and overall self-concepts (Jackson & Chen, 2008).

In our work in Fiji and Tonga, where the culture has traditionally valued larger and more robust body sizes, we also studied the extent to which adolescents were influenced by the media, peers, and the family using both interviews (McCabe et al. 2011; Williams, Ricciardelli, & McCabe, 2006) and surveys (Ricciardelli & McCabe, 2010). In our interviews with boys, we found that sociocultural influences were important for Indigenous Fijians, Indo-Fijians and Tongans, who reported messages from fathers, other family members and friends about attaining an ideal muscular body (McCabe et al., 2011).

Fijian girls reported experienced messages that promoted thinness from their family members and peer but also messages that promoted a larger body size (Williams et al., 2006). Thus, suggesting that they are influenced by both their traditional culture but also by Western style thinness ideals.

We also examined the nature and source of the sociocultural messages in more depth in our survey study (Ricciardelli & McCabe, 2010). Interestingly, irrespective of weight status and gender, we found that Tongan adolescents perceived more messages than the Indigenous Fijians, Indo-Fijians, and Australians to gain weight from both male and female adult relatives, younger family members, peers, and the media. We also found that Tongans reported more messages about increasing muscles than each of the other three groups, and the messages to increase muscles were consistently relayed across each of examined sources: adult male relatives, adult female relatives, older brothers/male cousins, older sisters/female cousins, male peers, female peers, and the media. In addition, boys perceived more messages to increase muscles than girls, and this was found across each of the four cultural groups.

We had not expected to find that Tongans would perceive more messages to increase weight and muscles than Indigenous Fijians; however, some of our interview work with Tongan and Indigenous Fijian adolescent boys did suggest that one of the main reasons that Tongans place a lot of importance on muscularity was because of the physical work they are required to do, and this was a more salient theme among Tongans than Indigenous Fijians (Ricciardelli, McCabe, Mavoa et al., 2007). Physical work is highly valued in Tonga, and many rely on farming and livestock for their living; most adolescent Tongan males assist with cultivating the land.

Indigenous Fijians and Indo-Fijians did not differ in the messages they perceived about increasing muscles, and both groups perceived more messages to attain muscularity from all sources in comparison to Australian adolescents. In our previous study, we also found that muscularity was important to both Indigenous Fijians and Indo-Fijians boys (Ricciardelli, McCabe, Mavoa et al. 2007). However, the reasons were different. Indigenous Fijians were more interested in attaining muscularity to play sport and for physical work. In contrast, Indo-Fijians, who tended to have smaller body builds, were more likely to focus on the importance of a more muscular body so that they could dominate, intimidate, and avoid being bullied or teased by others.

We also found that Tongan adolescents in the healthy weight range perceived more messages to lose weight from adult relatives than the other three cultural groups. These findings suggest that Tongan adult male relatives are transmitting more modern messages to lose weight, which are a direct contrast to the messages being transmitted about gaining weight. It is interesting that this result was only found for Tongans in the healthy weight range. It may be that adult relatives are aware of the potential to gain weight, and thus these messages are serving as an early warning. Adolescents in the healthy weight range would stand out even more than ones who are overweight so they may be receiving encouragement to maintain their current body size. However, as they are perceived messages, they may also be reflecting adolescents' concerns about gaining weight rather than the actual messages by adults. Clearly, further study of Pacific cultural groups is important as they are influenced by traditional messages, which focus more on the importance of a large body size, but at the same time they are also receiving messages which are a promoting thinness and weight loss.

South America

McArthur, Holbert, and Peña, (2005) studied adolescents from six South American cities: Buenos Aires (Argentina), Guatemala City (Guatemala), Havana (Cuba), Lima (Peru), Panama City (Panama), and Santiago (Chile). Adolescents in all cities were dissatisfied with their bodies, but the largest percentage of adolescents desiring to be thinner was found in Buenos Aires, Argentina, the most affluent country of the six. Argentineans often differentiate themselves from other Latin Americans in that they believe that they are more acculturated to European ways than any other Latin Americans (Holmqvist & Frisén, 2010). Another study that compared Argentineans with Swedish adolescents found that the two groups did not differ in their levels of body dissatisfaction (Holmqvist, Lunde, & Frisén, 2007).

Mellor, McCabe, Ricciardelli, and Merino (2008) also investigated body dissatisfaction and body change strategies among Chilean adolescents aged 12 to 18 years. Girls were found to report higher levels of body dissatisfaction and higher levels of perceived pressure to lose weight from the media than boys. On the other hand, boys reported greater perceived pressure from peers to lose weight than girls and more pressure than girls from all sources to increase muscles.

South Korea

Jung, Forbes, and Lee (2009) found greater levels of body dissatisfaction in their sample of adolescent girls and boys from South Korea than from American adolescents. Moreover, boys in South Korea displayed substantially higher body image concerns than boys from the U.S., while girls' body image concerns were more similar across the two countries. These findings are in line with several other studies that have shown that males in rapidly changing countries are more at risk of body image concerns and disordered eating (Ricciardelli,

McCabe, Williams, & Thompson, 2007). These differences may reflect in part the changing status quo and power relations for men, which are in line with feminist theories (Jung et al., 2009). Although usually applied to women, Jung et al. have also applied this theory to men who live in counties with rapid social changes, as these changes affect men more than women.

Other Western Countries

Although the majority of the research reviewed in this book comes from the U.S., U.K., and Australia, some of the studies have been conducted in other Western countries, which include France (Ferron, 1997), Sweden (Frisén & Holmqvist, 2010), and Switzerland (Knauss, Paxton, & Alsaker, 2008). Overall, body image concerns and their correlates have been found to be similar across countries. As concluded by Knauss et al. (2008), "Switzerland is a Western culture and, therefore, there is no particular reason to assume that the findings could not be generalised to other Western cultures" (p. 642).

Other researchers have highlighted that there are 'cultural nuances' across different countries. However, these are difficult to measure and may be too subtle to detect unless examined qualitatively. For example, in a qualitative study of American and French adolescents, girls in both countries were dissatisfied with their fat, but they had different ideas about which features formed the ideal face (Ferron, 1997). American girls aimed for more 'dramatic looks' with thick lips and pronounced cheek-bones, while French girls aimed for the 'baby-face', the long eye lashes and the clear complexion. In addition, French boys were more dissatisfied with their bodies than American boys.

Comparisons across Countries

McCabe et al. (2012) compared body image across countries using the Body Image Satisfaction Scale (see Chapter 2), which has been validated among different adolescent cultural groups (Fuller-Tyszkiewicz et al., 2012). In the majority of the countries, Australia, Chile, Fiji, Malaysia and Tonga, the boys reported higher levels of body satisfaction than the girls. However, there were no gender differences in China or among the Tongans from New Zealand. Unexpectedly, boys in Greece reported lower body satisfaction than girls. This latter finding could not be explained and thus needs replication. However, the finding may be reflecting the increasing focus that males are placing on body image, and this is consistent with other work that shows that Greek adult women show a preference for men with a smaller overall body weight than British women (Swami et al., 2007). It was also interesting to note that body satisfaction was lower in Greece, China, and Malaysia but higher in

Chile and among Indigenous Fijians. An in-depth study of the inter- and intra-cultural factors to account for these differences is now needed.

In another recent study that included both girls and boys, Japanese adolescents, in comparison to Chinese, Malaysian, Australian, Tongan, and Indigenous Fijian adolescents, were found to have the highest level body dissatisfaction despite lower BMIs (Brockhoff et al., 2014). This is consistent with other work that has shown that Japanese males prefer images of women with significantly lower BMIs than Britons (Swami, Caprario, Tovée, & Furnham, 2006). Traditionally Japanese culture has valued an extremely thin body ideal for women, which is now being reinforced by Western influences (Swami et al., 2006).

Minority Cultural Groups Living in Western Countries

A large number of studies have examined minority cultural groups living in Western countries, however, most of these studies have focused on adults rather than adolescents (see reviews by Grabe & Hyde, 2006; Ricciardelli, McCabe, Williams, & Thompson, 2007; Roberts et al., 2006). Grabe and Hyde (2006) found in one review that focused on women and included 13 studies with adolescents, that White girls and women reported higher levels of body dissatisfaction than Black girls and women, and that these differences were largest during adolescence. Hispanic women also reported higher levels of body dissatisfaction than Black women, but this effect was very small. Last, it was interesting to note that older studies showed greater differences than more recent studies.

The results of another review by Roberts et al. (2006), which specifically focused on the differences between Black and White women, "suggest that the relationship between Black-White ethnicity and body image is more complex than previously suggested" (p. 1121). Greater differences between Blacks and Whites were found when global assessments of body image were evaluated, that is, where the focus was not just on weight or shape but included facial features, hair, or overall appearance. Moreover, the studies that examined more global measures showed that the degree of differences between Blacks and Whites has continued to increase rather than decrease in more recent studies. The review by Roberts et al. also showed that body image differences were largest at age 25 and non-existent around age 40. However, only four of the reviewed studies included adolescents, with three of these showing large differences and one showing no difference. A more recent study, which included a range of measures, found higher body image concerns among adolescent Black girls in comparison to White girls (Jung & Forbes, 2012). This included body dissatisfaction as assessed using figure ratings, body esteem, and appearance evaluation.

Black adolescent girls have been found to be less influenced by their peers but more influenced by adult role models who are less likely to promote weight loss behaviours (Parnell et al., 1996). In addition, Black girls have been found to be less affected by media messages, as the media tend to portray a limited view of what is considered attractive for women (Duke, 2000). Moreover, content analyses reveal that television programs targeting Black youth tend to incorporate a broader range of body sizes (Schooler, Ward, Merriwether, & Caruthers, 2004). Further studies of magazines targeting Black women in the U.S. found that 76% of the cover models were in the healthy weight range and only 6% were underweight which is in stark contrast with the models in magazines targeting white women (Thompson-Brenner, Boisseau, & St. Paul, 2011) and therefore young women who were exposed to black-oriented media were found to have higher levels of body image (Schooler et al., 2004). Some research with adult women has also found that Black women do not compare themselves to the predominantly White images that they see in the media, and so therefore, they might be protected (DeBraganza & Hausenblas, 2010).

In our review that specifically focused on males, we found that the majority of studies showed that males from minority groups demonstrated more body dissatisfaction than Whites (Ricciardelli, McCabe, Williams, & Thompson, 2007). We argued that these differences may in part reflect the changing status quo and power relations for males and/or the higher level of social isolation of men in minority groups when compared to the dominant cultural group(s). In particular, men more than women are worse off in a climate of emerging acculturation and modernisation as they may have more to lose than to gain in their social status with changing social structures.

When studying differences across minority cultural groups, it is also important to take into account BMI differences and perceptions of whether one is overweight. Both of these factors have been found to vary in relation to body dissatisfaction and body change strategies across minority groups, but not always in the expected direction. In one study, Neumark-Sztainer et al. (2002) surveyed White, Black, Hispanic, Asian, and Native American adolescent boys and girls. Hispanic and Native American boys' body dissatisfaction and body change strategies were in line with their BMIs and weight perceptions. Hispanic boys had higher BMIs, were more likely to perceive themselves as overweight, were more likely to have high body dissatisfaction, and engaged in more weight loss behaviours and binge eating but were less likely to try to gain weight in comparison to White boys. Similarly, Native American boys were more overweight than White boys, were more likely to perceive themselves as overweight, were more likely to have high body dissatisfaction, and engaged in more weight loss behaviours than Whites. On the other hand, although Asian boys' BMI did not differ from Whites, they had higher body dissatisfaction and engaged in more weight loss behaviours than Whites. Asian males tend to have smaller builds and less muscular physiques than Whites (Kuo, 2005), but these differences may not be fully captured by measuring BMI. Last, Black boys were found to have lower body dissatisfaction than White boys, and although they were less likely to see themselves as overweight, they engaged in more weight loss behaviours and binge eating than White boys. Other research has suggested that Black boys are more proud of their bodies (Story et al., 1995), thus they may be using body change strategies to maintain and even improve their bodies.

Neumark-Sztainer et al. (2002) also found that Hispanic girls were more overweight and more likely to perceive themselves as overweight than White girls, and consistently they had the highest body dissatisfaction and were more likely to be trying to lose weight and reported more binge eating in comparison to White girls. Interestingly, there were no differences in body dissatisfaction among White, Asian, and Native American girls. However, comparable to what was found among boys, Native American girls, who were more overweight than White girls, were more likely to be trying to lose weight and reported higher levels of binge eating than White girls. Last, and in line with other studies reviewed above, Black girls, although more overweight than White girls, had the lowest body dissatisfaction.

While Neumark-Sztainer et al. (2002) found no differences in body dissatisfaction between Native American and White girls, in our research (Ricciardelli, McCabe, Ball & Mellor, 2004), we found Indigenous Australian adolescent girls to score lower than non-Indigenous girls on body dissatisfaction and body image importance. On the other hand, Indigenous Australian boys scored higher than non-Indigenous boys, and irrespective of gender, Indigenous adolescents reported significantly more strategies to lose weight and increase muscles than non-Indigenous adolescents. In a more recent study, Cinelli and O'Dea (2009) also showed that Indigenous Australian male adolescents were more dissatisfied with their weight that non-Indigenous boys; they were more likely to report a greater desire for weight gain and used strategies to gain weight and muscles. On the other hand, Indigenous Australian female adolescents were more satisfied with their weight than non-Indigenous girls and they were more likely to want to gain weight and to build muscles.

In our study we also examined perceived pressure to lose weight and/ or increase muscles from fathers, mothers, male friends, female friends, and the media in relation to body dissatisfaction, weight loss strategies and strategies to increase muscles (Ricciardelli et al., 2004). One of the main similarities across three of the four groups (Indigenous girls, Indigenous boys, and non-Indigenous girls) was the association between perceived pressure to lose weight from the media and strategies to decrease weight. These findings are consistent with those of other studies, which show that the media is viewed by White adolescent girls to be the strongest pressure that promotes the thin ideal, as we reviewed in Chapter 5.

For both Indigenous girls and boys there was a correlation between perceived pressure to lose weight from friends and strategies to decrease weight. For Indigenous girls, this included perceived pressure to lose weight from both male and female friends, whereas it was primarily messages from male friends for Indigenous boys. In addition, the main sociocultural influence associated with strategies to increase muscles across three of the four groups (Indigenous girls, Indigenous boys, and non-Indigenous boys) was perceived pressure from female friends. Overall, these findings are similar to those reported among adolescents in general, as reviewed in Chapter 6.

Only among Indigenous girls was there also a strong association between weight loss strategies and perceived pressure to lose weight and increase muscles from parents. Overall, we showed in Chapter 7 that parents are influential, but on the whole, they are less influential than peers and the media. Parental influences may be stronger in more traditional and non-Western cultures, which include Indigenous cultures; however, more studies are needed to test whether this is in fact the case.

The finding that none of the sociocultural influences were associated with Indigenous girls' body dissatisfaction or the importance they placed on body image, whereas 8 of the 10 subscales were associated with their strategies to lose weight, provides a striking discrepancy. A possible explanation for these findings is that Indigenous girls may have a very positive self-image and high self-esteem, which is more similar to non-Indigenous boys (Ricciardelli & McCabe, 2001; Ricciardelli et al., 2000). This positive self-image may protect Indigenous girls from the sociocultural messages that could increase their levels of body dissatisfaction and body image importance.

In contrast, perceived pressure from mother, male friend, and the media were associated with body image concerns for Indigenous boys. These findings are consistent with gender differences on self-esteem that have been found among minority groups. In contrast to White girls, who tend to report lower levels of self-esteem in comparison to White boys, minority girls demonstrate higher levels of self-esteem than minority boys (Twenge & Crocker, 2002).

Acculturation

One variable that has been proposed as a mediator of the relationship between body image concerns and culture is acculturation (Dunkel, Davidson, & Qurashi, 2010; Ricciardelli et al., 2007). 'Acculturation' is the term used to describe the modification of the culture of a group or individual as a result of contact with a different culture. It has been argued that acculturation to Western values and the adoption of the thin ideal has led to high levels of body image problems and eating disorders among women from non-Western cultures (Humphrey & Ricciardelli, 2004). However, there is no agreement as to how to best assess acculturation, and various measures have been used. These include the preference to speak English, participants' level of integration in the dominant culture, and the level of identity with the non-dominant cultural group. Some measures are unidimensional (Suinn, Ahuna, & Khoo, 1992), others are bi-dimensional (Ryder, Alden, & Paulhus, 2000), and more recently, Brockhoff et al. (2012) have argued for a tri-cultural scale, which assesses traditional versus modern values and Eastern versus Western values. Other researchers have focused on additional factors associated with the acculturation process, such as adjustment, length of residence in the new country and perceived discrimination (Swami, 2009; Swami, Arteche, Chamorro-Premuzic, & Furnham, 2010).

We located four studies that have examined the role of acculturation in relation to adolescents' body image (Brockhoff et al., 2012, 2014; Newman, Sontage, & Salvato, 2006; Nieri et al., 2005). The findings from two studies, which assessed acculturation as a unidimensional construct, showed there was no relationship for girls, but the findings were discrepant for boys. Nieri et al. (2005) found that less acculturated Hispanic boys reported higher body image concerns than acculturated Hispanic boys. On the other hand, Newman et al. (2006) found that less acculturated Native American boys reported a more positive body image than more acculturated Native Americans. Clearly more studies are needed to further investigate this relationship, and unidimensional constructs of acculturation are unlikely to fully capture the effects of acculturation.

In a more recent study, Brockhoff et al. (2012) examined the role of the independent and combined influences from traditional Japanese, modern Japanese, and Western values on body image and body change behaviours among adolescents living in Japan. Four 'acculturative' groups were identified: 'anti-modern', 'traditional', 'pro-modern/anti-traditional', and 'pro-Western/anti-Japanese'. Adolescents who were classified as pro-modern or pro-Western were the most dissatisfied with their bodies, and pro-Western adolescents were also more likely to report higher levels of weight loss behaviours. In an additional study, Brockhoff et al. (2014) found that a higher identification with traditional Japanese values but a lower identification with modern values was associated with less body dissatisfaction in girls. On the other hand, identification with modern Japanese values or with Western values was associated with increased body dissatisfaction by way of increased media influence among both girls and boys.

In terms of more fully understanding acculturation, an interesting comparison group who are shielded from much of Western culture and the media are the Amish. The Amish are a very conservative Protestant religious community living the U.S. who lives separately from Western society (Platte, Zeltan, & Stunkard, 2000). A study of the body image of males and females aged between 14 and 22 years demonstrated no body dissatisfaction among the Amish (Platte et al., 2000). This study suggests that communities that are less affected by Western culture may be protected from developing body dissatisfaction.

Socioeconomic Status (SES)

SES is another important sociocultural factor, as can it reflect wide ranging differences in individuals' lifestyles and values. One of the indicators of SES is wealth, and as concluded by Holmqvist and Frisén (2010) "body dissatisfaction is a phenomenon that appears to be more common in countries that are economically wealthier and where people have a more Western lifestyle" (p. 135). On the other hand, larger body sizes have been found to be popular in less affluent and non-Western countries (Holmqvist & Frisén, 2010). Individuals from more affluent countries have greater access to body-centred information through television, newspapers and Internet and so may experience more pressure to conform to body ideals. They also have more economic resources that they are able to spend on dieting foods, beauty products, and exercise equipment.

Holmqvist and Frisén's (2010) conclusions were confirmed by Swami et al. (2010) who examined body dissatisfaction among adult women in 26 countries across 10 world regions (Southeast Asia, East Asia, South and West Asia, Oceania, Western Europe, Eastern Europe, Scandinavia, Africa, North America, and South America). The preference for thinner bodies was found to be more prevalent in high SES settings such as in North America and Western Europe. On the other hand, heavier bodies were preferred in low SES settings in Malaysia and South Africa. In an earlier study, Jaeger et al. (2002) also showed that adult females in affluent Western countries, such as Sweden, Germany, Spain, France and Italy, were very dissatisfied with their bodies in comparison to females in less affluent non-Western countries such as Tunisia, Ghana, Gabon, and Indonesia. While the two above studies have been conducted with adults, SES has also been found to be one of the main predictors of body dissatisfaction in older adolescent girls and early adolescent boys from the U.S. (Paxton et al., 2006).

Consistent with the above findings are those from rural settings, where women have been found to rate heavier figures of men as more attractive while in more industrialised settings, males who are depicted with relatively slim figures and an "inverted triangle" shape are rated as more attractive (Swami & Tovée, 2005). These findings are consistent with the view that a heavier body weight in times of food scarcity and in less industrialised societies is a main indicator of high status. According to this view, men who have higher status would be seen as more desirable as potential partners to women, as this high status indicates that they have a greater ability to control economic resources.

Gender Roles

The study of gender roles, often referred to as masculinity and femininity, provides another way of studying sociocultural nuances, both within and between cultures. Masculinity and femininity have been conceptualised as multidimensional constructs that include gender role stereotypes; adherence to traditional gender role norms; gender role conflict; and gender role stress. These constructs reflect stereotypes about the beliefs and behaviours typically attributed to men and women that are acquired as they learn about the world and their roles in it (Basow, 1992; Deux & Major, 1987; Helgeson, 2012). Given that there are likely to be differences across cultures, they would be important factors to study in relation to body image concerns in different countries. However, only research conducted in Western countries was located, so the conclusions may not generalise to other countries and cultures.

One review of the literature was conducted by Gillen and Lefkowitz (2006, p. 27) and they concluded:

> Research demonstrates a link between femininity and appearance orientation in women (Jackson et al., 1988; Timko, Striegel-Moore, Silberstein, & Rodin, 1987), but less is known about this association in men. Although one study showed an association between femininity and appearance orientation in both men and women across the lifespan (ages 10 to 79; Pliner, Chaikem, & Flette, 1990), other work suggests that gender-typed men (i.e., men who are masculine) may be more orientated toward their appearance than other men are (Andersen & Bem, 1981).

The association between femininity and both body image concerns and disordered eating is well accepted. Sometimes referred to as the 'femininity hypothesis', this maintains that the identification with characteristics typically labelled as 'feminine', such as passivity, dependence and unassertiveness, reflect a need of approval from others and low self-esteem (Lakkis et al., 1999; Murnen & Smolak, 1997). Therefore, both women and men, who identify strongly with feminine traits, and in particular, negative feminine traits, are viewed as having negative body image and may use body change strategies and disordered eating to alleviate their low self-esteem and strive for the ideal-body form.

However, the conclusion that males who identify with higher levels of masculinity are the ones who are more concerned with their body image does not align with other reviews (Blashill, 2011; Lakkis et al., 1999; Ricciardelli &

Williams, 2011). In a more recent review by Blashill (2011), only two of the 47 studies which examining gender roles in relation to disordered eating and/ or body dissatisfaction among males included adolescents. One of these studies, which included a combined analysis of the girls and boys, showed that higher scores on femininity were associated with greater dissatisfaction with appearance and weight while higher scores on masculinity were associated with higher satisfaction (Bowker, Gadbois, & Cornock, 2003). The other study only examined masculinity, and this was found to be associated with higher satisfaction with appearance and weight for both girls and boys (Gadbois & Bowker, 2007).

All of the research that has been reviewed so far has examined femininity and masculinity using measures that assess gender role stereotypes. Other measures designed to assess other dimensions of femininity and masculinity include adherence to traditional gender role norms; gender role conflict; and gender role stress (Ricciardelli & Williams, 2011). However, none of these other measures has yet to be examined in relation to body image concerns among adolescents. Only one aspect of the traditional masculine gender role has been studied among adolescent boys. Smolak and Stein (2006) created a new 8-item scale to assess the investment adolescent boys (aged 11 to 15 years) have in the traditional masculine gender norms which focus on strength and athleticism (e.g., "Guys should be able to throw a ball farther than most girls can."). Consistent with expectations, the endorsement of these traditional masculine norms was associated with higher levels of drive for muscularity among boys. It is surprising though that a comparative study, which examines traditional feminine norms, has yet to be conducted with adolescent girls.

Conclusion

Overall, the nature of body image concerns among adolescents from non-Western countries is similar to those found among adolescents from the U.S., U.K., and Australia. Girls are often more preoccupied with thinness while boys are more concerned about their muscles. Overweight adolescents also consistently demonstrate higher levels of body dissatisfaction; and where examined, the media, peers and/or family have been found to be important influences. However, no conclusions about any differences among adolescents from different Western and non-Western countries can be drawn as too few studies have been conducted, and where differences have been found, there has been no examination of any of the inter- or intra- cultural factors that may account for the differences. Two factors that may moderate differences between countries are SES and gender roles, as both cultural factors have been found to be associated with body image concerns.

The majority of studies of minority groups living in Western countries have examined body image concerns among Blacks. Consistently, Black girls and boys from the U.S. have been found to display lower levels of body dissatisfaction than Whites. In the case of girls the differences have been attributed to the more protective messages they receive from their family and the broader range of body sizes of Black women depicted in the media. Other minority groups living in Western countries have received less study but some of the differences in their body image concerns have been attributed to differences in BMI, weight perceptions, and acculturation. Further studies are now needed to more systematically examine these factors across different minority groups. In addition, qualitative studies are needed to more clearly identify other factors that may be contributing to body image concerns in different cultural groups.

References

Andersen, S. M., & Bem, S. L. (1981). Sex typing and androgyny in dyadic interaction: Individual differences in responsiveness to physical attractiveness. *Journal of Personality and Social Psychology, 41*, 74–86.

Anderson-Frye, E.P. (2011). Body images in non-Western cultures. In T.F. Cash & L. Smolak (Eds.), *Body image: A Handbook of science, practice, and prevention* (2nd ed., pp. 244–52). New York, NY: Guilford Press.

Basow, S.A. (1992). *Gender stereotypes and roles*. (3rd ed.). Pacific Grove, CA: Brooks/Cole.

Becker, A. E., Burwell, R. A., Gilman, S. E., Herzog, D. B., & Hamburg, P. (2002). Eating behaviours following prolonged exposure to television among ethnic Fijian adolescent girls. *British Journal of Psychiatry, 180*, 509–514.

Blashill, A.J. (2011). Gender roles, eating pathology, and body dissatisfaction in men: A meta-analysis. *Body Image, 8*, 1–11.

Bowker, A., Gadbois, B., & Cornock, B. (2003). Sports participation and self-esteem: Variations as a function of gender and gender role orientation. *Sex Roles, 49*, 47–58.

Brokhoff, M., Mussap, A.J., Mellor, D., Skouteris, H., Ricciardelli, L.A., McCabe, M.P., & Fuller-Tyszkiewicz, M. (2012). Cultural influences on body dissatisfaction, body change behaviours and disordered eating of Japanese adolescents. *Asian Journal of Social Psychology, 15*, 238–48.

Brockhoff, M. Mussap, A.J., Mellor, D., Skouteris, H., Ricciardelli, L.A., McCabe, M. P., & Fuller-Tyszkiewicz, M. (2014). *Cultural influences on adolescents' body image: a comparison of adolescents in Japan with adolescents in China, Malaysia, Australia, Tonga and Fiji.* Deakin University, Melbourne. Manuscript submitted for publication.

Chen, H., & Jackson, T. (2009). Predictors of changes in weight esteem among mainland Chinese adolescents: A longitudinal analysis. *Developmental Psychology, 45*, 1618–29.

Chen, H. & Jackson, T. (2012). Gender and age group differences in mass media and interpersonal influences on body dissatisfaction among Chinese adolescents. *Sex Roles, 66*, 3–20.

Chisuwa, N., & O'Dea, J.A. (2010). Body image and eating disorders amongst Japanese adolescents. A review of the literature. *Appetite, 54*, 5–15.

Cinelli, R.L., & O'Dea, J.A. (2009). Body image and obesity among Australian adolescents from indigenous and Anglo-European backgrounds: Implications for health promotion and obesity prevention among Aboriginal youth. *Health Education Research, 24*, 1059–68.

DeBraganza, N., & Hausenblas, A. H. (2010). Media exposure of the ideal physique on women's body dissatisfaction and mood: The moderating effects of ethnicity. *Journal of Black Studies, 40,* 700–716.

Deux, K., & Major, B. (1987). Putting gender into context: An interactive model of gender-related behavior. *Psychological Review, 94,* 369–389.

Dounchis, J.Z., Hayden, H.A., & Wilfley, D.E. (2001). Obesity, body image, and eating disorders in ethnically diverse children and adolescents. In J.K. Thompson and L. Smolak (Eds.), *Body image, eating disorders, and obesity in youth* (pp. 67–98). Washington, DC: American Psychological Association.

Duke, L. (2000). Black in a blonde world: Race and girls' interpretations of the feminine ideal in teen magazines. *Journalism and Mass Communication Quarterly, 77,* 367–392.

Dunkel, T.M., Davidson, D., & Qurashi, S. (2010). Body satisfaction and pressure to be thin in younger and older Muslim and non-Muslin women: The role of Western and non-Western dress preferences. *Body Image, 7,* 56–65.

Ferron, C. (1997). Body image in adolescence: Cross-cultural research: Results of the preliminary phase of a quantitative survey. *Adolescence, 32,* 735–45.

Fuller-Tyszkiewicz, M., Skouteris, H., McCabe, M., Mussap, A., Mellor, D. & Ricciardelli, L. (2012). An evaluation of equivalence in body dissatisfaction measurement across cultures. *Journal of Personality Assessment, 94,* 410–17.

Gadbois, S., & Bowker, A. (2007). Gender differences in the relationships between extracurricular activities participation, self-description, and domain specific and general self-esteem. *Sex Roles, 56,* 675–89.

Gillen, M. M., & Lefkowitz, E. S. (2006). Gender role development and body image among male and female first year college students. *Sex Roles, 55,* 25–37.

Grabe, S. & Hyde, J.S. (2006). Ethnicity and body dissatisfaction among women in the United States: A meta-analysis. *Psychological Bulletin, 132,* 622–40.

Helgeson, V.S. (2012). *The psychology of gender* (4th ed.). Boston, MA: Pearson Education.

Holmqvist, K., & Frisén, A. (2010). Body dissatisfaction across cultures: Findings and research problems. *European Eating Disorders Review, 18,* 133–46.

Holmqvist, K., Lunde, C., & Frisén, A. (2007). Dieting behaviors, body shape perceptions, and body satisfaction: Cross-cultural differences in Argentinean and Swedish 13-year-old. *Body Image, 4,* 191–200.

Humphry, T.A., & Ricciardelli, L.A. (2004). The development of eating pathology in Chinese-Australian women. *International Journal of Eating Disorders, 35,* 579–588.

Jackson, L. A., Sullivan, L. A., & Rostker, R. (1988). Gender, gender role, and body image. *Sex Roles, 19,* 429–443.

Jackson, L. A. (2002). Physical attractiveness: A sociocultural perspective. In T. F. Cash & T. Pruzinsky (Eds.), Body image: A handbook of theory research and clinical practice (pp. 13–21). New York, NY: Guilford Press.

Jackson, T. & Chen, H. (2008). Sociocultural influences on body image concerns of young Chinese males. *Journal of Adolescent Research, 23,* 154–71.

Jaeger, B., Ruggiero, G.M., Edlund, B., Gomez-Perretta, C., Lang, F., Mohammadkhani, P. et al. (2002). Body dissatisfaction and its interrelations with other risk factors in bulimia nervosa in 12 countries. *Psychotherapy and Psychosomatics, 71,* 54–61.

Jung, J., & Forbes, G.B. (2012). Body dissatisfaction and characteristics of disordered eating among Black and White early adolescent girls and boys. *The Journal of Early Adolescence, 33,* 737–64.

Jung, J., Forbes, G.B., & Lee, Y. (2009). Body dissatisfaction and disordered eating among early adolescents from Korea and the US. *Sex Roles, 61*, 42–54.

Khor, G.L., Zalilah, M.S., Phan, Y.Y., Ang, M., Maznak, B., Norimah, A.K. (2009). Perceptions of body image among Malaysian male and female adolescents. *Singapore Medical Journal, 50*, 303–11.

Knauss, C., Paxton, S.J., & Alsaker, F. (2008). Body dissatisfaction in adolescent boys and girls: Objectified body consciousness, internalization of the media body ideal and perceived pressure from media. *Sex Roles, 59*, 633–43.

Kuo, W. (2005). Body image of Taiwanese men versus Western men. *The American Journal of Psychiatry, 162*, 1758.

Lakkis, J., Ricciardelli., L.A., & Williams, R.J. (1999). The role of sexual orientation and gender-related traits in disordered eating. *Sex Roles, 41*, 1–16.

Li, Y., Hu, X., Ma, W., Wu, J., & Ma, G. (2005). Body image perceptions among Chinese children and adolescents. *Body Image, 2*, 91–103.

Malete, L., Motlhoiwa, K., Shaibu, S., Wrotniak, B.H., Maruapula, S.D., Jackson, J., & Compher, C.W. (2013). Body dissatisfaction is increased in male and overweight/obese adolescents in Botswana. *Journal of Obesity*, Article ID 763624.

Matsumoto, D., & Juang, L. (2004). *Culture and psychology* (3rd ed.). Belmont, CA: Wadsworth.

McArthur, L.H., Holbert, D., & Peña, M. (2005). An exploration of the attitudinal and perceptual dimensions of body image among male and female adolescents from six Latin American cities. *Adolescence, 40*, 801–16.

McCabe, M.P., Ricciardelli, L., Waqa, G., Goundar, R., & Fotu, K. (2009). Body image and change strategies among adolescent males and females from Fiji, Tonga and Australia. *Body Image, 6*, 299–303.

McCabe, M.P., Mavoa, H., Ricciardelli, L., Waqa, G., Fotu, K., & Goundar, R. (2011) Sociocultural influences on body image among adolescent boys from Fiji, Tonga, and Australia. *Journal of Applied Social Psychology, 41*, 2708–22.

McCabe, M.P., Fuller-Tyszkiewicz, M, Mellor, D., Ricciardelli, L., Skouteris, H., & Mussap, A. (2012). Body satisfaction among adolescents in eight different countries. *Journal of Health Psychology, 17*, 693–701.

Mellor, D., McCabe, M., Ricciardelli, L., & Merino, M.E., (2008). Body dissatisfaction and body change behaviors in Chile: The role of sociocultural factors. *Body Image, 5*, 205–15.

Mellor, D., Ricciardelli, L.A., McCabe, M.P., Yeow, J., Mamat, N.H.b., & Hapidzal, N.F. b.M. (2010). Psychosocial correlates of body image and body change behaviors among Malaysian adolescent boys and girls. *Sex Roles, 63*, 386–98.

Mukai, T., (1996). Mothers, peers, and perceived pressure to diet among Japanese adolescent girls. *Journal of Research on Adolescence, 6*, 309–24.

Mukai, T., Crago, M., & Shisslak, C.M. (1994). Eating attitudes and weight preoccupation among female high-school students in Japan. *Journal of Child Psychology and Psychiatry and Allied Disciplines, 35*, 677–88.

Murnen, S.K., & Smolak, L. (1997). Femininity, masculinity, and disordered eating: A meta-analytic review. *International Journal of Eating Disorders, 22*, 231–42.

Neumark-Sztainer, D., Croll, J., Story, M., Hannan, P.J., French, S.A., & Perry, C. (2002). Ethnic/racial differences in weight-related concerns and behaviors among adolescent girls and boys: Findings from project EAT. *Journal of Psychosomatic Research, 53*, 963–74.

Newman, D.L., Sontage, L.M., & Salvato, R. (2006). Psychosocial aspects of body mass and body image among rural American Indian adolescents. *Journal of Youth and Adolescence, 35*, 281–91.

Nieri, T., Kulis, S., Keith, V. M., & Hurdle, D. (2005). Body image, acculturation, and substance abuse among boys and girls in the southwest. *American Journal of Drug and Alcohol Abuse, 31*, 617–39.

Parker, S., Nichter, M., Nichter, N., Vuckovic, N., Sims, C., & Ritenbaugh, C. (1995). Body image and weight concerns among African-American and White adolescent females: Differences that make a difference. *Human Organization, 54*, 103–14.

Parnell, K., Sargent, R., Thompson, S., Duhe, S., Valois, R., & Kemper, R. (1996). Black and White adolescent females' perceptions of ideal body size. *Journal of School Health, 66*, 112–18.

Paxton, S.J., Eisenberg, M.E., & Neumark-Sztainer, D. (2006). Prospective predictors of body dissatisfaction in adolescent girls and boys: A five-year longitudinal study. *Developmental Psychology, 42*, 888–99.

Platte, P., Zelten, J.F., & Stunkard, A. (2000). Body image in the old order Amish: A people separate from "the world". *International Journal of Eating Disorders, 28*, 408–44.

Pliner, P., Chaiken, S., & Flett, G.L. (1990). Gender differences in concern with body weight and physical appearances over the life-span. *Personality and Social Psychology Bulletin, 16*, 263–273.

Ricciardelli, L.A., & McCabe, M. P. (2001). Self-esteem and negative affect as moderators of sociocultural influences on body dissatisfaction, strategies to decrease weight, and strategies to increase muscles among adolescent boys and girls. *Sex Roles, 44*, 189–207.

Ricciardelli, L.A., & McCabe, M.P. (2010). *Perceived sociocultural messages to lose weight, gain weight and increase muscles among adolescent girls and boys from Tonga, Fiji and Australia.* Unpublished manuscript, Deakin University, Melbourne, Australia.

Ricciardelli, L.A., McCabe, M.P., Ball, K., & Mellor, D. (2004). Sociocultural influences on body image concerns and body change strategies among Indigenous and Non-Indigenous Australian adolescent girls and boys. *Sex Roles, 51*, 731–41.

Ricciardelli, L.A., McCabe, M.P., & Banfield, S. (2000). Body image and body change methods in adolescent boys: Role of parents, friends, and the media. *Journal of Psychosomatic Research, 49*, 189–97.

Ricciardelli, L., McCabe, M.P., Mavoa, H., Fotu, K, Groundar, R., Schultz, J., Waqa, G., & Swinburn, B. (2007). The pursuit of muscularity among adolescent boys in Fiji and Tonga. *Body Image, 4*, 361–371.

Ricciardelli, L.A, McCabe, M.P., Williams, R.J., & Thompson, J.K. (2007). The role of ethnicity and culture in body image and disordered eating among males. *Clinical Psychology Review, 27*, 582–606.

Roberts, A., Cash, T.F., Feingold, A., & Johnson, B.T. (2006). Are Black-White differences in females' body dissatisfaction decreasing? A meta-analytic review. *Journal of Consulting and Clinical Psychology, 74*, 112–31.

Ryder, A., Alden, L. E., & Paulhus, D. L. (2000). Is acculturation unidimensional or bidimensional? A head-to-head comparison in the prediction of personality, self-identity, and adjustment. *Journal of Personality and Social Psychology, 79*, 49–65.

Schooler, D., Ward, L. M., Merriwether, A., & Caruthers, A. (2004). Who's that girl: Television's role in the body image development of young White and Black women. *Psychology of Women Quarterly, 28*, 38–47.

Smolak, L., & Stein, J.A. (2006). The relationship of drive of muscularity, sociocultural factors, self-esteem, physical attractiveness gender role, and social comparisons in middle school boys. *Body Image, 2,* 121–29.

Story, M., French, S.A., Resnick, M.D., & Blum, R.W. (1995). Ethnic/racial and socioeconomic differences in dieting behaviors and body image perceptions in adolescents. *International Journal of Eating Disorders, 18,* 173–79.

Suinn, R. M., Ahuna, C., & Khoo, G. (1992). The Suinn-Lew Asian Self-Identity Acculturation Scale: Concurrent and factorial validation. *Educational and Psychological Measurements, 52,* 1041–1046.

Swami, V. (2009). Predictors of sociocultural adjustment among sojourning Malaysian students in Britain. *International Journal of Psychology, 44,* 266–73.

Swami, V., Arteche, A., Chamorro-Premuzic, T., & Furnham, A. (2010). Sociocultural adjustment among sojourning Malaysian students in Britain: A replication and path analytic extension. *Social Psychiatry and Psychiatric Epidemiology, 45,* 57–65.

Swami, V., Caprario, C., Tovée, M.J., & Furnham, A. (2006). Female physical attractiveness in Britain and Japan: A cross-cultural study. *European Journal of Personality, 20,* 69–81.

Swami, V., Frederick, D.A., Aavik, T., Alcalay, L., Allik, J., Anderson, D., … & Zivcic-Becirevic, I. (2010). The attractive female body weight and female body dissatisfaction in 26 countries across 10 world regions: Results of the international body project. *Personality and Social Psychology Bulletin, 36,* 309–25.

Swami, V., Smith, J., Tsiokris, A., Georgiades, C., Sangareau, Y., Tovée, M.J., & Furnham, A. (2007). Male physical attractiveness in Britain and Greece: A cross-cultural study. *The Journal of Social Psychology, 147,* 15–26.

Swami, V., & Tovée, M.J. (2005). Male physical attractiveness in Britain and Malaysia: A cross-cultural study. *Body Image, 2,* 383–93.

Thompson-Brenner, H., Boisseau, C. L., & St Paul, M. S. (2011). Representation of ideal figure size in Ebony magazine: A content analysis. *Body Image, 8,* 373–78.

Tiggemann, M. (2012). Sociocultural perspectives on body image. In T.F. Cash, (Ed.), *Encyclopedia of body image and human appearance, Volume 2* (pp. 758–65). London: Elsevier.

Timko, C., Striegel-Moore, R.H., Silberstein, L.R., & Rodin, J. (1987). Femininity/masculinity and disordered eating in women: How are they related? *International Journal of Eating Disorders, 6,* 701–712.

Twenge, J.M., & Crocker, J. (2002). Race and self-esteem: Meta-analyses comparing Whites, Blacks, Hispanics, Asians, and American Indians, and comment on Gray-Little and Hafdahl (2000). *Psychological Bulletin, 128,* 371–408.

Xu, X., Mellor, D., Kiehne, M., Ricciardelli, L.A., McCabe, M.P., & Xu, Y. (2010). Body dissatisfaction, engagement in body change behaviors and sociocultural influences on body image among Chinese adolescents. *Body Image, 7,* 156–164.

Wildes, J.E., Emery, R.E., & Simons, A.D. (2001). The roles of ethnicity and culture in the development of eating disturbance and body dissatisfaction: A meta-analytic review. *Clinical Psychology Review, 21,* 521–51.

Williams, L., Ricciardelli, L.A., & McCabe, M.P. (2006). A comparison of the sources and nature of body image messages perceived by Indigenous Fijian and European Australian adolescent girls. *Sex Roles, 55,* 555–66.

9
INDIVIDUAL FACTORS

In this chapter we examine the main individual factors that have been found to contribute to body image among adolescents. These include the internalisation of societal ideals of attractiveness, negative affect and self-esteem, perfectionism, and sexual orientation. More research in this area has been done with girls than boys. However, increasingly studies show that similar factors are associated with body image concerns among boys.

In addition, we examine the body image of adolescents with visible differences. Visible differences can result from congenital conditions, such as a cleft of the lip, or they may result from illnesses and their treatment, such as cancer, or injuries like burns (Rumsey & Harcourt, 2007).

Psychological Factors that Contribute to Body Dissatisfaction
Internalisation of Societal Ideals of Attractiveness

Internalisation of societal ideals of attractiveness, also usually referred to as simply 'internalisation', is one of the most robust risk factors of body dissatisfaction and disordered eating (Karazsia, van Dulmen, Wong, & Crowther, 2013). Internalisation involves adopting the societal ideals of body image as personal goals and standards, including being thin for women and muscular for men. An item that has been used to assess internalisation for both girls and boys is "I would like my body to look like the models which appear in magazines" (e.g., Mitchell, Petrie, Greenleaf, & Martin, 2012; Rodgers, Ganchou, Franko, & Chabrol, 2012).

Internalisation is a main component of Stice's Dual-Pathway Model of Bulimic Behaviour (1994), the Tripartite Influence Model (Thompson, Heinberg, Altabe, & Tantleff-Dunn, 1999), and self-objectification theory (Fredrickson & Roberts, 1997). As we saw in Chapters 5, 6, and 7, pressures to adopt societal ideals are relayed by the media, family, and peers. However, not everyone who is exposed to these pressures develops body image concerns. According to the current theoretical models, adolescents and adults with higher levels of internalisation are at risk, as they believe that they should strive to look like the thin or muscular ideals that are ubiquitous in the media, and the same ideals are reinforced by other sources such as peers and the family. Moreover, when adolescents compare themselves with these ideals, they generally find themselves to be less attractive, and become dissatisfied with their appearance. It is important to note that some researchers examine internalisation and social comparisons together as a single factor, as the two constructs have been found to be highly correlated, and both are viewed as mediating the relationship between sociocultural influences and body dissatisfaction (e.g., Rodgers et al., 2012; Rodgers, Paxton, & McLean, 2014). Peer comparisons are reviewed in Chapter 6.

Strong support for the importance of internalisation was demonstrated in a meta-analysis by Cafri, Yamamiya, Brannick, and Thompson (2005). This meta-analysis, which examined only studies with women, showed that internalisation of the thin ideal was moderately and significantly related to body image, with effect sizes from cross-sectional studies being larger than both longitudinal and experimental studies. Eleven of the 35 reviewed studies were conducted with adolescents, including adolescents from other cultural groups. More recent studies have also shown internalisation to be one of the main predictors of body image concerns among girls (e.g., McLean, Paxton, & Wertheim, 2013; Mitchell, Petrie, Greenleaf, & Martin, 2012; Rodgers et al., 2014) and among boys (e.g., Petrie, Greenleaf, & Martin, 2010; Rodgers et al., 2012). However, what is still debated is the extent to which internalisation mediates different sociocultural influences, as these relationships have been found to vary across studies (e.g., Mitchell et al., 2012). In addition, the role of other factors such as negative affect needs to be taken into account (Rodgers et al., 2014).

Negative Affect and Self-Esteem

Negative affect encompasses mood states such as depression, anxiety, stress, shame, inadequacy, guilt, and helplessness and is closely associated with self-esteem and other self-concepts (Ricciardelli & McCabe, 2001). Several studies have shown that adolescent girls and boys who display higher levels of negative affect also demonstrate more body image concerns. A number of theorists and researchers have argued that body change strategies that result from body dissatisfaction are used to regulate and/or alleviate negative affect. Other researchers have argued that negative affect is associated with a negative information-processing bias that may result when one evaluates his/her body negatively (Stice & Whitenton, 2002). Increasingly, the evidence, as reviewed below, is suggesting that negative affect may be both a risk factor and a resulting consequence of body image concerns.

Several correlational studies have demonstrated that higher levels of negative affect, lower levels of self-esteem, and other negative self-concepts, are associated with higher body dissatisfaction in girls (Almedia, Severo, Araújo, Lopes, & Ramos, 2012; Brausch & Gutierrez, 2009; Mitchell et al., 2012; Petrie et al., 2010; Rodgers et al., 2014) and boys (Almedia et al., 2012; Brausch & Gutierrez, 2009; Petrie et al., 2010). These relationships tend to be weaker among boys (Petrie et al., 2010); however, when more sensitive and validated measures to assess boys' body image concerns are used, the relationships are more consistently found among adolescent boys (Brunet, Sabiston, Dorsch, & McCreary, 2010; Cafri, van den Berg, & Thompson, 2006; McCreary & Sasse, 2000).

In our own work (Ricciardelli & McCabe, 2009, Appendix 2 at the end of Chapter 4), we found that negative affect predicted strategies to decrease weight, increase muscles and weight cross-sectionally, and body image importance over an 8-month period among adolescent boys. In each case, higher levels of negative affect predicted body change strategies and the importance placed on the body. Moreover, in a longer term follow-up, we found that depressive symptoms predicted the use of food supplements among adolescent boys, which may be used to increase muscle size over a 16-month period (McCabe & Ricciardelli, 2006).

It is not clear whether negative affect is also associated with muscle concerns among girls. In one of our studies we found that depression predicted adolescent girls' use of food supplements (such as protein powder), which included a large focus on increasing muscles (McCabe & Ricciardelli, 2006). However, other researchers have not found the same kind of associations among girls (e.g., McCreary & Sasse, 2000; McVey, Tweed, & Blackmore, 2005).

The longitudinal evidence for the relation of negative affect and/or self-esteem to body image concerns is less consistent and in some studies varies according to gender. For example, some studies have shown that negative affect or depressive symptoms predicted increases in body dissatisfaction among boys over a one-year period (Martin et al., 2000; Presnell, Bearman, & Stice 2004) but not among girls (Martin et al., 2000; Presnell et al., 2004; Stice & Whitenton, 2002). On the other hand, one study that only included girls showed that lower self-esteem predicted increases in body dissatisfaction over a one-year period (Wojtowicz & von Ranson, 2012). Interestingly, another recent study controlled for gender and showed that stress was a predictor of body dissatisfaction over a one-year period (Murray, Rieger, & Byrne, 2013).

Some longer-term longitudinal studies suggest that the age of the adolescents is another important factor to consider. For example, in one study Holsen, Kraft, and Roysamb (2001), after controlling for initial levels in body dissatisfaction, found that depression did not predict any changes in body dissatisfaction over a five-year period, among girls or boys. On the other hand, Paxton, Eisenberg, and Neumark-Sztainer (2006) found that lower self-esteem predicted body dissatisfaction in early adolescent girls while depressive symptoms predicted body dissatisfaction among older adolescent boys over a five-year period. However, neither self-esteem nor depression predicted body dissatisfaction among early adolescent boys or older adolescent girls.

Self-esteem may be more important for early adolescent girls as they are experiencing more physical developmental changes and there are more pressures to conform and be accepted by friends and peers. The relationship between self-esteem and body image is more established by later adolescence and thus may not be as easy to detect. On the other hand, negative affect may be more important for older adolescent boys who experience physical developmental changes later than girls (Paxton, Neumark-Sztainer et al., 2006).

Longer term follow-ups are needed to more fully evaluate all the relationships. Low self-esteem may contribute to an increase in negative evaluation generally and lead to a negative of evaluation of the body. In addition, low self-esteem over an extended period may make girls vulnerable to more proximal pressures, such as environmental pressures to be the thin and contribute to girls being more likely to internalise cultural ideals of success, including the beauty ideal, and engage in social comparisons that increase their vulnerability to increases in body dissatisfaction (Paxton, Eisenberg, & Neumark-Sztainer, 2006). The same applies to depressive symptoms that typically involve negative feelings about self and are likely over time to include negative feelings about body image. Moreover, as with self-esteem, depression may increase one's vulnerability to real or perceived criticism and pressures to achieve the ideal body.

Much of the focus is on depression and self-esteem as predictors of body dissatisfaction. However, the opposite relationships have also been tested. Body dissatisfaction has been found to be a predictor of depression in a study of adolescent girls over a two-year period (Bearman & Stice, 2008). In addition, body dissatisfaction has been found to be a predictor of both depression and self-esteem in early adolescent girls and older adolescent boys over a two-year period (Paxton, Neumark-Sztainer et al., 2006). Therefore, it has been argued that body dissatisfaction may contribute to depressive mood and low self-esteem, which may in turn further increase body dissatisfaction. It is also possible to conceive that in some adolescents the nature of the relation between body dissatisfaction and negative affect is in one direction, whereas in others it may be in the opposite (Paxton, Neumark-Sztainer et al., 2006). Longitudinal studies that track the direction and stability of this relationship over time are required.

Perfectionism

Perfectionism is another individual factor that has been often been found to be related to body dissatisfaction and disordered eating among adult women (e.g., Sherry et al., 2009; Welch, Miller, Ghaderi, & Vaillancourt, 2009) and men (e.g., Grammas & Schwartz, 2009; Sherry et al., 2009). Given that perfectionists display extreme efforts to achieve often unattainable ideals, it is understandable that these characteristics often underlie their body image concerns and body change strategies. To date, only a handful of studies have examined perfectionism in relation to body image concerns among adolescents, and the findings are inconsistent. Thus, additional studies are needed before any conclusions can be drawn.

One model of perfectionism that has been studied among adolescents highlights four different components: personal high standards, concern over mistakes, parental criticisms, and parental expectations (Frost, Marten, Lahart, & Rosenblate, 1990).

- Personal high standards: involves the setting of high standards (e.g., "If I do not set the highest standards for myself, I am likely to end up a second rate person")
- Concern over mistakes: assesses the tendency to interpret mistakes as equivalent to failure (e.g., "If I fail at work/school, I am a failure as a person")
- Parental criticisms: focuses on the tendency of parents to give critical evaluations of their child (e.g., "As a child, I was punished for doing things less than perfect")
- Parental expectations: assesses the parents' tendency to give critical evaluations and the child's tendency to place considerable importance on these evaluations (e.g., "Only outstanding performance is good enough in my family")

In their cross-sectional study of adolescent girls, Ruggiero, Levi, Ciuna, and Sassardi (2003) found that both concern over mistakes and parental criticism were related to body dissatisfaction. In another study, evaluative concerns perfectionism (this assessed concern over mistakes and doubts about actions) was found to be associated with body dissatisfaction cross-sectionally, but it did not predict increases in body dissatisfaction longitudinally in a three-year wave study (Boone, Soenens, & Braet, 2011). On the other hand, personal standards perfectionism was not related to body dissatisfaction either cross-sectionally or longitudinally (Boone et al., 2011). However, indirect paths showed that personal standards perfectionism was related to the thin ideal internalisation, and evaluative concerns perfectionism was related to pressure to be thin. All relationships were found to be similar for both girls and boys. More research is needed to further examine these indirect effects.

Another model of perfectionism distinguishes maladaptive from adaptive perfectionism (Slaney, Rice, Mobley, Trippi, & Ashby, 2001). Maladaptive perfectionism is defined as the self-prescription of unrealistic fixed standards and an inability to cope with the failure to achieve these standards. It is argued that perfectionists' inability to cope with failure leads to negative evaluations of self (Dour & Theran, 2011). In their cross-sectional study, Dour and Theran (2011) found that maladaptive perfectionism was related to body esteem among both girls and boys. However, a study that examined maladaptive perfectionism as a one-year predictor of body dissatisfaction among adolescent girls found no support for this relationship longitudinally (Wojtowicz & von Ranson, 2012). Rather than perfectionism, two of the other examined factors, self-esteem and BMI, were found to predict increases in girls' body dissatisfaction.

Sexual Orientation

In addition to the normative challenges in their transition to adulthood, gay, lesbian, and bisexual adolescents face additional challenges related to their sexual orientation (Coker, Austin, & Schuster, 2010). It has been argued that the stigma associated with sexuality and sexual orientation may induce psychosocial stress that leads to increased health risk behaviours and poorer health outcomes (Coker et al., 2010; Saewyc, Bearinger, Heinz, Blum, & Resnick, 1998). These might include emotional difficulties, problems in school, verbal abuse from peers, physical assaults. sexual abuse, conflict with the law, substance use, eating disorders, and suicide attempts (Saewyc et al., 1998). One review has shown "compelling evidence" that gay, lesbian and bisexual youth "have an increased likelihood of a range of negative health indicators compared" with non-gay, non-lesbian, and non-bisexual youth (Coker et al., 2010, p. 468). These include substance use, suicidality, sexual behaviours, and violence and victimisation. In addition, gay youth, in particular, are viewed to be at risk of developing higher body dissatisfaction and disordered eating given that male gay subculture places great emphasis on the lean and muscular body ideal, appearance, and fashion (Ricciardelli & McCabe, 2004).

Sexual orientation is one of the other main and consistent variables found to be associated with body image concerns and disordered eating among adult males (McCabe & Ricciardelli, 2004; Ricciardelli & McCabe, 2004). However, this relationship has only been studied in a handful of studies with adolescents. In an early study, French, Story, Remafedi, Resnick and Blum (1996) found a weak effect showing that gay adolescent boys from 7th to 12th grade were more likely to report weight concerns, poorer body image, dieting, binge eating, and purging than non-gay boys. In another study, gay/bisexual boys reported making a greater effort to look like boys and men in the media than heterosexual boys (Austin et al., 2004). However, Lock et al. (2001) found no association between sexual orientation and disordered eating for adolescent boys aged between 12 and 19 years.

In contrast to research with adult males, the findings from research on sexual orientation and body image concerns and related behaviours among adult females have been inconsistent. Some studies suggest that lesbians are less concerned with body weight and shape and diet and binge less frequently than heterosexual women (Bankoff & Pantalone, 2014; Lakkis, Ricciardelli, & Williams, 1999). Other studies have found that for women, gender "trumps" sexual orientation on a range of disordered eating attitudes and behaviours (Bankoff & Pantalone, 2014; Lakkis et al., 1999). Overall the data suggest that even though lesbian subculture may be more flexible and tolerant of diverse body sizes and shapes, it may be insufficient to reverse media and societal messages that promote thinness and attractiveness, as women have been exposed to these messages from childhood. In line with some of the adult studies, Austin et al. (2004) found that lesbian/bisexual girls were happier with their bodies and less likely to report trying to look like images of women in the media that heterosexual girls.

Physical Factors: Visible Differences

Mainstream body image research tends to focus on how adolescents feel about the way that they look, and focuses on body weight and shape as the main things adolescents would be dissatisfied with. However, a small proportion of adolescents have congenital conditions, injuries, or other conditions that do actually make them look different and vary from societal ideals. For full details of this extensive area of research, see Rumsey and Harcourt (2012), *The Oxford Handbook of the Psychology of Appearance*. Here, we provide an overview of the body image research that has been conducted with adolescents with visible differences.

Congenital conditions are a main cause for visible differences. These are physical conditions existing pre-memory; the adolescent has no experience of what life was like without them (Feragen, 2012). They include craniofacial conditions, which involve the head and neck, the most common being a cleft of the lip and/or palate. Other conditions include the failure by a part of the face or head to develop, absence of an ear or an eye, underdevelopment of cheek and jaw bones, and premature fusion of the structure lines of the skull. Also included are conditions that involve the nervous system such as neurofibromatosis type 1, which causes neural crest cells to proliferate excessively throughout the body, forming tumours on body nerves. One such condition is characterised by visible 'café au lait' patches, peripheral neurofibromas, and deformed bones. Congenital conditions may also involve vascular development such as vascular tumours, which usually disappear completely before a child is 10 years old, and vascular malformations, which are lesions that occur in visible locations on the head or neck. Other congenital conditions involve body parts such that part of the limb fails to develop; there may be a missing breast, hand, or foot or a shape anomaly; there may be a failure of the fingers and toes to separate, or there may be growth of extra fingers.

Overall, research shows that the body image of adolescents with congenital conditions does not differ from adolescents without congenital conditions (Pinquart, 2013). Moreover, the range of body image emotions, cognitions, and behaviours of individuals with congenital conditions is comparable to that found in individuals who are generally dissatisfied with their normal appearance, and most individuals with a congenital condition cope well (Feragen, 2012). In addition, the degree of visible difference associated with a congenital condition does not seem to predict level of psychological distress, self-perceptions, and satisfaction with appearance. Rather, the best predictor of psychological adjustment is the individual's subjective appearance satisfaction and the extent to which he or she believes that the condition is visible to others (Feragen, 2012). The family environment is another important factor, as some parents report more concerns about their child's appearance and body image than their children do, and these in turn affect children's emotional well-being (Feragen, 2012). Also important are others' responses to the visible differences, which include teasing and staring by peers. Such peer harassment has been found to mediate the relationship between cleft visibility and dissatisfaction with appearance among girls (Feragen & Borge, 2010).

Cancer and its treatment are also associated with distinct visible differences, as there are often aggressive side-effects that affect adolescents' physical appearance and lead to hair loss and changes in body weight (Fan & Eiser, 2009; Varni, Katz Colegrove, & Dolgin, 1995). The overall relationship between cancer and body image has been found to be weak (Pinquart,

2013), and several studies have found no differences regarding body image between adolescents with cancer and healthy controls (Fan & Eiser, 2009). However, body image concerns have been found to be particularly high while adolescents undergo chemotherapy (Fan & Eiser, 2009), and these concerns were highlighted in an in-depth interview study of adolescents being treated for acute lymphoblastic leukemia and/or a range of cancers at various stage of treatment (Williamson, Harcourt, Halliwell, Frith, & Wallace, 2010). Adolescents described their appearance as "different" or "unusual" and perceived this as unattractive, "ugly", aged, or ill-looking. Many felt anxious and self-conscious and were reluctant to reveal appearance changes in public, as they reported staring, teasing, and inappropriate questioning. In addition, the need to look 'normal' was the greatest drive for those who employed techniques to conceal or enhance their appearance.

As found with adolescents who have congenital conditions, adolescents with cancer worry about how other people judge them, and this affects their desires to interact with others and establish intimate relationships (Lee et al., 2012). This has been found to lead to withdrawal, feeling different, losing touch with peers, and feeling lost at school or behind in their work. Moreover, in one study, children with leukaemia cited being teased from hair loss or weight gain or loss as worse than the physical pain from the disease or the diagnostic and treatment procedures (Varni et al., 1995). Other findings show that a more positive body image is associated with lower anxiety and loneliness and greater self-worth, but again the degree of visible physical impairment is not associated with psychological adjustment (Fan & Eiser, 2009).

Survivors of burns also live with a range of visible differences that can include long-term scarring, changes in skin colour, and loss of fingers, toes, ears, or hair (Pope, Solomons, Done, Cohn, & Possamai, 2007). However, survivors of burns have not been found to display more body image concerns. One study of adolescents who had had burns as children found that they reported more positive general feelings about their appearance, more positive weight satisfaction, more positive evaluation of how others viewed their appearance, and a higher quality of life (Pope et al., 2007). Similarly, another study of adolescents who were more than one year post-burn found that male burn survivors did not differ on body image from the comparison group while female burn survivors had a more positive body image than comparison group (Lawrence, Rosenberg, & Fauerbach, 2007). However, body image was weakly correlated with number of surgeries, number of body parts with scars, and overall severity and scar visibility and moderately with perceived stigmatisation and feeling less comfortable in social situations.

The main finding that visible differences are not associated with higher body image concerns is often viewed as unexpected (Fan & Eiser, 2009).

This is because individuals without visible differences often believe that those with visible differences are preoccupied with their differences and that these concerns prevent a 'normal' life (Lawrence et al., 2007). On the contrary, researchers have highlighted the high level of resilience developed by children and adolescents with visible differences (Fan & Eiser, 2009). Resilience focuses on "the strengths and abilities of those who can 'bounce back' from stress and challenges"; "strategies to minimise the effects of BI [body image] change, for example wearing a hat to disguise hair loss; or long trousers to high an affected limb"; and the reinterpretation of "their experiences in order to hasten the process of 'getting back to normal'" (Fan & Eiser, 2009, p. 255). It has also been suggested that young people with visible differences have developed healthy coping skills that enable them to see beyond appearance concerns (Pope et al., 2007). Likewise, it has been suggested that survivors of severe burns who have lived through a "life-altering experience may cause some to have a deeper appreciation for life and drop the need to prove oneself" (Lawrence et al., 2007, 376), which again may draw adolescents away from a focus on appearance.

Conclusion

Internalisation of the societal ideals of attractiveness has been consistently found to be related to body image concerns. Adolescents who internalise societal ideals of attractiveness are more likely to report increased levels of body dissatisfaction and engage in body-change strategies. Negative affect and self-esteem have also been shown to be related to body image; however, increasingly the evidence suggests that the relationship is bidirectional, in that negative affect might contribute to the development of body dissatisfaction, and those with body image concerns might also experience low mood states as a result of their dissatisfaction. There have been fewer studies examining perfectionism and sexual orientation among adolescents; however, these factors have been found to be important among adults. Last, although, negotiating body image and appearance concerns can be more challenging for adolescents who have visible differences, their body image, overall, has been found to be similar to that of adolescents without visible differences.

References

Almeida, S., Severo, M., Araujo, J., Lopes, C., & Ramos, E. (2012). Body image and depressive symptoms in 13-year-old adolescents. *Journal of Paediatrics and Child Health, 48*, E165-E171.

Austin, S.B., Ziyadeh, N., Kahn, J.A., Camargo, C.A., Colditz, G.A., & Field, A.E. (2004). Sexual orientation, weight concerns, and eating-disordered behaviors in adolescent girls and boys. *Journal of the American Academy of Child and Adolescent Psychiatry, 43*, 1115–23.

Bankoff, S.M., & Pantalone, D.W. (2014). Patterns of disordered eating behaviour in women by sexual orientation: A review of the literature. *Eating Disorders, 22*, 261–74.

Bearman, S.K., & Stice, E. (2008). Testing a gender additive model: The role of body image in adolescent depression. *Journal of Abnormal Child Psychology, 36*, 1251–63.

Boone, L., Soenens, B., & Braet, C. (2011). Perfectionism, body dissatisfaction, and bulimic symptoms: The intervening role of perceived pressure to be thin and thin ideal internalization. *Journal of Social and Clinical Psychology, 30*, 1043–68.

Brausch, A.M., & Gutierrez, P.M. (2009). The role of body image and disordered eating as risk factors for depression and suicidal ideation in adolescents. *Suicide and Life-Threatening Behavior, 39*, 58–71.

Brunet, J., Sabiston, C.M., Dorsch, K.D., & McCreary, D.R. (2010). Exploring a model linking social physique anxiety, drive for muscularity, drive for thinness and self-esteem among adolescent boys and girls. *Body Image, 7*, 137–142.

Cafri, G., van den Berg, P., & Thompson, J.K. (2006). Pursuit of muscularity in adolescent boys: Relations among biopsychosocial variables and clinical outcomes. *Journal of Clinical Child and Adolescent Psychology, 35*, 283–291.

Cafri, G., Yamamiya, Y., Brannick, M., & Thompson, J.K. (2005). The influence of sociocultural factors on body image: A meta-analysis. *Clinical Psychology: Science and Practice, 12*, 421–33.

Coker, T.R., Austin, S.B., & Schuster, M.A. (2010). The health and health care of lesbian, gay, and bisexual adolescents. *Annual Review of Public Health, 31*, 457–77.

Dour, H.J., & Theran, S.A. (2011). The interaction between the superhero ideal and maladaptive perfectionism as predictors of unhealthy eating attitudes and body esteem. *Body Image, 8*, 93–96.

Grammas, D.L., & Schwartz, J.P. (2009). Internalization of messages from society and perfectionism as predictors of male body image. *Body Image, 6*, 31–36.

Fan, S., & Eiser, C. (2009). Body image of children and adolescents with cancer: A systematic review. *Body Image, 6*, 247–56.

Feragen, K.B. (2012). Congenital conditions. In N. Rumsey and D. Harcourt (Eds.), *The Oxford Handbook of the Psychology of Appearance* (pp. 353–71). Oxford: Oxford Press.

Feragen, K.B., & Borge, A.I.H. (2010). Peer harassment and satisfaction with appearance in children with and without a facial difference. *Body Image, 7*, 97–105.

Fredrickson, B.L., & Roberts, T.A. (1997). Objectification theory: Toward understanding women's lived experiences and mental health risks. *Psychology of Women Quarterly, 21*, 173–206.

French, S.A., Story, M., Remafedi, G., Resnick, M.D., & Blum, R.W. (1996) Sexual orientation and prevalence of body dissatisfaction and eating disordered behaviors: a population-based study of adolescents. *International Journal of Eating Disorders, 19*, 119–26.

Frost, R.O., Marten, P., Lahart, C., & Rosenblate, R. (1990). The dimensions of perfectionism. *Cognitive Theory and Research, 14*, 449–468.

Holsen, I., Kraft, P., & Roysamb, E. (2001). The relationship between body image and depressed mood in adolescence: A five-year longitudinal panel study. *Journal of Health Psychology, 6*, 613–27.

Karazsia, B.T., van Dulmen, M.H.M, Wong, K., & Crowther, J.H. (2013). Thinking meta-theoretically about the role of internalization in the development of body dissatisfaction and body change behaviors. *Body Image, 10*, 433–41.

Lakkis, J., Ricciardelli, L.A., & Williams, R.J. (1999). The role of sexual orientation and gender-related traits in disordered eating. *Sex Roles, 41*, 1–16.

Lawrence, J.W., Rosenberg, L.E., & Fauerbach, J.A. (2007). Comparing the body esteem of pediatric survivors of burn injury with the body esteem of an age-matched comparison group without burns. *Rehabilitation Psychology, 52*, 370–79.

Lee, M., Mu, P. Tsay, S., Chou, S., Chen, Y., & Wong, T. (2012). Body image of children and adolescents with cancer: A metasynthesis on qualitative research findings. *Nursing and Health Sciences, 14*, 381–90.

Lock, J., Reisel, B., & Steiner, H. (2001). Associated health risks of adolescents with disordered eating: How different are they from their peers? Results from a high school survey. *Child Psychiatry and Human Development, 31*, 249–65.

Martin, G.C., Wertheim. E.H., Prior, M., Smart, D., Sanson, A., & Oberklaid, F. (2000). A longitudinal study of the role of childhood temperament in the later development of eating concerns. *International Journal of Eating Disorders, 27*, 150–62.

McCabe, M.P., & Ricciardelli, L.A. (2004). Body image dissatisfaction among males across the lifespan: A review of past literature. *Journal of Psychosomatic Research, 56*, 675–85.

McCabe, M.P. & Ricciardelli, L.A. (2006). Prospective study of extreme weight change behaviors among adolescent boys and girls. *Journal of Youth and Adolescence, 35*, 425–34.

McCreary, D. & Sasse, D. (2000). An exploration of the drive for muscularity in adolescent boys and girls. *Journal of American College Health, 48*, 297–304.

McLean, S.A., Paxton, S.J., & Wertheim, E.H. (2013). Mediators of the relationship between media literacy and body dissatisfaction in early adolescent girls: Implications for prevention. *Body Image, 10*, 282–89.

McVey, G., Tweed, S., & Blackmore, E. (2005). Correlates of weight loss and muscle-gaining behavior in 10 to 14-year-old males and females. *Preventive Medicine, 40*, 1–9.

Mitchell, S.H., Petrie, T.A., Greenleaf, C.A., & Martin, S.B. (2012). Moderators of the internalization-body dissatisfaction relationship in middle school girls. *Body Image, 9*, 431–40.

Murray, K., Rieger, E., & Byrne, D. (2013). A longitudinal investigation of the mediating role of self-esteem and body importance in the relationship between stress and body dissatisfaction in adolescent females and males. *Body Image, 10*, 544–51.

Paxton, S.J., Eisenberg, M.E., & Neumark-Sztainer, D. (2006). Prospective predictors of body dissatisfaction in adolescent girls and boys: A five-year longitudinal study. *Developmental Psychology, 42*, 888–99.

Paxton, S.J., Neumark-Sztainer, D., Hannan, P.J., & Eisenberg, M.E. (2006). Body dissatisfaction prospectively predicts depressive mood and low self-esteem in adolescent girls and boys. *Journal of Clinical Child and Adolescent Psychology, 35*, 539–49.

Petrie, T.A., Greenleaf, C., & Martin, S. (2010). Biopsychosocial and physical correlates of middle school boys' and girls' body satisfaction. *Sex Roles, 63*, 631–44.

Pinquart, M. (2013). Body image of children and adolescents with chronic illness: A meta-analytic comparison with healthy peers. *Body Image, 10*, 141–48.

Pope, S.J., Solomons, W.R., Done, D.J., Cohn, N., & Possamai, A.M. (2007). Body image, mood and quality of life in young burn survivors. *Burns, 33*, 747–55.

Presnell, K., Bearman, S.K., & Stice, E. (2004). Risk factors for body dissatisfaction in adolescent boys and girls: A prospective study. *International Journal of Eating Disorders, 36*, 389–401.

Ricciardelli, L.A., & McCabe, M.P. (2001). Self-esteem and negative affect as moderators of sociocultural influences on body dissatisfaction, strategies to decrease weight, and strategies to increase muscles among adolescent boys and girls. *Sex Roles, 44*, 189–207.

Ricciardelli, L.A., & McCabe, M.P. (2004). A biopsychosocial model of disordered eating and the pursuit of muscularity in adolescent boys. *Psychological Bulletin, 130*, 179–205.

Ricciardelli, L.A. & McCabe, M.P. (2009). *Study of adolescent health risk behaviours.* Unpublished manuscript, Deakin University.

Rodgers, R.F., Ganchou, C., Franko, D.L., & Chabrol, H. (2012). Drive for muscularity and disordered eating among French adolescent boys: A sociocultural model. *Body Image, 9*, 318–23.

Rodgers, R.F., Paxton, S.J., & McLean, S.A. (2014). A biopsychosocial model of body image concerns and disordered eating in early adolescent girls. *Journal of Youth and Adolescence, 43*, 814–23.

Ruggiero, G.M., Levi, D., Ciuna, A., & Sassardi, S. (2003). Stress situation reveals an association between perfectionism and drive for thinness. *International Journal of Eating Disorders, 34*, 220–26.

Rumsey, N., & Harcourt, D. (2007). Visible difference amongst children and adolescents: Issues and interventions. *Developmental Neurorehabilitation, 10*, 113–23.

Rumsey, N., & Harcourt, D. (2012). (Eds.), *The Oxford Handbook of the Psychology of Appearance.* Oxford: Oxford Press.

Saewyc, E.M., Bearinger, L.H., Heinz, P.A., Blum, R.W., & Resnick, M.D. (1998). Gender differences in health and risk behaviors among bisexual and homosexual adolescents. *Journal of Adolescent Health, 23*, 181–88.

Sherry, S.B., Vriend, J.L., Hewitt, P.L., Sherry, D.L., Flett, G.L., & Wardrop, A.A. (2009). Perfectionism dimensions, appearance schemas, and body image disturbance in community members and university students. *Body Image, 6*, 83–89.

Slaney, R.B., Rice, K.G., Mobley, M., Trippi, J., & Ashby, J.S. (2001). The Revised Almost Perfect Scale. *Measurement and Evaluation in Counselling and Development, 34*, 130–45.

Stice, E. (1994). Review of the evidence for a sociocultural model of bulimia nervosa and an exploration of the mechanisms of action. *Clinical Psychology Review, 16*, 633–61.

Stice, E., & Whitenton, K. (2002). Risk factors for body dissatisfaction in adolescent girls: A longitudinal investigation. *Developmental Psychology, 38*, 669–78.

Thompson, J.K., Heinberg, L.J., Altabe, M.N., & Tantleff-Dunn, S. (1999). *Exacting beauty: Theory, assessment, and treatment of body image disturbance.* Washington, DC: American Psychological Association.

Varni, J.W., Katz, E.R., Colegrove, R., & Dolgin, M. (1995). Perceived physical appearance and adjustment of children with newly diagnosed cancer: A path analytic model. *Journal of Behavioral Medicine, 18,* 261–78.

Welch, E., Miller, J.L., Ghaderi, A., & Vaillancourt, T. (2009). Does perfectionism mediate or moderate the relation between body dissatisfaction and disordered eating attitudes and behaviors? *Eating Behaviors, 10,* 168–75.

Williamson, H., Harcourt, D., Halliwell, E., Frith, H., & Wallace, M. (2010). Adolescents' and parents' experiences of managing the psychosocial impact of appearance change during cancer treatment. *Journal of Pediatric Oncology Nursing, 27,* 168–75.

Wojtowicz, A.E., & von Ranson, K.M. (2012). Weighing in on risk factors for body dissatisfaction: A one-year prospective study of middle-adolescent girls. *Body Image, 9,* 20–30.

10
SPORT

Sport provides an important environment and sociocultural context for studying adolescent body image among boys and girls. Sport naturally draws adolescents' attention to their bodies, and it can help shift the attention away from the focus on 'looks' to how the body moves and functions and what the body can 'do' (Abbott & Baber, 2010). Sport also helps adolescents develop a range of skills such as self-discipline, leadership, and self-confidence, which facilitate the development of positive self-esteem and self-concept. However, there is also the negative side of sport, as its environment can heighten adolescents' risk of developing disordered eating (Ricciardelli & McCabe, 2004). As early as 1980, Garner and Garfinkel drew attention to the fact that involvement in activities such as sports, that demand more attention and control over body image is a risk factor for the development of eating disorders.

More recently, both the positive and negative aspects of sport have been highlighted in Galli and Rell's (2009) qualitative study of 10 male athletes. These men were simultaneously proud and self-critical of their bodies. Most of the athletes wanted to be taller, heavier, or stronger, but they also reported an overall feeling of confidence in the appearance and performance capability of their bodies. Langdon (2012) has also highlighted both positives and negatives associated with dance for girls. Dance is a positive experience because it promotes exercise, therapy and self-expression; however, it is also a negative force as it often takes place in an environment that constantly emphasises appearance. The positive and negative aspects of sport are further evident in the studies in the field, which overall show that athletes have lower levels of body dissatisfaction than non-athletes but at the same time display higher levels of disordered eating than non-athletes.

In this chapter we will review the meaning and the experiences associated with sport for boys and girls. We examine how sport is associated with a more positive body image but higher levels of disordered eating among athletes. We will also address the reasons for athletes' more positive body image and aspects of sport environment, which heighten their risk for disordered eating.

Sport for Boys and Girls

Sport is especially central to the lives of boys as it takes up a lot of their time; boys derive great enjoyment from sport; and sport provides boys with a supportive social environment for developing friendships (Coleman, 2011; Ricciardelli, McCabe, & Ridge, 2006). Participation in any kind of sport for boys is related to higher self-esteem (Holland & Andre, 1994), and adolescent boys more than girls perceive that the function of sport participation is to increase their social status and peer popularity (White, Duda, & Keller, 1998). In addition, the sporting context is the main forum that Western males have for demonstrating various aspects of masculinity, which are closely aligned with the pursuit of muscularity. These include athletic strength and superiority, competitiveness, toughness, endurance, leadership, status, power, and authority (Connell, 1995; Drummond, 2002).

In an early study, Grogan and Richards (2002) showed that there are limited contexts where adolescents and other males feel at ease in discussing their body image concerns. In their focus group study of preadolescent, adolescent, and adult males, Grogan and Richards found that males in all age groups viewed discussions of muscularity acceptable in relation to fitness and athleticism. Moreover, although males gave primarily cosmetic reasons for wanting to attain the lean and muscular look, men and boys in all age groups resisted representing men's bodies as objects of aesthetic interest by shifting their discussions to how bodies looked in relation to function, fitness, and/ or health. Similarly, we found in our interviews with adolescents that the majority of adolescent boys were reluctant to focus on their body per se, but through their talk about sport, the boys openly discussed what they liked and did not like about their bodies (Ricciardelli et al., 2006). In addition, our research showed that what boys liked about their bodies and the aspects they wanted to improve were synonymous with the attributes associated with being successful at sport. These included functional aspects of the body such as overall size, height, speed, strength, fitness, and endurance.

Sport is also often used as a forum for competing with other boys, on the playing field and by using sport performance to make favourable social comparisons about their own body size. For example, in our interviews boys talked about being "the best on the field", "the strongest in the class", and "wanting to be bigger than their friends" (Ricciardelli et al., 2006). This emphasis on competition among males is also viewed as having a strong and adaptive evolutionary function in promoting the survival of males and may be used by boys to maintain a more positive body image.

Although sport is less central in the lives of girls, several researchers have highlighted the positive potential effects of sports for girls. For example, Fredrickson and Roberts (1997) have argued that one way girls can resist the internalisation of messages to attain the thin ideal is to encourage sports participation and related forms of physical activity. A focus on sport promotes an active, instrumental experience of the self and therefore may be less likely to promote self-objectification (Fredrickson & Roberts, 1997; Tiggemann, 2001). In this way the focus is more on function and what the body can do rather than what the body looks like. In line with this view, one recent study with adolescent girls demonstrated that any involvement in sporting activities was associated with a more functional view of their body image than found among girls not involved in sport (Abbott & Barber, 2011). Sport also provides girls with opportunities to learn teamwork, goal-setting, and perseverance (Varnes et al., 2013). In support of this view, female participation in sports has been linked to improved academic performance and enhanced self-esteem, as well as reductions in depression and better physical health (Varnes et al., 2013).

However, some of the experiences associated with sport and physical participation for girls also present a dilemma and are more negative than those found with boys. Girls during adolescence in comparison to boys are more likely to cease playing sport, often citing the reason that it is not 'cool' or feminine (Slater & Tiggemann, 2011). In order to be successful at sport they need to develop characteristics associated with masculinity such as strength, competitiveness, assertiveness, and independence (Steinfeldt, Zakrajsek, Carter, & Steinfeldt, 2011). This is consistent with the finding that female athletes often report being conflicted about their body image, as the muscular body required to be successful in sport does not fit in with cultural norms of what a feminine body should be like (Steinfeldt, Zakrajsek, Bodey, Middendorf, & Martin, 2013). As noted by Markula (1995, p. 424), female athletes are required to be "firm but shapely, fit but sexy, strong but thin", and this is not easy to achieve. Girls are also more likely to drop out of sport due to the higher level of teasing in comparison to boys that they experience while playing sport and during other physical activities (Slater & Tiggemann, 2011). These experiences include being stared at because of how they look, being made fun of/laughed at because of how they look, being teased about being uncoordinated, and being called names relating to size or weight.

Sport and Body Image

Researchers have drawn attention to the fact that certain sports dictate different kinds of bodies (Petrie & Greenleaf, 2012) and a unique set of demands related to body weight, shape, and size (Reel, Petrie, SooHoo, & Anderson, 2013). For example, figure skating tends to dictate small, petite, thin bodies; football players need to be big, strong, and powerful; basketball players are required to be tall; and gymnasts need to be tiny and light. On the other hand, some types of sports dictate a physique that is close to societal ideals for males: muscular, lean, and powerful as in wrestling, volleyball, lacrosse, and swimming. However, differences in body image across different sporting groups have generally not been found (Hausenblas & Downs, 2001; Varnes et al., 2013).

The main focus of studies in the field has been on examining body image concerns between athletes and non-athletes. Overall, studies have shown that athletes report a more positive body image than non-athletes. In a meta-analysis, which summarised 78 studies (38 with adolescents), Hausenblas and Downs (2001) found a small effect indicating that athletes had a more positive body image compared to non-athletes. There were no differences between the female athletes and the male athletes; no differences between different types of sports (aesthetic, endurance, and ball game sports); and no differences by age or BMI. The only significant differences related to the post hoc analyses, which indicated that college athletes had significantly more positive body image than the club/recreational athletes. Another meta-analysis that focused exclusively on female athletes conducted by Smolak, Murnen and Ruble (2000), also showed that athletes overall had a more positive body image than non-athletes.

The majority of studies conducted since the above meta-analyses have continued to demonstrate that adolescents who participate in sport demonstrate lower levels of body dissatisfaction (Tiggemann, 2001; Varnes et al., 2013). This finding has further been supported by a more recent meta-analysis that examined the relationship between body image and physical activity, which showed that both adolescent girls and boys with lower levels of body dissatisfaction, less appearance concerns, and more positive physical self-concepts were more physically active (Babic et al., 2014). However, the overall relationship was weak ($r = .14$), highlighting that some studies have found no relationship between sport participation and body image (e.g., Slatter & Tiggemann, 2011).

There is also emerging evidence that girls who participate in sports may be more conflicted about their body image, as they are confronted with messages from the sporting environment to be more athletic, but at the same time they are bombarded with the more general sociocultural messages to be slender and feminine (Abbott & Barber, 2011). Specifically in one study girls who participated in sport reported higher functional values (e.g., "How good I feel about my body depends a lot on what my body can do physically"), functional behavioural-investment (e.g., "I do physically active things often"), and functional satisfaction (e.g., "I feel really good about what I can do physically") with their body than girls who were not physically active (Abbott & Barber, 2011). However, the girls who participated in sport also reported higher aesthetic values (e.g., "How good I feel about my body depends a lot on how I look") and aesthetic behavioural-investment (e.g., "I always try to look the best I can) with their body.

Given the sexual objectification of female athletes in the media in recent years, with the focus on being both athletic and thin, Varnes et al. (2013) were especially interested in reviewing recent studies with adult female athletes. In 8 of the 10 studies, athletes overall were found to display a more positive body image. More specifically, three studies found that athletes competing in the endurance sports of swimming, track, and water polo experienced less body image concerns than non-athletes. Another study showed that golf and volleyball athletes experienced less weight preoccupation than non-athletes. Furthermore, athletes defined as participating in 'appearance-focused' sports (gymnastics and tennis) experienced lower body image concerns than athletes participating in 'non-appearance/non-lean' focused sports. On the other hand, three of the four studies that compared non-athletes to athletes in more feminine sports of gymnastics, tennis, and volleyball found no differences.

In one recent study, Karr, Davidson, Bryant, Balague, and Bohnert (2013) examined body dissatisfaction among adolescent females who played three different types of sports: gymnastics, which is considered a sport that focuses on aesthetics and leanness; cross-country running, which focuses on leanness but not aesthetics; and softball, which focuses on neither aesthetics nor leanness. In line with previous studies, the majority of athletes displayed low body dissatisfaction, but there were no overall differences in body dissatisfaction across the three groups. In addition, across all three groups, greater athletic self-efficacy predicted less body dissatisfaction, suggesting that when adolescents have strong positive beliefs about their performance they also hold strong positive beliefs about their bodies. BMI was also a predictor of body dissatisfaction with higher BMI associated with greater body dissatisfaction. Last, mothers' body dissatisfaction was related to daughters' body dissatisfaction among the cross-country runners and softball group but not among the gymnasts.

Another recent study conducted by Francisco, Narisco and Alarcão (2013) compared elite with non-elite adolescent athletes. Elite athletes were found to be more dissatisfied with their bodies than non-elite athletes. However, the predictors of body dissatisfaction in both groups were the same. These included: gender (girls displayed higher levels of body dissatisfaction), higher BMI, and higher perceived sociocultural pressures. The other examined variables, parent relationships, self-esteem and social support, were not found to be significant predictors.

The differences in body image among adolescents who play team sports versus individual sports have also been studied. Boys participating in team sports have been found to report lower body dissatisfaction than those in individual sports (Morano, Colella, & Caprancia, 2011). Similarly, girls who participate in team sports have been found to report a more positive body image than girls who participate in individual sports (Jaffe & Lutter, 1995). The focus in team sports is more likely to be on the group, so this may draw less attention to adolescents' abilities and their body image.

Hausenblas and Downs (2001) proposed possible explanations for why athletes, on the whole, have a more positive body image than non-athletes. These explanations have been reiterated by Petrie and Greenleaf (2012). These researchers argue that athletes may have a more positive image than non-athletes because their high physical activity levels combined with rigorous training may assist in bringing athletes closer to the ideal of a 'thin/lean and fit physique' for females and a 'lean and muscular physique' for males than is the case for non-athletes. In addition, physical activity participation is associated with increases in positive psychological characteristics (e.g., increased self-esteem, decreased mood disturbance), and these help to promote a positive body image. However, it is also possible that individuals with a positive body image choose to participate in sport. Clearly, longitudinal studies are needed to test these different hypotheses. In addition, more studies are needed to more fully examine some of the nuances of different sporting environments (e.g., college and elite) and how these can impact on body image.

It is also important to address the motives for sport, physical activity and exercise. Physical activity and exercise are often individual pursuits that may be undertaken as a quest to improve fitness and health but also for appearance-related motives (Abbott & Barber, 2011). When these are undertaken for fitness and health there is an association with lower levels of body dissatisfaction. Similarly, when dance is for self-expression, it is associated with a more positive self-image, but when one's dance performance or outcome is determined by judges or an audience, it is associated with a more negative body image (Langdon, 2012). There are also differences between one's participation in sports and one's participation in physical activity. Abbott and Barber (2011) found that girls who played sports valued and invested in the functional body to a greater extent than did physically active girls. In addition, girls who played sports were more satisfied with their functional bodies than both physically active and non-physically active girls (Abbott & Barber, 2011).

Sport and Disordered Eating

Although athletes have been found to have a more positive body image than non-athletes, they have been shown to display higher levels of disordered eating. However, the prevalence of disordered eating among athletes and different subgroups of athletes varies across studies. These are due to different sampling procedures, sizes, and criteria used to define eating disorders (Ricciardelli & McCabe, 2004, 2015), but they are also likely to reflect the different culture of the sporting clubs and different training programs (Voelker, Gould, & Reel, 2014).

The estimates in an early study showed that 1.6% of male athletes and 4.2% of female athletes aged between 16 and 25 years satisfied the DSM III-R criteria for anorexia nervosa, and 14.3% of male athletes and 39.2% of female athletes met the DSM III-R criteria for bulimia nervosa (Burckes-Miller & Black, 1988). Another survey of elite college athletes (average age = 19.9 years) showed that only 1.1% of females met the full DSM-IV criteria for bulimia nervosa, while no athlete met the criteria for anorexia nervosa (Johnson, Powers, & Dick, 1999). However, in the same study, 9.2% of the female and .005% of the male athletes were identified as having clinically significant symptoms of bulimia nervosa, and 2.85 % of females were considered to have clinically significant symptoms of anorexia nervosa. In addition, another 25% of the female and 9.5% of the male athletes were considered at risk of anorexia nervosa, while 58% of the female and 38% of the male athletes were considered at risk for bulimia nervosa (Johnson et al., 1999). Other estimates suggest that subclinical levels of eating disorders among elite athletes are 10 to 50 times higher than those found in the general population (Glazer, 2008).

In a comprehensive meta-analysis, Hausenblas and Carron (1999) examined the relationship between the type of sport and disordered eating, which included 17 studies with males (16.9% of the reviewed studies). The meta-analysis showed that adolescent and adult male athletes across all categories of sport, but particularly athletes who participated in sports where there was a strong emphasis on aesthetics and sports that required weight restrictions, reported more disordered eating than comparison groups. In addition, the difference between male athletes and male controls was found to be greater than the difference between female athletes and controls. However, the overall effects were small to moderate in size.

The other comprehensive meta-analysis that specifically focused on female athletes and eating problems was conducted by Smolak et al. (2000). Fifteen of the 44 reviewed studies were with adolescents. Although athletes showed significantly more eating problems than non-athletes the effect size was very small. This difference was larger among college student samples but non-significant among high school students. Elite athletes were found to demonstrate higher levels of eating problems than non-elite athletes, as were athletes participating in lean sports. In addition, athletes participating in elite, lean sports were especially at higher risk, as were females participating in various forms of dance or performance sports. These included ballet, aerobic instruction, and cheerleading.

Studies have continued to highlight the higher levels of disordered eating among sporting groups where the focus is on leanness and aesthetics. This includes ballet dancers and women who participate in other aesthetic and competitive sports such as gymnastics, figure skating, cheerleading, and synchronised swimming (Langdon, 2012). Ballet dancers have been specifically found to demonstrate significantly higher disordered eating symptoms than basketball players among adolescent girls (Monthuy-Blanc, Maiano, & Therme, 2010). In another study female athletes who participated in either ballet or figure skating (average age of 14.5 years) displayed higher drive for thinness, bulimic symptoms, dieting behaviour, and more concerns about weight and shape compared to normative data (van Durme, Goossens, & Braet, 2012). In addition, the time spent on aesthetic activities such as ballet, gymnastics and exercising at the gym has been found to be positively related to disordered eating for both girls and boys (Slater & Tiggemann, 2011).

Sports for boys have also been found to be associated with body change strategies, in particular, muscle-enhancing behaviours. In our 8-month longitudinal study (Ricciardelli & McCabe, 2009, Appendix 2 in Chapter 4), we devised three questions to assess the importance of sport to adolescent boys in terms of the appearance of their bodies and their relationships with their friends ("How important is it for you to be good at sports?"; "How important is your best male friend's view of your ability at sport?"; and "How important is your best female friend's view of your ability at sport?"). At 8 months we found that a focus on sport predicted body image importance, strategies to decrease weight, strategies to increase muscles, and strategies to increase weight. In each case, a higher focus on sport predicted a greater importance placed on the body and body change strategies. In another study, participation in sports was found to be associated with muscle-enhancing behaviours, including eating patterns, exercise, and protein powders, in both adolescent boys and girls (Eisenberg, Wall, Neumark-Sztainer, 2012). In addition, participation in power sports for adolescent boys has been found to be a risk factor for using anabolic steroids. These include sports such as athletics, cycling, hockey, football (Sagoe, Andreassen, & Pallesen, 2014), field events, weightlifting (Wichstrom & Pedersen, 2001), and bodybuilding (Blouin & Goldfield, 1995). Adolescents resort to using anabolic steroids to improve their appearance but also to increase their strength and size, and to improve their sporting performance (Sagoe et al., 2014).

There are several dimensions of the sport environment that heighten athletes' risk for disordered eating. It has long been argued that the sport environment, with its emphasis on obtaining an optimal weight for athletic performance, promotes a subculture with intensified pressures to be lean, and this increases athletes' risk of developing eating disorders and disordered eating (Ricciardelli & McCabe, 2004). The specific desire to be leaner to improve sports performance was one of the four factors examined in relation to disordered eating among adolescent male and female athletes from aesthetic sports over a one-year period by Krentz and Warschburger (2013). The other factors were body dissatisfaction, emotional distress from missed exercise sessions, and social pressure from the sports environment. Only increased desire to be leaner to improve sports performance predicted disordered eating.

Two other aspects of the sporting environment have been found to be associated with higher levels of body dissatisfaction and more disordered eating among adolescent and adult female athletes (Reel et al., 2013). One aspect was assessed by the scale that focused on pressures from coaches and weight requirements for sport and included questions such as "My coach encourages athletes on my team to drop pounds"; "Body weight and appearance are important to my coach"; "My team/sport has a weight requirement to try out or compete"; and "There are pressures with my sport to maintain a below average weight" (Reel et al., 2013). The other aspect was assessed by the scale that highlighted other pressures regarding appearance and performance and included questions such as "My workout/competition attire makes me more conscious of my bodily appearance"; "Spectators make me more concerned about my weight and appearance"; "Any of my body flaws are readily apparent in my workout/competition attire" and "My teammates notice if I put on weight" (Reel et al., 2013).

Given that coaches work closely with athletes, Coppola, Ward and Freysinger (2014), conducted an in-depth study of eight elite female athletes' experiences of their coaches' communication of sport body image. This more fully showed how coaches can influence athletes' body image and their eating behaviours in both positive and negative ways. On the whole, coaches were very encouraging in promoting a healthy, fit body through nutrition and physical activity. The athletes found discussions about diet and exercise habits helpful, and wanted more input from their coaches about healthy eating. However, coaches' comparisons and criticisms of athletes' bodies were found to be upsetting and unhelpful. Many of the coaches' critical comments regarding body weight and shape were viewed as irrelevant and unhelpful as the athletes were healthy and performing well. More valuable to the athletes were coaches' discussions about ways to achieve body change, and they espe-cially valued individual feedback from coaches as they viewed the impor-tance of recognising individual differences when developing training plans because all athletes' bodies are unique. However, they also commented on the importance of coaches' sensitively communicating body change strategies to individual athletes.

The requirement of wearing revealing uniforms is another aspect that can promote more focus on appearance and lead to higher levels of disordered eating for female athletes, especially for aesthetic sports like ballet dancing, gymnastics, figure skating, cheerleading, diving, and volleyball (Langdon, 2012; Steinfeld et al., 2013; Thompson & Digsby, 2004; Voelker et al., 2014). The revealing uniforms females are required to wear are often tight and uncomfortable, distract players from the game, and contribute to feelings of increased self-consciousness (Steinfeld et al., 2013). This was highlighted in an in-depth study of nine female college student athletes who played volley-ball at the elite level (Steinfeld et al., 2013). Although the women reported feeling pride and confidence in their athletic bodies, they also reported feel-ing concerned with how their bodies looked in their revealing spandex sports uniforms. In another study, self-consciousness of weight and appearance, which was in part attributed to the wearing of revealing uniforms, was found to be the main predictor of disordered eating among female figure skaters (mean age 15 years) (Voelker et al., 2014).

It has been argued that athletes' vulnerability to eating disorders may be increased because several individual characteristics (e.g., perfectionism, com-pulsiveness, self-motivation, high achievement expectations) thought to be advantageous for athletic performance are the same characteristics commonly found in individuals with eating disorders (Hausenblas & Carron, 1999). Thus, it is not clear whether higher levels of disordered eating found among athletes are due to sociocultural pressures from the environment or whether individuals with certain traits and attitudes self-select into particular sport (Langdon, 2012).

In addition, one of the problems with studying disordered eating among athletes is that many of the extreme weight loss behaviours that are con-sidered symptoms of disordered eating are also essential to athletes' optimal performance; they are sanctioned by the athletic culture and are viewed as athletic drive (Chung, 2001; Enns, Drewnowski, & Grinker, 1987). As many athletes may only use extreme weight loss strategies before tournaments and on a very short-term basis, it has been questioned whether these should be viewed as indicators of disordered eating (Chung, 2001; Dale & Landers, 1999; Enns et al., 1987).

Conclusion

Overall, studies show that sport participation is associated with a more positive body image but higher levels of disordered eating. Some of the factors associated with higher body image concerns and/or disordered eating among athletes are the same as those found among adolescents in general. These include being female, a higher BMI, greater perceived sociocultural pressures, and mothers' body dissatisfaction. However, other factors are more specific to the sporting environment. These include desire for leanness to improve sport performance, pressures from coaches and weight requirements for sport, and revealing sports uniforms. More in-depth studies are needed to more fully examine some of the nuances of different sporting environments and how these are experienced by athletes.

References

Abbott, B.D., & Barber, B.L. (2010). Embodied image: Gender differences in functional and aesthetic body image among Australian adolescents. *Body Image, 7*, 22–31.

Abbott, B.D., & Barber, B.L. (2011). Differences in functional and aesthetic body image between sedentary girls and girls involved in sports and physical activity: Does sport type make a difference. *Psychology of Sport and Exercise, 12*, 333–42.

Babic, M.J., Morgan, P.J., Plotnikoff, R.C., Lonsdale, C., White, R.L., & Lubans, D.R. (2014). Physical activity and physical self-concept in youth: Systematic review and meta-analysis. *Sports Medicine, 44*, 1589–1601.

Blouin, A.G., & Goldfield, G.S. (1995). Body image and steroid use in male bodybuilders. *International Journal of Eating Disorders, 18*, 159–65.

Burckes-Miller, M.E., & Black, D.R. (1988). Male and female college athletes: Prevalence of anorexia nervosa and bulimia nervosa. *Athletic Training, 23*, 137–40.

Chung, B. (2001). Muscle dysmorphia: A critical review of the proposed criteria. *Perspectives in Biology and Medicine, 44*, 565–74.

Coleman, J.C. (2011). *The nature of adolescence* (4th ed.). London: Routledge.

Connell, R. (1995). *Masculinities*. Cambridge: Polity.

Coppola, A.M., Ward, R.M., & Freysinger, V.J. (2014). Coaches' communication of sport body image: experiences of female athletes. *Journal of Applied Sport Psychology, 26*, 1–16.

Dale, K.S., & Landers, D.M. (1999). Weight control in wrestling: Eating disorders or disordered eating. *Medicine and Science in Sports and Exercise, 31*, 1382–89.

Drummond, M.J.N. (2002). Sport and images of masculinity: The meaning of relationships in the life course of "elite" male athletes. *The Journal of Men's Studies, 10*, 129–41.

Eisenberg, M.E., Wall, M. & Neumark-Sztainer, D. (2012). Muscle-enhancing behaviors among adolescent girls and boys. *Pediatrics, 130*, 1019–26.

Enns, M.P., Drewnowski, A., & Grinker, J.A. (1987) Body composition, body size estimation and *attitudes towards eating in male college athletes. Psychosomatic Medicine, 49*, 56–64.

Frederickson, B.L., & Roberts, T.A. (1997). Objectification theory: Toward understanding women's lived experiences and mental health risks. *Psychology of Women Quarterly, 21,* 173–206.

Francisco, R., Narisco, I., & Alarcão, M. (2013). Individual and relational risk factors for the development of eating disorders in adolescent aesthetic athletes and general adolescents. *Eating and Weight Disorders, 18,* 403–11.

Hausenblas, H.A., & Carron, A.V. (1999). Eating disorder indices and athletes: An integration. *Journal of Sport and Exercise Psychology, 21,* 230–58.

Hausenblas, H.A., & Downs, D.S. (2001). Comparison of body image between athletes and nonathletes: A meta-analytic review. *Journal of Applied Sport Psychology, 13,* 323–39.

Holland, A., & Andre, T. (1994). Athletic participation and the social status of adolescent males and females. *Youth and Society, 25,* 388–407.

Galli, N., & Rell, J. (2009). Adonis or Hephaestus? Exploring body image in male athletes. *9,* 95–108.

Garner, D.M., & Garfinkel, P.E. (1980). Socio-cultural factors in the development of anorexia nervosa. *Psychological Medicine, 10,* 647–56.

Glazer, J.L. (2008). Eating disorders among male athletes. *Current Sports Medicine Reports, 7,* 332–37.

Grogan, S., & Richards, H. (2002). Body image: Focus groups with boys and men. *Men and Masculinities, 4,* 219–32.

Jaffe, L., & Lutter, J.M. (1995). Adolescent girls: Factors affecting low and high body image. *Melpomene Journal, 14,* 14–22.

Johnson, C., Powers, P.S., & Dick, R. (1999). Athletes and eating disorders: The national collegiate athletic association study. *International Journal of Eating Disorders, 26,* 179–88.

Langdon, S.W. (2012). Body image in dance and aesthetic sports. In T.F. Cash, (Ed.), *Encyclopedia of body image and human appearance, Volume 1* (pp. 226–32). London: Elsevier.

Karr, T.M., Davidson, D., Bryant, F.B., Balague, G., & Bohnert, A.M. (2013). Sport type and interpersonal and intrapersonal predictors of body dissatisfaction in high school female sport participants. *Body Image, 10,* 210–19.

Krentz, E.M., & Warschburger, P. (2013). A longitudinal investigation of sports-related risk factors for disordered eating in aesthetic sports. *Scandinavian Journal of Medicine and Science in Sports, 23,* 303–10.

Monthuy-Blanc, J., Maiano, C., & Therme, P. (2010). Prevalence of eating disorder symptoms in nonelite ballet dancers and basketball players: An exploratory and controlled study among French adolescent girls. *Revue d'Epidemiologie et de Sante Publique, 58,* 415–24.

Morano, M., Colella, D., & Capranicia, L. (2011). Body image, perceived and actual physical abilities in normal-weight and overweight boys involved in individual and team sports. *Journal of Sports Sciences, 29,* 355–62.

Petrie, T.A., & Greenleaf, C. (2012). Body image and sports/athletes. In T.F. Cash, (Ed.), *Encyclopedia of body image and human appearance, Volume 1* (pp. 160–65). London: Elsevier.

Reel, J.J., Petrie, T.A., SooHoo, S., & Anderson, C.M. (2013). Weight pressure in sport: Examining the factor structure and incremental validity of the weight pressures in sport-Females. *Eating Behaviors, 14*, 137–44.

Ricciardelli, L.A., & McCabe, M.P. (2004). A biopsychosocial model of disordered eating and the pursuit of muscularity in adolescent boys. *Psychological Bulletin, 130*, 179–205.

Ricciardelli, L.A. & McCabe, M.P. (2009). *Study of adolescent health risk behaviours.* Unpublished manuscript, Deakin University.

Ricciardelli, L.A., McCabe, M.P., & Ridge, D. (2006). The construction of the adolescent male body through sport. *Journal of Health Psychology, 11*, 577–87.

Sagoe, D., Andreassen, C.S., & Pallesen, S. (2014). The aetiology and trajectory of anabolic-androgenic steroid use initiation: A systematic review and synthesis of qualitative research. *Substance Abuse Treatment, Prevention, and Policy, 9*, 27.

Slater, A., & Tiggemann, M. (2011). Gender differences in adolescent sport participation, teasing, self-objectification and body image concerns. *Journal of Adolescence, 34*, 455–63.

Smolak, L., Murnen, S.K., & Ruble, A.E. (2000). Female athletes and eating problems: A meta-analysis. *International Journal of Eating Disorders, 27*, 371–80.

Steinfeldt, J.A., Zakrajsek, R., Bodey, K.J., Middendorf, K.G., & Martin, S.B. (2013). Role of uniforms in the body image of college volleyball players. *The Counselling Psychologist, 41*, 791–819.

Steinfeldt, J.A., Zakrajsek, R., Carter, H., & Steinfeldt, M.C. (2011). Conformity to gender norms among female-student-athletes: Implications for body image. *Psychology of Men and Masculinity, 12*, 401–16.

Thompson, S.H., & Digsby, S. (2004). A preliminary survey of dieting, body dissatisfaction, and eating problems among high school cheerleaders. *Journal of School Health, 74*, 85–90.

Tiggemann, M. (2001). The impact of adolescent girls' life concerns and leisure activities on body dissatisfaction, disordered eating, and self-esteem. *The Journal of Genetic Psychology, 162*, 133–42.

van Durme, K., Goossens, L., & Braet, C. (2012). Adolescent aesthetic athletes: A group at risk for eating pathology? *Eating Behaviors, 13*, 119–22.

Varnes, J.R., Stellefson, M.L., Janelle, C.M., Dorman, S.M., Dodd, V., & Miller, M.D. (2013). A systematic review of studies comparing body image concerns among female college athletes and non-athletes, 1997–2012. *Body Image, 10*, 421–32.

Voelker, D.K., Gould, D., & Reel, J.J. (2014). Prevalence and correlates of disordered eating in female figure skaters. *Psychology of Sport and Exercise, 15*, 696–704.

White, S.A., Duda, J.L., & Keller, M.R. (1998). The relationship between goal orientation and perceived purposes of sport among youth sport participants. *Journal of Sport Behavior, 21*, 475–83.

Wichstrom, L., & Pedersen, W. (2001). Use of anabolic-androgenic steroids in adolescence: Winning, looking good or being bad? *Journal of Studies on Alcohol, 62*, 5–13.

11

THE IMPACT OF SCHOOLS AND TEACHERS ON BODY IMAGE

Adolescents spend the majority of their time in schools, so this is the setting where the majority of peer influences on body image takes place. Group norms relating to weight, appearance, dieting, and exercise are developed and reinforced in this unique environment. While the predominant peer influence in a school is thought to be negative, schools also offer a unique opportunity to disseminate prevention programs and to make other changes to the physical and social environment to promote positive body image.

Numerous school-based programs designed to prevent the development of eating disorders have been implemented since the 1980s (Neumark-Sztainer et al., 2006). Several lessons have been learned from the first generation of eating disorder prevention programs, and newer school-based programs have been more successful in terms of improving body image and reducing disordered eating pathology. Although many exciting developments have been made in the area of school-based body image programs, widespread and complete effectiveness and dissemination have not been achieved. The school environment is particularly challenging for prevention research due to issues of appropriateness and relevance of program content, teacher's adherence to program content, and effectiveness of standardised measures in 'normal' populations or those not particularly at risk. In addition, there is evidence of 'research fatigue' in certain areas as schools are bombarded with requests for research participation and are less likely to participate due to time constraints and parental concern.

In this chapter we outline the way in which schools might contribute to the development of body image issues, and how they might be involved in approaches to prevent the development of body dissatisfaction. We include some recent research on current school practice in terms of implementing a whole school approach to the promotion of positive body image and how teachers and researchers can work together to promote positive body image. A discussion of the strategies that are not recommended in schools is also included.

Development of Body Dissatisfaction in Schools

Schools are a setting where many of the risk factors for the development of body dissatisfaction impact on young people, including the influence of peers, weight-based teasing, and media use. The school setting is generally the main source of interactions between friends and peers (Brown, Bakken, Ameringer, & Mahon, 2008). We specifically discuss the influence of peers on body image in Chapter 8. The culture of each school is influenced by the appearance conversations, appearance-based teasing from peers, and use of appearance-focused media within the school environment (Jones, Vigfusdottir, & Lee, 2004). For example, girls regularly bring fashion and celebrity magazines to school, and the process of jointly reading and looking at these magazines with friends may prompt appearance-related conversations and 'fat talk' among friends, as well as social comparisons with the images and the peers involved. These complex environments involve an interplay of the different influences on body image, and this is recognised by adolescent girls, who report that appearance, weight, and diet-based conversations are prevalent in schools (Carey, Donaghue, & Broderick, 2010).

Several studies have demonstrated that girls in single-sex schools are more likely to desire a thinner body and have poor body image (Dyer & Tiggemann, 1996; Granleese & Joseph, 1993). A study of Australian adolescent girls showed that those in single-sex schools were significantly more likely to have a thinner ideal or preferred figure and display disordered eating behaviours (Dyer & Tiggemann, 1996). However, others have not replicated these findings among adolescent girls (Tiggemann, 2001) or women in college settings (Spencer, Barrett, Storti, & Cole, 2013). Some researchers argue that girls in single-sex schools might demonstrate higher levels of body dissatisfaction due to the larger number of female peers with whom they can compare themselves (Spencer et al., 2013). Other researchers argue that this difference is due to conflicting gender role pressures (Mensinger, 2001).

Research found that there were significant similarities in body image and dieting behaviour within friendship cliques of girls attending single-sex but not mixed-sex schools (Carey, Donaghue, & Broderick, 2013). Although some research has indicated a protective effect of platonic relationships with boys during early adolescent years (Compian, Gowen, & Hayward, 2004), no boys were reported as members of friendship cliques in this study, so the differences were not due to mixed-sex friendship groups (Carey et al., 2013). Overall, this research suggests that there are fundamental differences between girls attending mixed and single-sex schools that need to be explored further. In addition, the differences in body image among boys attending single, or mixed sex schools needs to be examined.

Promoting Positive Body Image in Schools

There are many opportunities for schools to engage in activities to promote body image, from the taught curriculum to the school environment and policy. A large range of curriculum-based programs to promote body image and prevent eating disorders have been tested and implemented in the school setting. Those that have been most successful in improving body image in the secondary school setting have focused on reducing the risk factors for the development of body dissatisfaction, including peers and the media. The two programs that have had the greatest impact are *Happy Being Me* and *Media Smart* (see Yager et al., 2013, for a full review). These Australian programs are described in Chapter 12. Whole school approaches to the prevention of body image and disordered eating problems go beyond the provision of a content-based curriculum to address the sociocultural environment in which these problems develop (Levine & Smolak, 2006).

Using a Whole School Approach to Promote Body Image

Whole school approaches to the prevention of eating disorders gained popularity throughout the late 1990s, after the first generation of eating disorder prevention programs that focused on psycho-educational content and didactic delivery failed to improve disordered eating outcomes. Similar whole school approaches have been proposed to the promotion of positive body image in the school environment. While curricular content focusing on the individual and behaviour change are recognised as being necessary, they are unlikely to be all that is required to reverse the extensive and long-term exposure to the media, peers, and other factors that are known to contribute to body dissatisfaction. Therefore, in a whole school approach, curricular initiatives are supported by changes in the school environment and policy that are able to support the promotion of positive body image.

Before discussing this approach, we must first address issues of terminology. While researchers might refer to environmental or ecological approaches (Evans, Roy, Geiger, Werner, & Burnett, 2008; Levine & Smolak, 2006; Neumark-Sztainer et al., 2006), schools might be more familiar with the terms 'Whole School Approach', 'Healthy Schools' (U.K.), 'Health Promoting Schools' (Australia, Germany) or the 'Coordinated School Health Approach' (U.S.). Broadly, all of these different approaches are based on the premise that making changes within the physical and social environment, in addition to curriculum content that focuses on individual change, will lead to increased intervention effects. These programs usually incorporate some sort of formal curriculum but then also include some level of parental involvement, activities to change peer culture and ethos of the school, changes to the physical environment of a school, and modifications to school policy that support prevention initiatives. O'Dea and Maloney (2000) presented a suggested application of the Health Promoting Schools framework for eating disorder prevention in Australia, and Evans and colleagues (2008) have done the same for the Coordinated School Health Program in the U.S., but there have been no formal evaluations of these initiatives.

Body dissatisfaction and eating disorder prevention programs that have sought to take an ecological approach have generally done so in primary or middle school settings. For example, *Healthy Schools-Healthy Kids* [HS-HK] (McVey et al., 2007) aimed to prevent eating disorders over an eight-month period in a school-wide intervention for 12 to 13 year olds in Canada. Activities included a teacher-led curriculum, parent education through workshops and newsletters, watching a musical, peer support groups, on-message posters and school announcements each morning. As a result of this program, higher risk students had significant improvements in body satisfaction, and weight loss strategies were decreased among intervention girls but not boys (McVey, Tweed, & Blackmore, 2007). *Very Important Kids* [VIK] (Haines, Neumark-Sztainer, Perry, Hannan, & Levine, 2006) aimed to reduce weight-based teasing and unhealthy weight control behaviours among elementary school students in the U.S. This program included individual (after-school program, theatre program), school environment (e.g., staff training, no-teasing campaign), and family (e.g., family nights, parent postcards) components for students aged around 10 years. Evaluation of VIK found significant reductions in the level of teasing but no improvements in body dissatisfaction, dieting internalisation, or use of unhealthy weight control behaviours (Haines et al., 2006). These programs demonstrate that whole school approaches are feasible but also require substantial time, resources, and research commitment in order to properly implement programs of this nature. While there is widespread theoretical support for these programs, evaluations have not generally demonstrated significant improvements in body image as a result. This is interesting given that they theoretically address more dynamic risk factors than individual, classroom-based programs. Greater attention to measures and more trials of these programs are therefore required.

Minimum Involvement → Maximum Involvement

	Minimum Involvement			Maximum Involvement
Policy and School Environment	□ Takes action on appearance-related teasing, through school policy, prevention, and management strategies	□ Adheres to the mandated healthy canteen requirements and provides a balance of food options so that students can make healthy food choices	□ Provides opportunity for all students to engage in regular physical activity in a non-competitive, non-weight-loss focused, safe, secure environment	□ Ensures that students always feel comfortable in mandatory school clothing by having body image friendly school and sports uniforms	□ Displays public material and posters that include a wide diversity of body shapes and sizes and ethnicity	□ Includes a statement in the school mission about providing a body image friendly environment and celebrating diversity
Classroom Curriculum	□ Avoids activities that may inadvertently have a negative impact (see table on page 180)	□ Ensures that body image activities meet the needs of males and females and students from a variety of cultural backgrounds	□ Provides activities that promote students' self identity and self-esteem	□ Provides media literacy education that assists students in becoming more critical consumers of the media	□ Offers an evidence-based program for the development of positive body image	□ Offers an appropriate, targeted, evidence-based program to improve body image among high risk students
Staff Organisation and Professional Development	□ Encourages school staff to use body image friendly language in their interactions with students	□ Provides school staff with information about the potential for their formal and informal interactions with students to impact on their self-esteem and body image	□ Provides relevant school staff the opportunity to engage in professional development to effectively plan and implement a body image friendly curriculum	□ Provides an opportunity for interested school staff to engage in training to effectively implement a whole school approach to develop positive body image	□ Nominates a staff member to be a resource person for body image and eating problems, and educate that person accordingly	□ Supports relevant teaching and support staff in receiving training for the early identification and referral of serious body image problems and eating disorders
Partnerships with Parents and Services	□ Provides parents/guardians with links to information about healthy body image in the school newsletter and on the school website	□ Makes up-to-date printed information about how parents and guardians can support their child to develop positive body image available or emails it directly to parents.	□ Considers incorporating body image as a related issue if parent information nights about cyber-bullying, puberty and adolescence are held	□ Utilises body image community organisations as a resource for students, teachers, and parents	□ Presents talks and information nights for parents /guardians about body image issues and how to support their child	□ Offers longer workshops to empower parents and assist them in developing their children's body image and healthy eating and exercise behaviours

(Figure adapted from 'Checklist for promoting positive body image in schools' by Susan Paxton in the National Strategy for Positive Body Image report, 42–43).

FIGURE 11.1 Recommendations for Action to Develop Positive Body Image in Schools.

Taking a whole school approach also allows for programs to address a broader range of risk factors that might be common to a range of issues. The crowding of the school curriculum and the increased competition for implementation of interventions provide a strong rationale for combined programs with a broader health promotion focus (Catalano, Hawkins, Berglund, Pollard, & Arthur, 2002; Neumark-Sztainer et al., 2006). The most common of these combinations has been the dual focus on risk factors common to both obesity and eating disorders to reduce the broad spectrum of weight problems (Austin et al., 2007; Irving & Neumark-Sztainer, 2002; Neumark-Sztainer et al., 2006). Examples of such programs include *New Moves* (Gortmaker et al., 2000; Neumark-Sztainer, Story, Hannan, & Rex, 2003), an extended physical education class for adolescent girls that improved eating patterns, sedentary and unhealthy weight control behaviour, and body image. The evaluation of *Planet Health* (Austin et al., 2007), a widely disseminated health education program for middle schools in the U.S.: indicated improvements in disordered weight control behaviours and reduced television viewing. A multi-behavioural program that did not address body image, but did combine prevention for a range of health behaviours using a whole-school approach demonstrated both the need for, and success of, these broader programs (Busch, De Leeuw, & Schrijvers, 2013).

No one program has demonstrated widespread effectiveness in taking a whole school approach for the prevention of body image problems. However, it is recommended that schools make ecological changes to reduce the potential negative impact of the school environment on body dissatisfaction. Figure 1 depicts a range of actions that schools could take to promote positive body image.

Body Image Activities that are Not Recommended in Schools

Body image interventions are not likely to cause harm. However, we have learned some lessons in the early prevention programs that have led researchers to caution against the inclusion of some activities in intervention programs, particularly those that focus on eating disorders due to unintended negative effects from some programs (Carter, Stewart, Dunn, & Fairburn, 1997; O'Dea, 2002). Researchers and teachers are encouraged to "First, do no harm" when designing and implementing body image programs (O'Dea, 2000) as many approaches to teaching about these topics were found to cause unintended negative effects. Although many meta-analyses have refuted claims of unintended negative effects of eating disorder prevention programs (e.g., Fingeret, Warren, Cepeda-Benito, & Gleaves, 2006), there have not been any direct evaluations of potentially harmful activities.

We recommend that schools avoid the following (O'Dea, 2000, 2005; Yager, 2007).

- Using magazines, and images of 'ideal bodies' from media sources. Laboratory studies indicate that viewing these images causes immediate increases in body dissatisfaction. If images are to be used, it is recommended that students are 'primed' with media literacy first to reduce the impact of viewing the images.
- Using images of those suffering from eating disorders, as well as guest speakers, books or other reports of individuals who have recovered from eating disorders. These approaches have not been found to improve body image, or 'scare people off' developing an eating disorder, but may normalise and glamourise disordered eating and provide suggestive information to vulnerable young people.
- Research assignments focusing on eating disorders. These are often chosen by young people who are susceptible to these disorders and may facilitate access to information that they use to fuel their disorder.
- Asking students to record food intake for the purposes of nutrition analysis; as this is behaviour associated with strict control of diet.
- Weighing of students in class, and conducting fitness testing in non-controlled environments, as they may induce competition, social comparison, and embarrassment or prompt strict regimes to improve scores.

Very little research exists to describe the range of activities that schools engage in to promote positive body image, particularly those that fit within a whole-school approach. The following sections in this chapter describe our research into current school practice and willingness to implement a whole school approach to the promotion of positive body image.

RESEARCH FOCUS: CURRENT SCHOOL PRACTICE

In a research project commissioned by the State Government of Victoria (Australia) in 2010, we conducted surveys (n = 122) and interviews (n = 9) with teachers in Victoria to determine their current practice in terms of body image content and support for future action in a whole school approach for promoting positive body image. Please refer to Appendix 3 at the end of this chapter for the Methods for this research.

(Continued)

Current Practice

The results indicated that there was a high level of awareness of body image as an issue among teachers and the other participants, and some positive initiatives were already taking place. There was widespread support for the coverage of this issue in the school setting, and many schools had taken action in this area, with 84.4% of teachers agreeing or strongly agreeing that their school had good policies in place to support the development of positive body image, and this generally referred to bullying policies. However, 21% of teachers reported that their school did not include body image in the curriculum for each year level. Further, 42% of participants indicated "Not at All" when asked about their current access to training about body image, and only 10% of schools currently involved parents in relation to this issue.

Current Curriculum Initiatives

We asked teachers to indicate whether they used a range of approaches that were relevant to body image. Table 1 displays this information.

TABLE 1 Current approaches used to promote positive body image

Rank	Approaches used to teach about body image	Yes, used (%)	Don't know (%)
1	Encouraging students to participate in healthy eating and exercise	96.7	2.5
2	Building self-esteem	95.9	2.5
3	Teaching about acceptance of diversity	87.7	11.5
4	Increasing knowledge about obesity	86.1	13.9
5	Increasing knowledge about what body image is	85.2	13.9
6	Discussing societal influences on body image	82.8	16.4
7	Teaching about genetic influences on weight and shape	76.2	23.0
8	Encouraging a critical analysis of the media	74.6	22.1
9	Increasing knowledge about eating disorders including symptoms and causes	68.9	27.9
10	Teaching about body types (ectomorph, mesomorph, endomorph)	59.8	36.9
11	Using media reports of celebrities with eating disorders	49.2	45.1
12	Discussion of body image issues that may vary according in different cultural groups	48.4	49.2
13	Discussion of specific male body image issues	44.3	51.6
14	Dissonance-based programs	17.2	74.6
15	Using role plays of people with low body image	10.7	80.3
16	Other (please describe):	2.5	26.2

The most commonly reported approaches for improving body image through classroom initiatives were encouraging healthy eating and exercise behaviours, building self-esteem, and teaching about acceptance of diversity. These approaches are supported by the evidence from our systematic review (Yager, Diedrichs, Ricciardelli, & Halliwell, 2013). Defining body image, discussing societal influences on body image, and encouraging a critical analysis of the media are common features of effective programs to improve body image and prevent eating problems. It is therefore encouraging to find that these approaches also commonly feature in Victorian school classrooms.

However, teachers also indicated that they used activities that would not be recommended in schools. There is some evidence that teaching about the symptoms of eating disorders (ranked 9th, 69% used) and using media reports about celebrities with eating disorders (ranked 11th, 49%) may cause unintentional negative effects (Yager, 2007).In one interview, a young female HPE teacher shared a PowerPoint presentation that she had given to a year 8 class. She explained that the school nurse had 'done the Dove training' and therefore assisted the HPE teacher in preparing the three-week body image unit of which the PowerPoint presentation was the beginning. The PowerPoint contained at least 15 to 20 full slides of women with severe anorexia nervosa and one man, also with the disorder. These are the sorts of images that are found on 'pro-ana' websites for 'thinspiration', and although very thin, the images also looked very similar to regular catwalk or magazine images of fashion models. Viewing these sorts of images is known to promote disordered eating pathology among those already at risk for eating disorders due to the personality characteristics of perfectionism and competitiveness (O'Dea, 2000).Teachers also commonly reported using images and articles from popular magazines, and one teacher commented that magazines were used because they were seen as 'affordable and available resources' to teach about this topic.

The use of guest speakers was another common way to present information about body image and would not be recommended by researchers. Almost a quarter of participants responded 'yes' to the question: Does your school fund expert organisations to deliver seminars and discussions on body image? Teachers also rated guest speakers who have recovered from eating disorders (61.5%) or from professional organisations (such as the Butterfly Foundation; 63.1%) as being among the most effective strategies of teaching about body image. The use of guest speakers to promote positive body image in schools was explored further in the interviews with school staff. In most cases, teachers indicated that they found guest speakers to be effective in engaging large audiences for important topics in health education, including body image. Teachers seemed to think that part of the value of guest speakers was having 'someone new' in front of the class, and that the effect was greater if that person was 'an

(Continued)

expert' in the area that they were speaking about. Teachers described the engaging nature of guest speakers and the fact that they could 'get kids thinking' about the topic they presented. This also seemed to be a relatively easy way to 'cover' a topic in an hour for a whole year level at a time and to provide pedagogical variety in on a topic where they were not confident in their own professional expertise. Although popular, presentations by individuals who have recovered from an eating disorder are generally not recommended as being an effective tool for promoting body image in schools (Yager, 2007), as there is some evidence that this strategy may lead to unintended negative effects when used as combined primary and secondary prevention (Mann et al., 1997).

Dove *BodyThink* was reported to be the most commonly used program, and most participants reported using this resource with female students in grades 9 and 10 (approximately 15 to 16 years of age). This may be because this is the most widely and freely disseminated resource that is related to body image, as teachers and other school professionals have been offered free training sessions to use this program. Evaluations of this program when conducted in co-educational settings found improvements in body image among boys but not girls (Richardson, Paxton, & Thomson, 2009).

Potential for Implementation of a Whole School Approach

Participants were asked to indicate their responses to the question: "How willing would your school be to do this?" for the items relating to the implementation of a whole school approach to promoting positive body image. The results are presented in Table 2.

TABLE 2 Potential for implementation of a whole school approach

Strategies	Not at All % (n)	Not Really % (n)	A Little % (n)	A Lot % (n)	Very Much % (n)
1. Include a statement in the school mission about providing a body image friendly environment and celebrating diversity	0.8 (1)	0	2.5 (3)	14.8 (18)	**77.9** **(95)**
2. Prohibit appearance-related teasing, including cyber–bullying in school policy	0	1.6 (2)	14.8 (18)	27 (33)	**53.3** **(65)**
3. Makes body image friendly school and sports uniforms available	3.3 (4)	3.3 (4)	15.6 (19)	30.3 (37)	**41** **(50)**
4. Ensure there is no weighing, measuring or anthropometric assessment of students in any context	3.3 (4)	3.3 (4)	18 (22)	32 (39)	**35.2** **(43)**

Policy and Environment

(Continued)

Strategies	Not at All % (n)	Not Really % (n)	A Little % (n)	A Lot % (n)	Very Much % (n)
5. Provide opportunity for all students to engage in regular physical activity in a non-competitive, non–weight-loss focused, safe, secure environment	7.4 (9)	12.3 (15)	13.9 (17)	23.8 (29)	**32.8 (40)**
6. Provide a balance of food options from all food groups in the canteen	1.6 (2)	9.8 (12)	24.6 (30)	22.1 (27)	**32.8 (40)**
7. Display public material and posters that include a wide diversity of body shapes and sizes and ethnicity	2.5 (3)	9 (11)	**31.1 (38)**	23 (28)	23.8 (29)
8. Provide developmentally appropriate body image teachings at every year level	2.5 (3)	3.3 (4)	25.4 (31)	**33.6 (41)**	30.3 (37)
9. Train all relevant teaching staff in the early identification and referral of serious body image and eating disorders	4.1 (5)	8.2 (10)	**28.7 (35)**	**28.7 (35)**	19.7 (24)
10. Provide all teachers with training and information about the impact of body image issues on the wellbeing of young people and ways that body dissatisfaction are reinforced by social environments	4.1 (5)	12.3 (15)	**44.3 (54)**	24.6 (30)	5.7 (7)
11. Train teachers to use body friendly language in their interactions with students	6.6 (8)	10.7 (13)	**39.3 (48)**	24.6 (30)	9.8 (12)
12. Make available printed info about how parents/guardians can support their child to develop positive body image	2.5 (3)	5.7 (7)	**41 (50)**	29.5 (36)	13.1 (16)
13. Provide parents/guadians with links to information about body image and eating disorders on the school website	4.9 (6)	9 (11)	**34.4 (42)**	27 (33)	12.3 (15)
14. Present talks and information nights for parents /guardians about body image issues	10.7 (13)	17.2 (21)	**32 (39)**	20.5 (25)	9 (11)

The left margin labels (vertical): Curriculum, Staff Training, Parents and Guardians

(Continued)

Participants generally indicated that their school would be willing to implement the strategies that related to policy and the environment and these items generally correlated with the things that teachers reported that their schools were already doing. There was only a medium level of support for most initiatives relating to staff training and the involvement of parents.

Barriers to Implementing Whole School Approach

Teachers were asked to rate their agreement with a number of commonly reported barriers to health education and health promotion in relation to the development of positive body image by responding on a five-point Likert scale. The proportion of participants who selected each option is given in Table 3 below. Barriers were re-ordered to form a list in descending order of importance.

TABLE 3 Participant agreement with barriers to implementation of a whole school approach

Rank	Barrier	Strongly Disagree %	Disagree %	Neutral %	Agree %	Strongly Agree %
1	Lack of time in the curriculum	0.0	10.7	4.1	40.2	**43.4**
2	Lack of funding	0.8	15.6	13.1	**39.3**	28.7
3	Lack of staff expertise	4.9	23.8	13.1	**45.9**	11.5
4	Body image less important than obesity	5.7	**28.7**	23.0	32.0	9.8
5	Lack of support from principal	13.9	**42.6**	23.0	13.9	5.7
6	Lack of interest from the students	14.8	**43.4**	16.4	21.3	3.3
7	Lack of support from parents	11.5	**48.4**	24.6	12.3	1.6
8	Other (please briefly describe)	0	.8	**2.5**	0	1.6

The lack of time in the curriculum was the most commonly supported barrier to the implementation of initiatives to develop positive body image, followed by lack of funding and lack of staff expertise. It was interesting and encouraging to note that participants generally did not indicate that a lack of support from principals and parents were barriers to the implementation of body image programs. 'Other' barriers were generally related to a lack of awareness and dissemination of resources:

"Not knowing which organisations are the most reputable/reliable to cover this issue with students" or lack of interest from staff "to learn about body image and integrate into curriculum". In addition, 'other' barriers were related to health education curriculum and delivery, such as: "Area left up to health teachers to teach in their subject area, delivery can vary greatly" and "Classroom setting is not the right place". One participant also wrote that "Talking about body image, very difficult in classroom setting. Sensitive issue. Programs should be targeted at media and for parents to run".

When asked to elaborate on the potential barriers to the implementation of a whole school approach to promote positive body image in interviews, most participants indicated that the major hurdle would be "getting everyone on board". This comment could reflect a lack of knowledge among teachers as to what a whole school approach generally means as they seemed to assume that all teachers would need to incorporate body image strategies into their daily practice. Body image was also seen to be less of a priority in schools, with literacy, numeracy and academic issues seen as more important for whole school action than body image. Where health was seen as a priority, other issues such as alcohol and drug use, child protection, and student welfare were higher priorities than the promotion of positive body image. This 'competition' between health issues supports the implementation of an ecological approach that might facilitate action on a range of related health issues.

Resource and Training Needs

We asked teachers to rate the types of activities that could be used to teach about body image in terms of their perceived ease of use and effectiveness in the classroom. Teachers endorsed videos, discussion questions (72.0%), and activities that you can photocopy from textbooks (60.6%) as the easiest activities to use, followed by speakers from professional organisations (55.8%) and guest speakers who had recovered from eating disorders (50.8%).

Interestingly, activities that could be photocopied from textbooks were ranked far lower (in 9th place out of 11 options) in terms of teachers' perceptions of effective activities. Here, the most effective approaches were videos and discussion questions (74.6%), guest speakers from organisations (63.1%), and guest speakers who had recovered from eating disorders (61.5%), followed by evidence-based programs (54.1%).

In the teacher questionnaire, staff members were asked: "To what extent would you like to see more of these types of resources?" Responses are presented in Table 4 in order from most to least requested resources.

(*Continued*)

TABLE 4　Teachers' Requests for Body Image Resources

Rank	Resources	Not at All %(n)	Not Really % (n)	A Little %(n)	A Lot % (n)	Very Much % (n)
1	Activities that you can photocopy from textbooks	3.3 (4)	3.3 (4)	30.3 (37)	26.2 (32)	**50 (61)**
2	Videos and discussion questions	0 (0)	.8 (1)	13.1 (16)	26.2 (32)	**48.4 (59)**
3	Guest speakers from organisations	0 (0)	1.6 (2)	19.7 (24)	18.9 (23)	**46.7 (57)**
4	Full programs that are usually based on evidence and come with all worksheets and teaching notes	1.6 (2)	0 (0)	10.7 (13)	23.8 (29)	**45.9 (56)**
5	Guest speakers who have recovered from eating disorders.	1.6 (2)	2.5 (3)	16.4 (20)	21.3 (26)	**42.6 (52)**
6	Individual activities from programs, but not the program in its entirety	.8 (1)	0 (0)	16.4 (20)	25.4 (31)	**38.5 (47)**
7	Websites	.8 (1)	.8 (1)	21.3 (26)	27 (33)	**37.7 (46)**
8	Interactive online quizzes	2.5 (3)	5.7 (7)	26.2 (32)	**27 (33)**	25.4 (31)
9	Song/lyric analysis	4.9 (6)	9 (11)	**32.8 (40)**	20.5 (25)	20.5 (25)
10	Books about eating disorders by those who have recovered from them	9.8 (12)	9 (11)	**30.3 (37)**	22.1 (27)	11.5 (14)
11	Popular magazines	5.7 (7)	7.4 (9)	**29.5 (36)**	23.8 (29)	19.7 (24)

Similar to their responses for the ease of use, perceived effectiveness and preparedness to use particular resources, videos and guest speakers were high on the list of requested resources. Surprisingly, 'activities that you can photocopy from textbooks' were the most requested type of resource, even though participants ranked these activities 2nd in terms of ease of use, 4th in terms of preparedness, and 9th in terms of effectiveness in previous items. In interviews, long programs were not seen as practical due to time constraints, and for shorter programs, teachers expressed a need to be able to adapt activities and lesson ideas 'to the needs of the class'. Teachers indicated that some class groups would not engage in discussion, and others are hard to stop talking. They indicated that some work well in small groups, whereas others require structured writing tasks. The 'needs of the class' seem to be a composition of classroom management considerations and learning needs, rather than relating to body image. Given that this is the way teachers currently work and will continue to work, it might be best to develop activities or stimulus materials with a range of suggestions for how they can best be used in class and to test each of these activities on its own to ensure that all options are evidence-based.

Finally, teachers were asked for their perceived needs and preferences relating to training about body image. There was strong support for workshop-based training (86.9%), videos (81.9%), and training sessions at the conference of the professional association (75.4%). Low proportions of teachers (~30–40%) indicated that they believed that these options were available to them. Other practical barriers to staff training arose in the interviews. Teachers are able to determine their own professional development needs, and often training relating to senior exams and literacy were priorities. Although they indicated that "leaving the school grounds" to immerse themselves in professional learning was an effective method of staff development for them, most said that they would not have the time or prioritise body image highly enough to warrant attendance at an external workshop. Therefore, it is recommended that some high quality forms of professional development are made available to staff online, so that they can improve their knowledge and skills in relation to the promotion of positive body image without having to leave the school grounds.

These data support the development of video-based resources. These were recommended as being easy to use and effective by teachers and could be developed by researchers in order to be informed by evidence. Video-based resources could also be developed in order to provide school staff with short professional development sessions that could boost their confidence to deliver materials about body image.

Summary

Through our questionnaire and interviews with teachers, we found a wide range of support for school-based action on body image. Teachers indicated that many initiatives relating to a whole-school approach to the promotion of positive body image were already taking place, and that they would be willing to implement these in their school. However, there was a general lack of knowledge about, and implementation of, evidence-based activities to improve body image. Guest speakers who had recovered from eating disorders, and images of people with eating disorders were used, and perceived to be effective by teachers even though these are thought to be potentially ineffective and harmful by body image researchers. Teachers supported the development of resources and training modules, particularly those that utilised video. If we are to succeed in the widespread dissemination of appropriate action to promote positive body image, it is important that we work with teachers and develop tools and resources that work practically within school systems, and regular classroom practice.

Working Together: Teachers and Researchers

If materials for the promotion of positive body image and prevention of the development of eating disorders are to be widely disseminated, schools need to be involved. The school curriculum in most countries has some sort of health education requirement. This means that existing members of staff within the school have the opportunity to deliver evidence-based body image or eating disorder prevention content. In our experience as both education professionals and researchers, we have come to identify several interesting observations that might assist researchers and teachers to work together effectively in the school setting. Teachers and researchers have the same overall aim: to improve the wellbeing of young people. However, they have very different ways of achieving these aims. It is important that researchers consider the way teachers and schools work when planning a trial of a school-based intervention.

Although theoretically possible and sustainable, there are some issues with the translation of research to practice that have so far limited the potential for prevention activities in the health curriculum (Yager, 2010). Most school-based body image prevention programs are developed and delivered by psychologists and research staff (Bergsma & Carney, 2008) with no education background. In many evaluations of prevention programs that utilise classroom teachers for program delivery, teacher training is limited or not provided at all. Even when professional development is provided, some evaluations report that teachers do not adhere to the program content (Levine, Smolak, & Schermer, 1996) thus reducing 'program fidelity'. However, it should not be surprising that teachers change program content, given that they are experts in delivery of education materials, whereas the researchers that developed the content are not. The majority of teachers' work and expertise is in adapting lessons to meet the needs of their students. The 'needs' of the class may be based on behavioural needs and classroom management. For example, teachers may have concerns that the class cannot be trusted to behave appropriately when performing a role-play; or the students in a particular class are too shy or quiet to engage in a discussion. Modifications might also be required for academic purposes, as some students might need more or less scaffolding in order to grasp concepts. Finally, teachers might modify content for practical purposes, due to the length of time and the resources that they have available. In teaching all other subject areas, teachers make these adaptations, and 'personalise' the curriculum (Prain et al., 2013). Thus, they are likely to modify body image materials.

Rather than restrict teachers by discouraging them from making program changes, we need to focus on utilising our expertise as researchers in order to develop prevention activities that allow teachers to use their expertise in this very important setting. We therefore suggest that researchers develop and test the efficacy of individual activities in terms of improving body image so that these can be recommended to teachers and schools. If we recommend four or five standard lessons (e.g., an 'airbrushing' lesson), teachers can implement them as possible within their programs. Rather than expecting teachers to adhere to manualised content, it is recommended that we provide guidelines around which teachers might adapt an activity to meet the needs of their students. By giving "do's" and "don'ts", teachers can adapt lessons to meet the needs of their students, and avoid approaches that are not recommended by researchers.

Conclusion

Adolescents spend a great deal of time in schools, and the sociocultural influences on body image are intensified in the school environment. In this chapter we have provided research that demonstrates that teachers and schools are willing to take action in this area but need guidance and resources in order to do so. We have outlined some of the effective strategies for schools, teachers, and researchers to implement in this area. If body image is considered to be a priority, if we use evidence-based approaches, and if there is collaboration between teachers and researchers, we are likely to succeed in making schools an environment that promote nurturing positive body image.

References

Austin, S. B., Kim, J., Wiecha, J., Troped, P.J., Feldman, H.A., & Peterson, K.E. (2007). School-based overweight preventive intervention lowers incidence of disordered weight-control behaviors in early adolescent girls. *Archives of Pediatrics & Adolescent Medicine, 161*(9), 865–69.

Bergsma, L.J., & Carney, M.E. (2008). Effectiveness of health-promoting media literacy education: A systematic review. *Health Education Research, 23*(3), 522–42.

Brown, B.B., Bakken, J.P., Ameringer, S.W., & Mahon, S.D. (2008). A comprehensive conceptualisation of the peer influence process in adolescence. In M.J. Prinstein & K.A. Dodge (Eds.), *Understanding peer influence in children and adolescence* (pp. 17–44). New York, NY: The Guilford Press.

Busch, V., De Leeuw, R.J.J., & Schrijvers, J.P. (2013). Results of a multibehavioral health-promoting school pilot intervention in a Dutch secondary school. *Journal of Adolescent Health, 52*, 400–406.

Carey, R., Donaghue, N., & Broderick, P. (2010). What you look like is such a big factor: interviews with adolescent girls about the appearance culture in an all-girls' school. *Feminism & Psychology, 21*(3), 299–316.

Carey, R., Donaghue, N., & Broderick, P. (2013). Peer culture and body image concern among Australian adolescent girls: A hierarchical linear modelling analysis. *Sex Roles, 69*(5–6), 250–63.

Carter, J., Stewart, A., Dunn, V., & Fairburn, C. (1997). Primary prevention of eating disorders: Might it do more harm than good? *International Journal of Eating Disorders, 22,* 167–72.

Catalano, R.F., Hawkins, J.D., Berglund, M.L., Pollard, J.A., & Arthur, M.W. (2002). Prevention science and positive youth development: Competitive or cooperative frameworks? *Journal of Adolescent Health, 31,* 230–39.

Compian, L., Gowen, L.K., & Hayward, C. (2004). Peripubertal girls' romantic and platonic involvement with boys: associations with body image and depression symptoms. *Journal of Research on Adolescence, 14*(1), 23–47.

Dyer, G., & Tiggemann, M. (1996). The effect of school environment on body concerns in adolescent women. *Sex Roles, 34*(1–2), 127–38.

Evans, R.R., Roy, J., Geiger, B.F., Werner, K.A., & Burnett, D. (2008). Ecological strategies to promote healthy body image among children. *Journal of School Health, 78*(7), 359–67.

Fingeret, M.C., Warren, C.S., Cepeda-Benito, C.S., & Gleaves, D.S. (2006). Eating disorder prevention research: A meta-analysis. *Eating Disorders: The Journal of Treatment and Prevention, 14,* 191–213.

Gortmaker, S.L., Peterson, K., Wiecha, J., Sobal, A. M., Dixit, S., Fox, M.K., & Laird, N. (2000). A school-based, interdisciplinary curriculum in grades 6 and 7 reduced obesity in girls. *Evidence-Based Nursing, 3,* 13.

Granleese, J., & Joseph, S. (1993). Self-perception profile of adolescent girls at a single-sex and a mixed-sex school. *Journal of Genetic Psychology, 155*(4), 487–92.

Haines, J., Neumark-Sztainer, D., Perry, C.L., Hannan, P.J., & Levine, M.P. (2006). V.I.K. (Very Important Kids): A school-based program designed to reduce teasing and unhealthy weight-control behaviors. *Health Education Research, 21*(6), 884–95.

Irving, L.M., & Neumark-Sztainer, D. (2002). Integrating the prevention of eating disorders and obesity: Feasible or futile? *Preventive medicine, 34,* 299–309.

Jones, D.C., Vigfusdottir, T.H., & Lee, Y. (2004). Body image and the appearance culture among adolescent girls and boys: An examination of friend conversations, peer criticism, appearance magazines, and the internalization of appearance ideals. *Journal of Adolescent Research, 19,* 323–39.

Levine, M.P., & Smolak, L. (2006). *The prevention of eating problems and eating disorders: Theory, research and practice.* Mahwah, NJ: Lawrence Erlbaum Associates.

Levine, M. P., Smolak, L., & Schermer, F. (1996). Media analysis and resistance by elementary school children in the primary prevention of eating problems. *Eating Disorders, 4*(4), 310–22.

McVey, G.L., Tweed, S., & Blackmore, E. (2007). Healthy schools-Healthy kids: A controlled evaluation of a comprehensive universal eating disorder prevention program. *Body Image, 4,* 115–36.

Mensinger, J. (2001). Conflicting gender role prescriptions and disordered eating in single-sex and coeducational school environments. *Gender and Education, 13,* 417–29.

Neumark-Sztainer, D., Levine, M., Paxton, S., Smolak, L., Piran, N., & Wertheim, E. (2006). Prevention of body dissatisfaction and disordered eating: What's next? *Eating Disorders, 14,* 265–85.

Neumark-Sztainer, D., Story, M., Hannan, P.J., & Rex, J. (2003). New Moves: A school-based obesity prevention program for adolescent girls. *Preventive Medicine, 37*(1), 41–51.

O'Dea, J. (2000). School-based interventions to prevent eating problems: First do no harm. *Eating Disorders, 8*, 123–30.

O'Dea, J. (2002). Can body image education programs be harmful to adolescent females? *Eating Disorders, 10*, 1–13.

O'Dea, J. (2005). Prevention of child obesity: First do no harm. *Health Education Research, 20*, 259–65.

O'Dea, J., & Maloney, D. (2000). Preventing eating and body image problems in children and adolescents using the Health Promoting Schools Framework. *The Journal of School Health, 70*(1), 18–22.

Prain, V., Cox, P., Deed, C., Dorman, J., Edwards, D., Farrelly, C., … Yager, Z. (2013). Personalised learning: Lessons to be learned. *British Educational Research Journal, 39*(4), 654–76.

Spencer, B., Barrett, C., Storti, G., & Cole, M. (2013). "Only girls who want fat legs take the elevator": Body image in single-sex and mixed-sex colleges. *Sex Roles, 69*, 469–79.

Tiggemann, M. (2001). Effect of gender composition of school on body concerns in adolescent women. *International Journal of Eating Disorders, 29*, 239–43.

Yager, Z. (2010). Issues of teacher training for eating disorder and child obesity prevention In J. O'Dea & M. Eriksen (Eds.), *Childhood obesity prevention-international research, controversies and intervention*. London: Oxford University Press.

Yager, Z. (2007). What not to do when teaching about eating disorders. *Journal of the Home Economics Institute of Australia, 14*(1), 28–33.

Yager, Z., Diedrichs, P.C., Ricciardelli, L.A., & Halliwell, E. (2013). What works in secondary schools? A systematic review of classroom-based body image programs. *Body Image, 10*, 271–81.

APPENDIX 3

METHODS FOR RESEARCH WITH SCHOOLS AND TEACHERS

Ethics approval was obtained from La Trobe University, the Catholic Education Office [CEO], and the Department of Education [DEECD]. An online questionnaire was administered between September and November 2010. Teacher participants were recruited to the study through contact with the professional association for Health and Physical Education [HPE] teachers—the Australian Council for Health, Physical Education and Recreation [ACHPER]. We targeted this group as HPE teachers are those most likely to be implementing body image content in Victorian schools. We sent out information about the study in an e-mail newsletter, and an e-mail was sent out through the ACHPER mailing list. Finally, the researchers set up a table at the conference for this professional association and recruited participants in person.

The questionnaire was designed to assess teachers' knowledge and attitudes about teaching about body image in schools, and implementing a range of strategies to create a Body Image Friendly School. The strategies for this whole school approach to promoting body image originated from a checklist that was developed for the National Strategy for Body Image (Australian Government, 2009). In the questionnaire, we asked teachers to respond to the question: "To what extent does your school currently do this?" and "How willing would your school be to do this" on a Likert scale (1–5) about each of the checklist items in the four areas of i) policy and environment, ii) school curricula, iii) parents/guardians, and iiii) staff training. We also asked a range of more detailed questions about the activities and resources that were currently used to teach about body image, as well as those that teachers would like to see more of. Questions about staff training and professional development needs, and attitudes about the interconnected nature of the issues of obesity and body image, were also included.

At the completion of the questionnaire, all participants were thanked for their time, and then asked if they would like to contribute further by volunteering to be contacted for an interview. In total, N = 61 teachers provided their details to indicate their willingness to participate in an interview. Teachers were selected for interviews at random in order to create a representative sample of schools within a two-hour driving distance of Melbourne CBD. Teachers at 24 schools were contacted regarding interviews, and included regional (Frankston, Werribee) and rural schools (Castlemaine, Daylesford, Ballarat), private schools, and schools from the South-East, Northern, and Western suburbs of Melbourne in order to obtain a spread of schools from all SES areas. In total, teachers and welfare staff from 9 schools were interviewed. Two participants were male, one was in the school welfare team, and one was a Physical Education [PE] specialist teacher in a primary school. The remaining five participants were young, female HPE teachers in secondary schools.

The semi-structured interview schedule was drawn from the teacher questionnaire and intended to obtain a more in-depth understanding of teachers' views, as well as obtaining data on the more sensitive aspects of this research, such as the inclusion of males and different cultural groups in programs to promote positive body image. The interviews focused on the following discussion topics:

1. Programs, activities, or resources that they currently use to teach about body image, what informs their decisions to use such programs, and whether they consider them to be effective.
2. Preferences and opinions regarding the types of programs and resources that would support their ability to promote positive body image in their school.
3. Current and perceived future action relating to a whole-school approach to the promotion of positive body image.
4. Barriers in the implementation of a whole-school approach to the promotion of positive body image and how they think that these barriers could be addressed.
5. Perceived resource and training needs of teachers and how these could be met.

Participants in the questionnaire study were all born between 1951 and 1988 and qualified as teachers between 1971 and 2010. The mean age of participants was 41 years. Twenty-two of the participants were male, and 100 were female. Most participants were classroom teachers, and other participants indicated that they were in roles that included assistant principal, welfare coordinator, and year level coordinator.

Respondents were predominantly Health and Physical Education [HPE] teachers. Fifty-eight of the teachers taught health education or health and human development, and 57 taught physical education. Other less common areas of teaching were science (6), maths (6), outdoor education (4), food technology (3), psychology (2), biology (2), English (2), English as second language (1) and VCAL (1).

12

PREVENTING BODY DISSATISFACTION AND PROMOTING POSITIVE BODY IMAGE

Psychological interventions to prevent the development of eating disorders have been conducted since the 1980s (Neumark-Sztainer et al., 2006). Many of these programs aimed to improve body image as a risk factor for disordered eating, but few programs specifically focused on improved body image as a primary outcome. The first generation of eating disorder prevention programs has produced some valuable lessons for the body image research community, and recently more programs have also been developed to specifically focus on the promotion of positive body image or prevention of body dissatisfaction.

Programs to improve body image have been conducted across a range of settings, from schools to community groups to online interventions. Schools are widely recognised as appropriate sites for interventions, as they offer the potential for sustained interactions with young people at a developmentally appropriate age, where they are already in a learning environment (Levine & Smolak, 2006). However, schools often do not have the time to implement a full program in its entirety, and the crowded curriculum, limits on funding and teacher expertise might limit the potential for effective program delivery. Community groups such as sporting teams and peer support groups or targeted interventions held outside of school have also been used for body image programs, with some success. Other programs have also targeted parents of adolescents in order to improve body image.

There is often some confusion as to what constitutes a successful outcome of a prevention program. In this chapter we use the guidelines set out by Levine and Smolak (2006). These authors define prevention as a delay of the development of a psychological disorder or unhealthy behaviour; protection of the current state of health and function; and promotion of greater wellbeing to further protect against future stressors (Albee, 1996; Bloom, 1996, cited by Levine & Smolak, 2006). Applied to body image, this means that programs aim to avoid the development of body dissatisfaction and promote the development of positive body image and body acceptance.

In this chapter, we provide empirical evidence of the success of widespread public policy initiatives that aim to promote positive body image, as this gives a sense of action at a population level. We then present an overview of the theoretical foundations of programs that focus on the individual and present a review of the body image programs that have been conducted with adolescents across a range of settings. We then discuss some of the major issues in this area and provide answers to a range of practical questions that those wanting to implement a body image program might want to learn.

Public Policy Initiatives to Promote Positive Body Image

The widespread negative impact of the media on body image is well known and widely accepted. This has prompted governments and other agencies to implement public policy initiatives in order to attempt to reduce the negative impact of the media, including banning underweight models, creating laws requiring the labeling of airbrushed images, or the introduction of voluntary regulatory codes of conduct. These initiatives have been designed to assist in changing the social environment in which adolescents develop body ideals. It is often quite difficult to obtain any evidence of the success of these initiatives, but we provide an overview in order to indicate future directions in this area.

Some governments and policy makers have introduced self-regulatory codes of conduct that might reduce the negative impact of the media on consumers. In 2009, the Australian government introduced a National Strategy for Body Image, which included a Voluntary Industry Code of Conduct on Body Image (Paxton, 2012). Similar voluntary codes of conduct for the media and fashion industries now also exist in Italy, France, and the providence of Quebec in Canada. Although it is difficult to evaluate the impact of such a broad approach, a small content analysis has evaluated the images and messages presented in the swimsuit editions of seven Australian women's magazines a year after the introduction of the voluntary media code that encouraged the use of models of diverse sizes, a reduction in the use of digital manipulation, and disclosure when images have been altered. Results indicated that one out of the seven magazines upheld all of the criteria in the code, and four used at least some models of diverse body sizes

(Boyd & Moncrieff-Boyd, 2011). While self-regulation is unlikely to have a widespread positive impact on body image, it might be a step in the right direction towards a less damaging media environment.

Labelling Airbrushed Images

Labelling airbrushed images with some sort of warning or disclaimer seems a simple and obvious initiative, given the known immediate and cumulative impact of viewing images featuring thin or muscular models that are often digitally altered. This suggestion was included in the Australian Voluntary Industry Code of Conduct for Body Image. French politicians introduced a bill to the French National Assembly in 2009, where the labeling of air-brushed images was proposed (Erlanger, 2009). Similar suggestions were made in an All-Party Parliamentary Inquiry [APPG] into Body Image in the U.K. in 2012 (APPG, 2012); and the American Medical Association recently introduced a policy to "discourage the altering of photographs in a manner that could promote unrealistic expectations" (AMA, 2011). In one Australian teen magazine, labels that indicate the amount of time spent preparing the model are used, while in another, they identify images that have not been air-brushed with a 'retouch free zone' label (Slater, Tiggemann, Firth, & Hawkins, 2012). However, these warnings are not provided for advertisements, which make up a substantial proportion of the images in the magazine.

While the impact of labeling airbrushed images is largely assumed to be positive, empirical research does not indicate consistent positive results. One study with college women found reduced body dissatisfaction among those who viewed advertisements with information about how the images had been digitally altered, compared to those who viewed the images without the warn-ing label (Slater et al., 2012). There was no negative effect on perceived adver-tising effectiveness and product recall, thus appeasing the concerns of advertisers. However another study by the same researchers reported that there was either no impact or a detrimental impact of warning labels on digitally altered images, particularly among those women with high levels of social comparison (Tiggemann, Slater, Bury, Hawkins, & Firth, 2013). These researchers argued that the labels actually increased social comparison among young women as they focused attention on the body of the models rather than the image as a whole. U.S.-based studies found no positive impact of either a disclaimer (i.e., "Retouched photograph aimed at changing a person's physical appearance.") or warning (i.e., "Warning: Trying to look as thin as this model may be dangerous to your health.") among college women (Ata, Thompson, & Small, 2013).

Two studies investigating the impact of warning labels have been con-ducted among adolescents. A U.S.-based study found that labelling an image as retouched resulted in increased objectified body consciousness and decreased physical self-esteem among adolescent boys and girls (mean age 15.43 years) (Harrison & Hefner, 2014). In that study, it was only the labelled airbrushed images that had the negative impact; the airbrushed images without the labels had no effect. A study in the Netherlands with 12- to 18-year-old girls only (mean age 14.54 years) compared the impact of images with information about the weight status of the model ("These models are underweight") was less harmful than the information combined with a warning label ("These models are underweight. Unconsciously, exposure to media models may negatively impact your self-image.") (Veldhuis, Konijn, & Seidell, 2014). Interestingly, the girls with lower levels of self-esteem had a more positive reaction to the information labels (Veldhuis et al., 2014). The evidence to date does not support the identification and labelling of airbrushed images; however, further research should continue to investigate the different types of information, warning, or label provided to determine whether some are more effective than others.

Advances in this area may indeed come from outside public health and psychology. Computer science researchers have built software that could detect the degree to which images have been altered, and assign a rating from one to five. Rather than relying on a generic dichotomous warning, using this system could mean that consumers are provided with much more information about the extent of the work, and could potentially create industry-wide change based on a desire to have low alteration ratings (Kee & Farid, 2011). The psychological impact of this more detailed rating system is yet to be tested.

Banning Underweight Models

Other public policy action includes a ban on models with a BMI that that is suggestive of an eating disorder. The benefits of bans are purported to be two-fold. Theoretically, there will be benefits for the health of the models themselves, as they will not be allowed to maintain an unhealthy and underweight body size. However, there should also be benefits for consumers, who will not be exposed to images that contain the very thin models to which they might compare themselves. Underweight (BMI<18.5) models have been banned from working in Madrid and Milan Fashion Week (Smith-Spark, 2006). Israel also recently passed body image laws that ban the use of models with a BMI of less than 18.5 (classifying them as underweight), and also enforced the disclosure of digital manipulation if it was used to make models look thinner (Sieczkowski, 2012). The laws in Israel came into effect at the start of 2013 and require models to produce medical proof that their BMI is in the healthy weight range. This approach is intended to create widespread change in an industry with a long history of focus on weight. However, critics from the fashion industry tend to argue that many models might naturally have a very low BMI and that by focusing on weight rather than health, the law arbitrarily disqualifies some models from working even if they are not suffering from an eating disorder (BBC, 2012).

While there is no empirical evidence of the success of underweight model bans, there has been research on the use of more diverse model sizes. One study found that using average-sized models in advertising is less harmful to the body image of consumers and would make them more likely to purchase the products advertised (Diedrichs & Lee, 2011). Further research is needed to determine whether banning underweight models is effective in improving body image.

There is some evidence that public policy initiatives that encourage the use of diverse-sized models are effective, but research on the impact of labelling airbrushed images or banning underweight models is still inconclusive. Further developments in broad-scale public policy initiatives to reduce the potential negative impact of the media on body image are encouraged and are likely to be more successful when combined with individual approaches to the improvement of body image.

Individual Approaches to Promote Positive Body Image

Interventions to prevent body dissatisfaction and promote the development of positive body image have been based upon a variety of theoretical frameworks. Here, we detail risk factor approaches, the Non-Specific Vulnerability Stressor Model, and Feminist frameworks that underpin the development of prevention programs.

Risk Factor Approaches

Risk Factor or Etiologic Approaches target sociocultural and individual risk factors for the development of body dissatisfaction. This approach is based on the theory that if you reduce the presence of modifiable, influential risk factors for the development of a problem, the problem itself is less likely to occur (Jacobi, Hayward, de Zwaan, Kraemer, & Agras, 2004; Mrazek & Haggerty, 1994). In the case of body image, we have discussed risk factors such as social comparisons in Chapter 6 and the Media in Chapter 5. Risk factor approaches target those such as the influence of peers and the media in order to reduce their impact and subsequent levels of body dissatisfaction. This approach is generally thought to be effective in promoting positive body image (Richardson & Paxton, 2010; Yager, Diedrichs, Ricciardelli, & Halliwell, 2013).

Interventions that focus on peers tend to target the risk factors of peer acceptance, appearance comparisons, and appearance conversations. Activities are generally interactive, and focus on changing perceptions of the importance of peers as well as changing the peer culture in the classroom. *Happy Being Me* (Richardson & Paxton, 2010) has been the most successful peer program among adolescent girls (Yager et al., 2013). This program was designed to focus on body comparison with peers, appearance conversations, and appearance teasing. Significant improvements on measures of all of these risk factors were found among the intervention group in comparison to the control group, and there were also significant improvements in body dissatisfaction and body satisfaction from pre to post test, and three-month follow up (Richardson & Paxton, 2010). This program was adapted to include boys, was trialled in the U.K. with a younger cohort (10–11 years), and achieved improvements in body satisfaction and appearance-related comparisons for girls and improvements in appearance-related conversations among boys and girls at post-test (Bird, Halliwell, Diedrichs, & Harcourt, 2013).

Media literacy is defined as the ability to access, analyse, evaluate, and create media in a variety of forms (Center for Media Literacy, 2011). Media literacy has been a particularly popular inclusion or focus of programs to improve body image, with the aim of reducing internalisation of the thin ideal by providing young people with skills to deconstruct and critique the media images and messages that they see. This approach targets the media as a risk factor, and Australian research recently confirmed that young people who are able to be more critical of the media are less likely to develop body dissatisfaction (McLean, Paxton, & Wertheim, 2013). Our review of secondary school body image programs (Yager et al., 2013) showed that the most effective media literacy program is *Media Smart* (Wilksch & Wade, 2009), an Australian program that consists of eight, 50-minute classroom lessons. Activities focus on media literacy, activism, and advocacy, including an exploration of the media's stereotypical portrayal of women and men in advertising, learning about airbrushing, and writing protest letters to the industry. Evaluation has found this program to be effective in reducing 13-year-old girls' and boys' concerns with, and over-evaluation of, body weight and shape, dieting, body dissatisfaction, and depression, and positive results were found to remain, even at 30 month follow-up (Wilksch & Wade, 2009). A subsequent investigation has compared *MediaSmart*, *LifeSmart* (a program focusing on shared risk factors for eating disorders and obesity), and *Helping, Encouraging, Listening, and Protecting Peers [HELPP]*, an extended, co-educational version of *Happy Being Me* among a large sample of 12 to 13-year-old boys and girls in Australia (Wilksch et al., 2014). This trial found that *MediaSmart* and

HELPP had a positive impact on the weight and shape concerns of girls at 12-month follow-up (but not immediate post-intervention), and that boys in the *MediaSmart* or *LifeSmart* groups improved on measures of body dissatisfaction at post-test (Wilksch et al., 2014). The pattern of results across all eating disorder risk factors revealed that *MediaSmart* had an more positive overall impact than the other interventions (Wilksch et al., 2014). However, an effectiveness trial of *MediaSmart,* where teachers delivered program materials, has not found the same positive results as when the program was delivered by the researchers, or graduate psychology students (Wilksch, 2013). This program is available through the research website: http://sparky.socsci.flinders.edu.au/researchonline/projects/5. Media literacy approaches have also been used in a variety of health promotion programs, including reducing violence and cigarette smoking as well as increased fruit and vegetable consumption (Bergsma & Carney, 2008).

Cognitive dissonance programs aim to reduce the risk factor of internalisation of the thin 'ideal' for females and muscular 'ideal' for males through counter-attitudinal activities that challenge these perceptions. There is a substantial amount of evidence supporting the success of this approach in *The Body Project* and *Reflections Body Image Program* among older adolescent girls (16 to 18 years) and young women (See Stice, Shaw, Becker, & Rohde, 2008). Cognitive dissonance interventions have had the greatest impact in targeted interventions with high-risk women (Stice, Marti, Spoor, Presnell, & Shaw, 2008; Stice, Shaw, Burton, & Wade, 2006; Stice, Trost, & Chase, 2003) and universal-selective interventions among women in sorority groups (Becker, Ciao, & Smith, 2008; Becker, Smith, & Ciao, 2005, 2006; Becker et al., 2010). A universal trial of a brief cognitive dissonance intervention based on *The Body Project* among adolescent girls in the U.K. was also successful in improving body image and internalisation of the thin ideal (Halliwell & Diedrichs, 2014). A modified version *of The Body Project* for middle school girls achieved significant pre-post improvements in pressure to be thin in one pilot trial, and in negative affect in another, but there were no other significant changes in outcome measures (Rohde et al., 2014).

The concept of prevention programs that target combined risk factors for eating disorders and obesity was raised in the 2000s and gathered some support (Austin, 2000; Neumark-Sztainer, 2009). Large scale projects such as *Planet Health* (Austin et al., 2012), and *New Moves* (Neumark-Sztainer et al., 2010) seemed to have a positive impact on risk factors for eating disorders and obesity. Subsequent trials in Australia, also included the universal *LifeSmart* program (Wilksch et al., 2014). The U.S.-based, selective, online, *Staying Fit* program is the most recent program of this kind, with a weight management intervention track for higher weight students and a Healthy Habits track for those below the 85th percentile of age-and-sex adjusted BMI (Jones et al., 2014). There was a significant reduction in weight concerns among high-risk participants in both intervention tracks in the *Staying Fit* project but no significant outcomes among the universal male and female participants (separate analysis by gender was not apparent) (Jones et al., 2014). The different responses to these programs by gender is apparent in the results from *LifeSmart*; there was a significant pre-post improvement in body image among the male participants, but also an increase in eating concerns at 12-month follow-up among the girls (Wilksch et al., 2014). These results suggest caution in the preparation of universal, co-educational programs that aim to reduce risk factors for obesity and eating disorders through an approach that targets body image.

Non-Specific Vulnerability Stressor Model

In contrast to targeting specific risk factors, the Non-Specific Vulnerability Stressor Model (Levine & Piran, 2001) targets broader, more general risk factors that might be common to the development of several disorders and diseases. This approach is based on the premise that individuals might have a range of risk factors that put them at risk for developing a range of physical and mental health issues, and that these issues are rarely isolated. Therefore, by addressing multiple areas of risk, such as self-esteem, resilience, social support, use of alcohol and other drugs, depression, and anxiety as well as improvement of body image and reduction of dieting, there might be broader health benefits (Levine & Smolak, 2006).

Two body image programs have targeted broader life skills, self-esteem, and communication rather than focusing on direct body image content. The Everybody's Different program (O'Dea, 2007; O'Dea & Abraham, 2000) utilised a 'content-free' curriculum to focus on stress reduction, building self-esteem, and improving relationship and communication skills in addition to some body image focused activities on exploring stereotypes in the media. Both the content of the program and the interactive, student centred approach in which it was presented, were purported to support the development of self-esteem, and therefore body image among the boys and girls in the study (O'Dea & Abraham, 2000). There was improvement on some measures of body image, and on drive for thinness, but not self-esteem and other measures of disordered eating pathology. Another program for adolescent boys involved a focus on adolescent adjustment, including communication skills, social skills, coping skills, and identifying unique personality traits (McCabe, Ricciardelli, & Karantzas, 2010). However, the evaluation of this program did not demonstrate any improvements for body image, self-esteem, drive for thinness, or body change strategies among adolescent boys.

Feminist Models

Finally, the Feminist-Empowerment Model is based on the idea that females are more vulnerable to body image issues, and because the experiences of the body are gendered, efforts to overcome body dissatisfaction should be based on empowerment against these stereotypes. These programs also draw on objectification theory, which claims that women's bodies are seen as passive objects to be admired while men's are active and for accomplishing tasks (Frederickson & Roberts, 1997). Programs based on this model aim to empower young girls to overcome these stereotypes within their own environments. Levine and Smolak (2006) detail several elements included in feminist programs, such as critical analysis of the gendered nature of body image, activism to create meaningful change within environments, and mentoring from adult women who facilitate the program rather than 'teach' the content. For example, a program titled *"Full of Ourselves": Advancing Girl Power, Health and Leadership* involves discussions about weightism as a social justice issue and uses creative writing and role play to explore topics such as body image, dieting, media influences and assertiveness (Steiner-Adair et al., 2002). While there were some improvements in knowledge, body image and disordered eating behaviours did not improve as a result of the program.

Prevention Research: A Review

Much research has now been devoted to the evaluation of programs designed to prevent eating disorders, and the majority of these include a specific focus on body image as the strongest risk EDs. While many systematic reviews and meta-analyses have evaluated the success of programs for disordered eating outcomes (e.g. Fingeret, Warren, Cepeda-Benito, & Gleaves, 2006; Stice & Shaw, 2004), very few have reviewed the research with the specific aim of determining the program features and approaches that have been most successful for body image outcomes. We conducted a systematic review in order to fill this gap in the literature and facilitate discussions about the next steps for body image prevention programs (Yager et al., 2013). The following is a report on an extension to that systematic review to include all body image programs, not just those conducted in schools.

The aim of this review was to assess the effectiveness of interventions in improving body image (our primary outcome), among adolescent boys and girls, at post-test (T1-T2) and at follow-up (T1-T3). In addition, we examine the effectiveness in improving modifiable factors related to body dissatisfaction during adolescence (our secondary outcomes), including self-esteem, internalisation of appearance ideals, appearance comparison, and drive for thinness, as well as knowledge and behaviours such as dieting or disordered eating. For more details about the methods used in this review, please see the Appendix 4 at the end of this chapter.

In total, we found 33 trials of 26 separate body image programs, presented in Table 1. The majority of these took place in the classroom setting in schools. We found 22 separate trials of 18 universal programs that were conducted during class time in schools, and three programs (evaluated in four trials, one was replicated) that were conducted outside of the regular classroom setting, but still took place in schools. There were two programs conducted in community settings that met the criteria for review. One was conducted in a gymnastics club, and the other was conducted only with mothers of middle school girls. Most of the programs were universal: only four trials evaluated three targeted programs (one was replicated), two of which took place in the school setting but were conducted online and tailored content to participant risk status.

There were some promising findings, as can be seen in Table 1: almost half of these programs were found to be effective in improving body image from pre to post, on at least one measure, with at least one gender. In total, 15 out of the 33 trials demonstrated significant improvements in the body image of adolescents in the intervention group, compared to the control group.

TABLE 1 Review of Body Image Programs Conducted with Adolescents after the Year 2000

Program	Participants			Body Image Outcomes	
	Mean Age	N	Gender	Improved body image at post?	Improved body image at Follow up?
School-based Programs Conducted in Classroom settings					
Happy Being Me (Richardson & Paxton, 2010) Aus	12.33	194	F	Y[a,b]	Y[a,b]
Dove BodyThink (Richardson et al., 2009) Aus	12.66	127	F	N[a,b]	N[a,b]
		150	M	Y[b] N[c]	Y[b] N[c]
The Body Project (Halliwell & Diedrichs, 2014) UK	12.07	104	F	Y[m]	–
MediaSmart (Wilksch & Wade, 2009a) Aus	13.62	273	F	N[a,d,e]	N[a] Y[d,e]
		267	M	Y[a] N[d,e]	Y[a,d,e]
Untitled (Stewart et al., 2001) UK [2]	13.40	860	F	Y[d] N[e]	N[d,e]

(Continued)

Program	Participants			Body Image Outcomes	
	Mean Age	N	Gender	Improved body image at post?	Improved body image at Follow up?
Everybody's Different (O'Dea & Abraham, 2000) Aus[3]	13.00	470	M/F	N[a]Y[i]	N
LifeSmart (Wilksch & Wade, 2013) Aus	12.71	51	F	Y[a,d,e]	–
		63	M	N[a,d,e]	–
Untitled (Stanford & McCabe, 2005) Aus	12.34	121	M	Y[j] N[k]	N
Adapted Go Girls! (Wade et al., 2003) Aus[1]	13.42	43	M/F	Y[e]N[f,d]	N
Girl's Group (Lobera et al., 2010) Spain[14]	14.72	174	F	Y[a]	–
Making Choices (Weiss & Wertheim, 2005) Aus [4]	14–16	197	M	Y[a]	–
Student Bodies (Bruning Brown et al., 2004) USA[5]	15.10	152	F	N[d,e]	N
Untitled (Wiseman et al., 2004) USA/Italy[6]	15–16	188	F[Italy]	N[a]	–
			F[USA]	N[a]	–
Full of Ourselves (Steiner-Adair et al., 2002) USA	12.59	411	F	N[g] N[h]	N
Untitled (Withers et al., 2002) Aus[7]	13.00	242	F	N[a,1]	N
Untitled (Rocco et al., 2001) Italy	16.07	112	F	N[a]	–
Healthy Body Image (McCabe et al., 2010) Aus	12.96	421	M	N[k]	N
Media Literacy Program (Wilksch et al., 2008) Aus[8]	15.00	20	F[6 Hi]	N[d,e]	N
		67	F[6 Lo]	N[d,e]	N

(Continued)

Program	Participants			Body Image Outcomes	
	Mean Age	N	Gender	Improved body image at post?	Improved body image at Follow up?
Everybody's Different (Replic:Wade et al., 2003) Aus	13.42	61	M/F	N[d,e,f]	N
Media Smart (teacher trial) (Wilksch, 2013) Aus	12.43	27	F	N[a,d,e]	N
		24	M	N[a,d,e]	N
In Favour of Myself (Golan et al., 2014) Israel	12–14	259	M/F	N[a]	N
Modified Student Bodies (Jones et al., 2014) USA	14.3	200	F	N[r]	–
		136	M	N[r]	
Programs Conducted in Schools but not in Classroom Settings					
Girl Talk/ (McVey et al., 2003a) CAN	12.5	214	F	Y[g]	Y[g]
Dance Curriculum (Burgess et al., 2008) USA	13.5	50	F	Y[p,q]	–
New Moves (Neumark-Sztainer et al., 2010) USA	15.8	356	F	N[n]	Y[n]
Girl Talk (McVey et al. 2003b) USA	12.3	282	F	N[g]	N[g]
Middle School Body Project (Rohde et al., 2014) USA	12.1	52	F	N[lm]	N
Community–based Programs					
BodySense (Bucholz et al., 2008)	13.4	62	F	N[g]	–
Healthy Girls Project (Corning et al., 2010) USA	13.16	31	F	N[a]Y[s]	N
Selected/Targeted Programs					
The Body Project -Efficacy trial (Stice Shaw et al., 2006)	17.0	481	F	Y[m]	Y[m]

(Continued)

Program	Participants			Body Image Outcomes	
	Mean Age	N	Gender	Improved body image at post?	Improved body image at Follow up?
The Body Project -Effectiveness trial (Stice, Rohde, et al., 2009)	15.7	306	F	Y[m]	Y[m]
My Body, My Life (Heinicke et al., 2007)	14.4	73	F	Y[o]	Y[o]
BodiMojo (Franko et al., 2013)	15.2	113	F	Y[a,g]	N
		65	M	N[a,g]	N

Key

- Participants: Mean age and number of participants are given, and a description of the sex; also includes risk status or country.
- Results: (Y/N) Improvements in body image among intervention participants compared to the control group at post-test or follow up. Details of the measures used are given in superscript (e.g., [a,b]) and provided in Table in Appendix 4 at end of this chapter.

Notes

1 Pre and post means and standard deviations were not presented so effect sizes could not be calculated.

2 Tests of significance were not provided for pre/post comparisons so effect sizes are provided for all analyses.

3 Results for this table were taken from analyses of group interaction effects for the group as a whole, not the analyses of effects among high-risk students. Effects for the measure of body image were presented as being significant for females.

4 Authors did not present means and standard deviations, so no effect sizes could be calculated.

5 This was a program delivered online but in the classroom setting and moderated by research assistants.

6 This program was conducted in co-educational classes of males and females, but questionnaires and evaluation were only conducted with the females.

7 This program was a 22- minute videotape.

8 Analyses were only given for high and low risk groups separately, and not the combined universal sample, but no significant change for either groups on the factors was reported.

9 A range of additional program components included 4 days of physical education lessons per week, individual counseling sessions, lunch-time get together and a parent outreach program. Program was run over nine months (an entire school year) with around 4 or 5 sessions per week, but this altered according to the stage of the program. Effect sizes could not be calculated as standard deviations were not provided for all scores.

10 This study compared a six week aerobic dance curriculum to the control condition of regular physical education lessons which was swimming lessons.

11 Two and three year follow up data was obtained from (Stice, Rohde, Shaw, & Gau, 2011).

12 Two and three year follow up data was obtained from (E Stice et al., 2008).

13 Participatory, ecological intervention also included parent and coach education, and changes to physical and social environment of gymnastics clubs.

14 The control group in this study received 10 90-minute sessions of psycho-education focusing on eating disorder prevention.

We will now discuss the results of this review by some of the characteristics of the programs, including the gender and age of the participants, approach and length of the program, the setting and facilitator, and the measures used in the evaluation of the program.

Gender

Most programs have been developed on the body image concerns of females, and the trials conducted outside of the class setting reflect this, as they, and the community programs, all targeted female adolescents. The majority of the targeted programs were also only trialled among girls, with the exception of *BodiMojo* (Franko, Cousineau, Rodgers, & Roehrig, 2013). In class settings, nine programs were conducted only among females, 10 included boys and girls, and two programs were implemented only with males.

We found that, when studies were conducted in a mixed-gender setting, body image was generally only improved among one gender. For example, only the boys improved on measures of body image in evaluations of *BodyThink* and *MediaSmart* (Richardson & Paxton, 2010; Wilksch & Wade, 2009), and only girls demonstrated body image improvement in the evaluation of *LifeSmart* (Wilksch & Wade, 2013). The exception is the Spanish replication of *Girls' Group* (Lobera et al., 2010), where improvements were seen among boys and girls, despite the fact that the program was clearly not designed to meet the needs of adolescent boys.

Happy Being Me (Richardson & Paxton, 2010) was the most effective of the classroom-based intervention conducted with girls. This was the only program to demonstrate significant improvements in body image at post-test and three month follow-up, as well as other factors related to body image, including self-esteem, internalisation, appearance comparisons, and disordered eating. Among boys, *MediaSmart* (Wilksch & Wade, 2009) was the most promising, as participants had significant improvements in body image at post-test and six months later, as well as improvements on dieting and disordered eating behaviours. The body image programs that were designed and conducted only among males were not particularly successful in improving outcomes on primary measures (McCabe et al., 2010; Stanford & McCabe, 2005). Clearly, we still do not fully understand how to meet the needs of young boys, and further research is required in order to develop suitable co-educational programs that result in improved outcomes for both genders.

Age

Nine of the 10 classroom-based programs that were identified as being effective in improving body image from pre- to post-test were conducted with younger participants 12 and 13 years of age (mean age range = 12.16 to 13.62 years). Again, the exception was the Spanish replication of *Girls' Group* (Lobera et al., 2010), where the program was conducted with four year levels in a secondary school, and the mean age was 14.72. None of the universal school-based programs for participants aged 15 to 16 years was effective in improving body image. However, the targeted programs were conducted among older students (mean age range = 14.4 to 17.0 years) and were all effective in improving body image, possibly because program materials could be adapted to suit those who had already developed high levels of body dissatisfaction.

Setting

The body image programs that were conducted in schools, but outside of the classroom setting, took place either in peer support settings or in physical education classes that involved physical activity rather than a classroom-based curriculum. There were mixed results among the programs conducted outside of classrooms in the school setting. *Girl Talk / Everybody is a Somebody* (McVey, Lieberman, Voorberg, Wardrope, & Blackmore, 2003) was successful in improving body image and other outcome measures in the original trial; however, a replication did not report the same positive findings. Another study compared an aerobic dance curriculum to swimming for physical education classes and found positive effects on body image (Buchholz, Mack, McVey, Feder, & Barrowman, 2008). Other approaches in the school setting included interventions involving exercise, such as *New Moves*, an all girls PE class with some supporting classroom materials, personal counselling sessions, and parent involvement reported improvements in body image at six month follow-up but not post test. The community program in the gymnastics club was not effective in improving body image (Buchholz et al., 2008); however, the intervention where mothers were provided with workshops about how to support their daughters' positive body image did produce some increases in a body image measure of daughters' body dissatisfaction that the researchers developed for the purposes of the research (Corning, Gondoli, Bucchianeri, & Blodgett Salafia, 2010). This limited range of evaluation studies conducted in community settings makes it difficult to determine the elements of success for programs that are to be implemented outside of the classroom curriculum.

Approach

Most interventions include a range of different approaches, with the most common being media literacy (present in 19 out of the 33 trials). Self-esteem (15 trials), body acceptance (12 trials), peer activities (11 trials), and those aiming to improve stress and coping (10 trials) were also common. Nine trials included a focus on healthy weight (by focusing on appropriate diet and exercise habits), six included psycho-education about body image, and six included psycho-education about eating disorders. Six programs included information about physical development and the impact of puberty on body shape and body image. Finally, four programs included cognitive dissonance.

Most effective programs utilised a combination of approaches and content. Effective programs tended to include activities that focused on media literacy, self-esteem, and peer influences. The variance in classification of activities, lack of information about activities in programs, and range of activities included in any one program make it difficult to ascertain trends in the effectiveness of program approaches.

As parents have a substantial influence on the body image of adolescents, it makes sense to involve them in prevention programs. Hart and colleagues provide an excellent systematic review of body image and eating disorder prevention programs that involve parents (Hart, Cornell, Damiano, & Paxton, 2014). Very few programs that we reviewed involved a parent component. The exception is the intervention conducted in the U.S. by Corning and colleagues, where the intervention consisted solely of workshops with mothers and then evaluated the impact on their middle-school daughters. Improvements in body image were seen as a result of this intervention, but only on a scale that was developed by the authors (and not standardised or validated), and the participant numbers were very low (Corning et al., 2010). Issues with parent interest in participating in body image programs, and in their low actual completion of program materials are reported as barriers to parent involvement (Hart et al., 2014) despite the potential benefits of having body image programs reinforced by family influences in the home environment.

Program Length

All of the classroom-based programs that were effective in improving body image included multiple sessions (two to 10), with a total program length that ranged from 80 to 900 minutes. The average total length of these effective classroom-based programs was 260 minutes, or just over four hours of program time. Among all programs, the range was much greater, from a single session of 22 minutes, to 27 hours of total program time. Targeted programs tended to be shorter and ranged from 180–540 minutes in length (Mean = 285 minutes). This leads us to conclude that the universal programs that were longer were not necessarily any more effective, and that targeted programs can be shorter and still achieve positive outcomes. Program length could not be determined for five out of the 33 trials, as the length of time for each session was not specified, which is a significant oversight in the reporting of intervention research.

Facilitator Characteristics

The details of the person facilitating body image programs (and in particular, their gender) were generally very poorly reported. Twelve out of 22 classroom-based trials were conducted by researchers, and only four were delivered by teachers. The remainder was delivered either through video, as online programs, and by other school staff. The majority of effective classroom-based trials was conducted by female researchers, with the exception of *MediaSmart*, that was effective in improving body image among young men, and was conducted by a male researcher (Wilksch & Wade, 2009). Programs in the school setting but conducted outside of the classroom were presented by school nurses and school counsellors, and only one out of the five trials was conducted by a researcher. Targeted programs tended to be facilitated online, and the community-based programs were generally conducted by researchers. The facilitator of research trials is a critical component in the success of the program, and these details need to be better reported in future body image intervention research.

Measures

Although the primary aim of this review was not to investigate the mechanisms of assessment of body image, it was quite concerning to discover that 19 different measures and variations of measures were used to evaluate the impact of body image programs (for a full list, please see the table in the Appendix 4 at the end of this chapter). This makes the comparison of results and effect sizes very difficult. We recommend that future research in this area give significant attention to the measures used and ensure that at least one measure of body image be standardised, validated for adolescents, and commonly used to determine the impact of body image interventions. Please see Chapter 2 for more details.

Recommendations for Future Prevention Research

Rather than concentrate on the development of new content, we suggest that future interventions focus on replicating the findings of those programs that score well in efficacy trials, which evaluate whether interventions are successful under experimental conditions, where the facilitators are methodically trained and supervised, and the intervention is typically delivered in controlled environments (Flay, 1986). Once programs have demonstrated success, and have been independently replicated, effectiveness trials are then essential to determine the generalisability and real-world application of a prevention program, as they evaluate success when conducted in regular conditions, in natural settings and by the providers who are generally facilitating those groups, e.g., by teachers in schools (Flay, 1986). Not all body image research has progressed through these stages, with some advancing straight to teacher-delivered programs. Cognitive dissonance programs have successfully progressed through these two stages of efficacy and effectiveness and meet the Standards of Criteria for Effective Interventions, as set out by the Society for Prevention (Marchland, Stice, Rohde, & Becker, 2011; Stice, Rohde, Shaw, & Gau, 2011).

While efficacy and effectiveness trials are important for the more widespread testing of complete programs, we also recommend that dismantling studies determine which aspects of these full programs are most effective on their own. Many schools do not have the time to commit three, four, or eight lessons to a complete body image program, particularly if the content of some of the lessons seems to overlap with other areas of the taught curriculum. Dismantling studies could tease apart the separate activities in a prevention program and be tested individually with groups of students to identify whether some activities are more effective than others. This would assist in making curriculum recommendations to schools.

It is also important to consider the needs of the target audience for prevention. Interventions are often developed by researchers, based on evidence, and delivered *to* young people. Some participatory approaches to eating disorder prevention have taken place (Levine & Piran, 2001), but these are rare. Sharpe and colleagues (2013) held focus groups with adolescent girls to determine their suggestions for prevention. Young girls recommended that programs focus on media literacy and educate about eating disorders (Sharpe, Damazer, Treasure, & Schmidt, 2013). They also suggested building sources of support about body image issues. In particular, they recommended the availability of anonymous support structures such as telephone hotlines or Internet-based services, where they can discuss concerns and receive help from professionals. This was seen as beneficial as they would receive accurate information, rather than endangering their relationship with parents, friends, and teachers, who might not know what to do to help them (Sharpe et al., 2013).

Conclusion

A good deal of evidence now supports a range of intervention options to improve body image through a variety of settings. Programs need not be lengthy or expensive, but they do need to be implemented among young people as early as possible, before they reach mid-adolescence and body dissatisfaction has become too well entrenched. Broad access to these programs and resources for adolescents and young adults, whether in online, school, or community settings, is urgently required to reduce the prevalence of body dissatisfaction and associated problems. The design, evaluation, and broad dissemination of materials that can easily be delivered by endogenous providers who are already in the position to influence young people, such as teachers, school counsellors, sports coaches, community group leaders, and parents will make this infinitely more possible. Changes to public policy and school and community environment and ethos would further support these efforts and lead to improvements in body image among adolescents around the world.

References

Albee, G.W. (1996). Revolutions and counter revolutions in prevention. *American Psychologist, 51*, 1130–1133.

All Party Parliamentary Group [APPG]. (2012). Reflections on Body Image. Report of the All Party Parliamentary Group. Retrieved from http://www.ymca.co.uk/bodyimage/report.

American Medical Association [AMA]. (2011). AMA Adopts New Policies at Annual Meeting. http://www.ama-assn.org/ama/pub/news/news/a11-new-policies.page.

British Broadcasting Corporation [BBC]. (2012). Israel passes law banning use of underweight models. Retrieved from http://www.bbc.co.uk/news/world-middle-east-17450275.

Ata, R.N., Thompson, J.K., & Small, B.J. (2013). Effects of exposure to thin-ideal media images on body dissatisfaction: Testing the inclusion of a disclaimer versus warning label. *Body Image, 10*, 472–80.

Austin, S.B. (2000). Prevention research in eating disorders: Theory and new directions. *Psychological Medicine, 30*, 1249–62.

Becker, C.B., Ciao, A.C., & Smith, L.M. (2008). Moving from efficacy to effectiveness in eating disorders prevention: The sorority body image program. *Cognitive and Behavioral Practice, 15*, 18–27.

Becker, C.B., Smith, L.M., & Ciao, A.C. (2005). Reducing eating disorder risk factors in sorority members: A randomized trial. *Behavior Therapy, 36*(3), 245–53.

Becker, C.B., Smith, L.M., & Ciao, A.C. (2006). Peer-facilitated eating disorder prevention: A randomized efficacy trial of cognitive dissonance and media advocacy *Journal of Counseling Psychology, 53*(4), 550–55.

Becker, C.B., Wilson, C., Williams, A., Kelly, M., McDaniel, L., & Elmquist, J. (2010). Peer-facilitated cognitive dissonance versus healthy weight eating disorders prevention: A randomized comparison. *Body Image, 7*, 280–88.

Bergsma, L.J., & Carney, M.E. (2008). Effectiveness of health-promoting media literacy education: A systematic review. *Health Education Research, 23*(3), 522–42.

Bird, E., Halliwell, E., Diedrichs, P.C., & Harcourt, D. (2013). Happy Being Me in the UK: A controlled evaluation of a body image intervention with pre-adolescent children. *Body Image, 10*(3), 326–34.

Boyd, E.R., & Moncrieff-Boyd, J. (2011). Swimsuit issues: Promoting positive body image in young women's magazines. *Health Promotion Journal of Australia, 22*(2), 102–106.

Buchholz, A., Mack, H., McVey, G.L., Feder, S., & Barrowman, N. (2008). BodySense: An evaluation of a positive body image intervention on sport climate for athetes. *Eating Disorders, 16*, 308–21.

Corning, A.F., Gondoli, D.M., Bucchianeri, M.M., & Blodgett Salafia, E.H. (2010). Preventing the development of body issues in adolescent girls through an intervention with their mothers. *Body Image, 7*(4), 289–95.

Cousineau, T., Franko, D., Trant, M., Rancourt, D., Ainscough, J., Chaudhuri, A., & Brevard, J. (2010). Teaching adolescents about changing bodies: Randomized controlled trial of an internet puberty education and body dissatisfaction prevention program. *Body Image, 7*(4), 296–300.

Diedrichs, P.C., & Lee, C. (2011). Waif goodbye! Average-size female models promote positive body image and appeal to consumers. *Psychology and Health, 26*(10), 1273–91.

Dunstan, C.J., Paxton, S., McLean, S.A., & Gregg, K. (2014). A school-based body image intervention for young girls: is co-educational or single-sex delivery more effective? *Journal of Eating Disorders, 2(Supplement 1)*, 01.

Erlanger, S. (2009). Point, shoot, retouch and label? *The New York Times*. Retrieved from http://www.nytimes.com/2009/12/03/fashion/03Boyer.html?pagewanted= all&_r=0.

Evans, E.H., Tovée, M.J., Boothroyd, L.G., & Drewett, R.F. (2013). Body dissatisfaction and disordered eating attitudes in 7- to 11-year-old girls: Testing a sociocultural model. *Body Image, 10*, 8–15.

Fingeret, M.C., Warren, C.S., Cepeda-Benito, C.S., & Gleaves, D.S. (2006). Eating disorder prevention research: A Meta analysis. *Eating Disorders: The Journal of Treatment and Prevention, 14*, 191–213.

Flay, R.R. (1986). Efficacy and effectiveness trials (an other phases of research) in the development of health promotion programs. *Preventive Medicine, 15*, 451–74.

Franko, D., Cousineau, T., Rodgers, R., & Roehrig, J. (2013). BodiMojo: Effective internet-based promotion of positive body image in adolescent girls. *Body Image*.

Frederickson, B.L., & Roberts, T.A. (1997). Objectification theory: Toward understanding women's lived experiences and mental health risks. *Psychology of Women Quarterly, 21*, 173–206.

Halliwell, E., & Diedrichs, P. (2014). Testing a dissonance body image intervention among young girls. *Health Psychology, 33*(2), 201–204.

Halliwell, E., Easun, A., & Harcourt, D. (2010). Body dissatisfaction: Can a short media literacy message reduce negative media exposure effects among adolescent girls? *British Journal of Health Psychology, 16*, 396–403.

Harrison, K., & Hefner, V. (2014). Virtually perfect: Image retouching and adolescent body image. *Media Psychology, 17*(2), 134–53.

Hart, L.M., Cornell, C., Damiano, S.R., & Paxton, S.J. (2014). Parents and prevention: A systematic review of interventions Involving parents that aim to prevent body dissatisfaction or eating disorders. *International Journal of Eating Disorders*.

Holt, K.E., & Ricciardelli, L.A. (2008). Weight concerns among elementary school children: A review of prevention programs. *Body Image, 5*, 233–43.

Jacobi, C., Hayward, C., de Zwaan, M., Kraemer, H.C., & Agras, W.S. (2004). Coming to terms with risk factors for eating disorders: Application of risk terminology and suggestions for a general taxonomy. *Psychological Bulletin, 130*(1), 19–65.

Jones, D.C. (2004). Body image among adolescent girls and boys: A longitudinal study. *Developmental Psychology, 40*(5), 823–35.

Jones, M., Taylor Lynch, K., Kass, A.E., Burrows, A., Williams, J., Wilfley, D., & Taylor, C.B. (2014). Healthy weight regulation and eating disorder prevention in high school students: A universal and targeted web-based intervention. *Journal of Medical Internet Research, 16*(2), e57–71.

Kee, E., & Farid, H. (2011). A perceptual metric for photo retouching *Proceedings of the National Academy of Sciences of America, 108*(50), 19907–12.

Levine, M.P., & Piran, N. (2001). The prevention of eating disorders: Towards a participatory ecology of knowledge, action, and advocacy. In R.H. Striegel-Moore & L. Smolak (Eds.), *Eating disorders: New directions for research and practice.* Philadelphia, PA: Brunner/Mazel.

Levine, M.P., & Smolak, L. (2006). *The prevention of eating problems and eating disorders: Theory, research and practice.* Mahwah, NJ: Lawrence Erlbaum Associates.

Lobera, I.J., Lozano, P.L., Rios, P.B., Candau, J.R., Lebreros, G.S.V., Millan, M.T.M., … Sanchez, N.V. (2010). Traditional and new strategies in the primary prevention of eating disorders: A comparative study in Spanish adolescents. *International Journal of General Medicine, 3*, 263–72.

Marchland, E., Stice, E., Rohde, P., & Becker, C. (2011). Moving from efficacy to effectiveness trials in prevention research. *Behaviour Research and Therapy, 49*, 32–41.

McCabe, M.P., Ricciardelli, L.A., & Karantzas, G. (2010). Impact of a healthy body image program among adolescent boys on body image, negative affect, and body change strategies. *Body Image, 7*(2), 117–23.

McLean, S.A., Paxton, S.J., & Wertheim, E.H. (2013). Mediators of the relationship between media literacy and body dissatisfaction in early adolescent girls: Implications for prevention. *Body Image, 10*(3), 282–89.

McVey, G.L., Lieberman, M., Voorberg, N., Wardrope, D., & Blackmore, E. (2003). School-based peer support groups: A new approach to the prevention of disordered eating. *Eating Disorders, 11*, 169–85.

Mrazek, P.J., & Haggerty, R.J. (1994). *Redcing risks for mental disorders: Frontiers for preventive intervention research.* Washington, DC: National Academy Press.

Neumark-Sztainer, D. (2009). The interface between the eating disorders and obesity fields: Moving toward a model of shared knowledge and collaboration. *Eating and Weight Disorders, 14*, 51–58.

Neumark-Sztainer, D., Friend, S.E., Flattum, C.F., Hannan, P.J., Story, M., Bauer, K. W., … Petrich, C.A. (2010). New moves: Preventing weight-related problems in adolescent girls: A group-randomised study. *American Journal of Preventive Medicine, 39*(5), 421–32.

Neumark-Sztainer, D., Levine, M., Paxton, S., Smolak, L., Piran, N., & Wertheim, E. (2006). Prevention of body dissatisfaction and disordered eating: What's next? *Eating Disorders, 14*, 265–85.

O'Dea, J. (2007). *Everybody's different: A positive approach to teaching about health, puberty, body image, nutrition, self-esteem and obesity prevention.* Melbourne: Australian Council for Educational Research [ACER] Press.

O'Dea, J., & Abraham, S.F. (2000). Improving the body image, eating attitudes, and behaviours of young male and female adolescents: A new educational approach that focuses on self-esteem. *International Journal of Eating Disorders, 28*, 43–57.

Paxton, S. (1993). A prevention program for disturbed eating and body dissatisfaction in adolescent girls: A 1 year follow-up. *Health Education Research, 8*, 43–51.

Paxton, S. (2012). Public policy approaches to prevention. In T.F. Cash & L. Smolak (Eds.), *Body image: A handbook of science, practice, and prevention (2nd Edition)*. New York, NY: Guilford Press.

Richardson, S.M., & Paxton, S.J. (2010). An evaluation of a body image intervention based on risk factors for body dissatisfaction: A controlled study with adolescent girls. *International Journal of Eating Disorders, 43*(2), 112–22. doi: 10.1002/eat.20682.

Rohde, P., Auslander, B.A., Shaw, H., Raineri, K.M., Gau, J.M., & Stice, E. (2014). Dissonance-based prevention of eating disorder risk factors in middle school girls: Results from two pilot trials. *International Journal of Eating Disorders, 47*, 483–94.

Rohde, P., Stice, E., & Marti, C.N. (2014). Development and predictive effects of eating disorder risk factors during adolescence: Implications for prevention efforts. *International Journal of Eating Disorders*. doi:10.1002/eat.22270.

Sharpe, H., Damazer, K., Treasure, J., & Schmidt, U. (2013). What are adolescents' experiences of body dissatisfaction and dieting, and what do they recommend for prevention? A qualitative study. *Eating and Weight Disorders*. doi:10.1007/s40519-013-0023-1.

Sieczkowski, C. (2012). Supermodels without photoshop: Israel's 'Photoshop Law' puts focus on digitally altered images. *International Business Times*. Retrieved from http://www.ibtimes.com/supermodels-without-photoshop-israels-photoshop-law-puts-focus-digitally-altered-images-photos.

Slater, A., Tiggemann, M., Firth, B., & Hawkins, K. (2012). Reality check: An experimental investigation of the addition of warning labels to fashion magazine images on women's mood and body dissatisfaction. *Journal of Social and Clinical Psychology, 31*(2), 105–22.

Smith-Spark, L. (2006). Is ultra-thin going out of fashion? *BBC*. Retrieved from http://news.bbc.co.uk/2/hi/europe/5384106.stm.

Stanford, J., & McCabe, M.P. (2005). Sociocultural influences on adolescent boys' body image and body change strategies. *Body Image, 2*, 105–13.

Steiner-Adair, C., Sjostrom, L., Franko, D., Seeta, P., Tucker, R., Becker, A., & Herzog, D. (2002). Primary prevention of risk factors for eating disorders in adolescent girls: Learning from practice. *International Journal of Eating Disorders, 32*, 401–41.

Stice, E., Marti, C.N., Spoor, S., Presnell, K., & Shaw, H. (2008). Dissonance and healthy weight eating disorder prevention programs: Long-term effects from a randomized efficacy trial. *Journal of Consulting and Clinical Psychology, 76*(2), 329–40.

Stice, E., Rohde, P., Shaw, H., & Gau, J. (2011). An effectiveness trial of selected dissonance-based eating disorder prevention program for female high school students: Long-term effects. *Journal of Consulting and Clinical Psychology, 79*(4), 500–508.

Stice, E., & Shaw, H. (2004). Eating disorder prevention programs: A meta-analytic review. *Psychological Bulletin, 130*(2), 206–27.

Stice, E., Shaw, H., Becker, C.B., & Rohde, P. (2008). Dissonance-based interventions for the prevention of eating disorders: Using persuasion principles to promote health. *Preventive Science, 9*, 114–28.

Stice, E., Shaw, H., Burton, E., & Wade, E. (2006). Dissonance and healthy weight eating disorder prevention programs: A randomized efficacy trial. *Journal of Consulting and Clinical Psychology, 74*, 263–75.

Stice, E., Trost, A., & Chase, A. (2003). Healthy weight control and dissonance-based eating disorder prevention programs: Results from a controlled trial. *International Journal of Eating Disorders, 33*, 10–21.

Tiggemann, M., Slater, A., Bury, B., Hawkins, K., & Firth, B. (2013). Disclaimer labels on fashion magazine advertisements: Effects on social comparison and body dissatisfaction. *Body Image, 10*, 45–53.

Veldhuis, J., Konijn, E.A., & Seidell, J.C. (2014). Counteracting media's thin-body ideal for adolescent girls: Informing is more effective than warning. *Media Psychology, 17*(2), 154–84.

Wilksch, S.M. (2013). School-based eating disorder prevention: a pilot effectiveness trial of teacher-delivered Media Smart. *Early Intervention in Psychiatry*.

Wilksch, S.M., Paxton, S.J., Byrne, S.M., Austin, S.B., McLean, S.A., Thompson, K.M., ... Wade, T.D. (2014). Prevention across the spectrum: a randomized controlled trial of three programs to reduce risk factors for both eating disorders and obesity. *Psychological Medicine*. doi: http://0-dx.doi.org.library.vu.edu.au/10.1017/S003329171400289X.

Wilksch, S.M., & Wade, T.D. (2013). Life Smart: A pilot study of a school-based program to reduce the risk of both eating disorders and obesity in young adolescent girls and boys. *Journal of Pediatric Psychology*. doi: 10.1093/jpepsy/jst036.

Wilksch, S.M., & Wade, T.D. (2009). Reduction of shape and weight concern in young adolescents: A 30-month controlled evaluation of a media literacy program. *Journal of the American Academy of Child and Adolescent Psychiatry, 48*(6), 652–61.

Yager, Z., Diedrichs, P., & Drummond, M.J.N. (2013). Understanding the role of gender in body image research settings: Participant gender preferences for researchers and co-participants in interviews, focus groups, and interventions. *Body Image, 10*(4), 574–82.

Yager, Z., Diedrichs, P.C., Ricciardelli, L.A., & Halliwell, E. (2013). What works in secondary schools? A systematic review of classroom-based body image programs. *Body Image, 10*, 271–81.

APPENDIX 4
METHODS FOR PREVENTION REVIEW RESEARCH

In order to conduct this review, two researchers independently searched electronic databases [EBSCOhost, Medline, PsycINFO, Current Contents, Google Scholar] using the following keywords: 'body image', 'body dissatisfaction', 'disordered eating', 'eating disorder', 'interventions', and 'prevention programs'. In addition, the 2008–2013 issues of the journals *Body Image*, *International Journal of Eating Disorders*, and *Eating Disorders: The Journal of Treatment and Prevention* were searched manually for relevant articles. Finally, all previous review papers (i.e., systematic and unsystematic reviews, and meta-analyses identified during the database searches) were scanned for additional published articles. Book chapters and theses were not included as their peer review status is not always reported, and they are often not readily accessible. Each article was read in full to determine whether it fit the inclusion criteria for the review, and two of the authors met to agree on the inclusion and exclusion of each study.

We used a strict set of inclusion criteria in order to meet our specific aims of identifying effective classroom-based body-image programs and to facilitate stronger comparisons between the programs that were identified. The inclusion criteria, and justification and explanation for each are provided below.

1. Studies were included if published as peer-reviewed journal articles, post-2000, in order to provide a current review of rigorous research.
2. In order to provide a review of programs conducted with adolescents, we included studies where the mean age of participants was reported as being older than 12.0 years and younger than 18.0 years.
3. We limited studies to those that evaluated a program that aimed to improve body image (even as a risk factor for eating disorders) and/or included

body image in program materials in order to review only those programs that focused on our primary outcome. Programs were only included in this review if they used, and reported the results of, at least one measure of body image or body dissatisfaction that was validated for adolescents (as reported by the authors of the evaluation) at pre and post test.

4. Finally, we included a methodological requirement that studies were controlled. This meant that the intervention groups were compared to a comparison condition that might have been a wait-list control, engaged in an alternative intervention, or usual classroom activities. Random allocation was not required.

Universal preventive interventions were defined as those that are "for general population groups not identified as having specific risk factors" (Weisz, Sandler, Durlak, & Anton, 2005, p. 631) and selected prevention is defined as "a strategy that targets groups who are identified because they share a significant risk factor" (Weisz et al., 2005, p. 632). Targeted preventive interventions are tailored to high-risk individuals who are identified as having 'significant symptoms of disorder' (Weisz et al., 2005, p. 632).

The name of each program, study authors, and country in which the study was conducted were obtained from the published reports. The approach of each intervention program was classified into 10 sub-types by the review authors, based upon the information provided in the published studies. We classified body image and eating disorder prevention programs into the following subtypes according to previous reviews and our own improvements for clarity (Holt & Ricciardelli, 2008; Stice & Shaw, 2004). Details of the professional background and gender of the facilitator were obtained from the methods, as were the number and length of sessions to determine the dose. The mean age of participants was obtained from the studies, or a range was used if a mean was not provided. Participant numbers were determined by adding the number of participants in the control and intervention conditions, as reported by the study authors, for males and females separately.

For each of the outcomes, intervention programs were classified as having achieved significant improvements if the analyses indicated that the intervention group improved on scores of the primary or secondary outcome measures from pre to post test, relative to the control group ($p<.05$). The same procedure was used to determine whether programs achieved, or maintained, significant improvements on the primary outcome measure of body image at follow-up (T1-T3). The measures used to determine changes in body image and body dissatisfaction were recorded using superscript, and are presented in Table 1 below.

TABLE 1 Details of the measures used to determine change on body image and body dissatisfaction

Measure
[1a] Body Dissatisfaction Subscale of Eating Disorders Inventory [EDI] (Garner, Olmstead, & Polivy, 1983).
[1b] Body Satisfaction Visual Analogue Scale [BSVAS] (Durkin & Paxton, 2002).
[1c] Adapted version of the Body Dissatisfaction Subscale of the EDI that is modified to represent the common areas of male body dissatisfaction (Jones, 2004).
[1d] Shape Concerns subscale of the Eating Disorder Examination [EDE] (Fairburn & Cooper, 1993).
[1e] Weight Concerns subscale of the Eating Disorder Examination [EDE] (Fairburn & Cooper, 1993).
[1f] Stunkard Figure rating scale- discrepancy score (Stunkard, Sorenson, & Schulsinger, 1983).
[1g] Weight Subscale of the Body Esteem Scale [BES] for adolescents and young adults (Mendelson, Mendelson, & White, 2001).
[1h] Body Areas Satisfaction Scale [BASS] of Multidimensional Body Self Relations Questionnaire [MBSRQ] (Cash, 2000).
[1i] 'Self' Physical Appearance Ratings [PAR] (O'Dea, Abraham, & Heard, 1996).
[1j] Satisfaction with muscles subscale of the Body Satisfaction Subscale of the Body Satisfaction and Body Change Inventory [BS&BCI] (Ricciardelli & McCabe, 2002).
[1k] Satisfaction with weight Subscale of the Body Satisfaction and Body Change Inventory [BS&BCI] (Ricciardelli & McCabe, 2000).
[1l] Size discrepancy on the Contour Drawing Rating Scale (Thompson & Gray, 1995).
[1m] Body Parts Scale (Berscheid, Walster, & Bohrnstedt, 1973).
[1n] Body Satisfaction scale adapted from the Body Shape Satisfaction Scale (Pingitore, Spring, & Garfield, 1997) and Body Cathexis Scale (Secord & Jourard, 1953).
[1o] Body Shape Questionnaire (Evans & Dolan, 1993).
[1p] Feeling Fat subscales of the Body Attitudes Questionnaire [BAQ] (Ben-Tovim & Walker, 1991).
[1q] Physical Self Worth subscales of the Children and Youth Physical Self Perception Profile [CYPSPP] (Whitehead, 1995).
[1r] Weight Concerns Scale (Killen et al., 1994).
[1s] Body Parts Dissatisfaction Scale- (developed by Corning et al., 2010).

13
WHAT NEXT? RECOMMENDATIONS FOR FUTURE RESEARCH

A great deal of research has examined the development of body image among adolescents. This has helped us understand how body image and body change strategies impact on many aspects of adolescents' lives. The volume and quality of this work is very encouraging. However, there is still much that we need to know.

In order to more fully reflect relevant and significant issues for adolescents, their body image needs to be studied in relation to everyday meaningful experiences. The use of participant-centred, qualitative and participatory methods is needed (Barter & Renold, 2000; Devine, 2002; Lightfoot & Sloper, 2002). These will allow the development and an in-depth exploration of the views and experiences from the perspective of the adolescents themselves, and also incorporate other factors that will emerge from the data. As was noted in Chapter 2, much of the work in the field is limited by the use of structured questionnaires, which have been adapted from research with adults. Such measures do not fully capture adolescents' experiences and perspectives. They also include references to complex constructs that may be misunderstood by adolescents.

In Chapter 2 we reviewed a large number of measurement tools that have been developed to quantify levels of body dissatisfaction. The most common measures that have demonstrated good psychometric properties with male and female adolescents are attitudinal measures that provide an indication of the extent of body dissatisfaction, but not whether adolescents are making inaccurate assessment of their body size (perceptual measures) or engaging in behaviours due to their negative body image (behavioural measures). While it is important that these standardised, commonly used measures are incorporated into future research to aid comparisons across studies, the current measures tend to be quite lengthy. There will be advantages to the development of new measures that are equally as accurate, but more concise, in order to reduce participant fatigue and facilitate more widespread collaboration and collection of body image data in related research fields across countries.

We reviewed a wide array of body change strategies and body modification methods used by adolescents in Chapter 3. However, we still need to know more about how these strategies are used by adolescents to enhance their body image and appearance and the other motives underlying some of these behaviours that are becoming more normative among adolescents, such as body piercing and tattooing. Many adolescents with high levels of body dissatisfaction also engage in a range of health-risk behaviours, which include substance use and unsafe sexual practices. Thus it is important that we track adolescents with body image concerns and ensure that they have supportive environments to reduce the health-risk behaviours.

As we showed in Chapter 4, physical and biological factors make a unique contribution to the development of body image and are particularly heightened for adolescents. Research has consistently indicated that a high BMI is one of the strongest predictors of the development of body dissatisfaction, for male and female adolescents. Research that has focused on the impact of puberty on body image has found that male and female adolescents are affected in very different ways. After going through puberty, girls are more and boys are less likely to be dissatisfied with their bodies; going through puberty earlier than peers is more likely to lead to increased levels of body dissatisfaction in girls and decreased body dissatisfaction in boys. Although less amenable to change as a target of prevention programming, understanding more about the impact of physical and biological factors will assist researchers in targeting intervention programs to more accurately address the concerns of adolescents at different weights or stages of puberty.

The media has been blamed for the development of negative body image for some time. A great deal of research has focused on investigating the impact of the media on body image and body dissatisfaction of adolescents and has generally been found to have a negative effect, particularly for adolescent girls. In Chapter 5, we provided a review of this research, conducted in correlational, experimental, and longitudinal studies. We also discussed new research that has focussed on less traditional forms of media such as the Internet, social media, and reality television, as these areas have received less research attention. In the near future, effective public policy initiatives to the promotion of positive body image such as the consideration of airbrushed images, and industry standards (discussed in Chapter 12) may be implemented to reduce the negative impact of the media. If this were to be complemented with intervention and prevention programs that focus on increasing media literacy, we might be able to reduce the impact of the media on adolescent body image.

Interview and more in-depth qualitative studies are also needed to further our understanding of the different factors that impact on adolescent body image. These include peers (Chapter 6), the family (Chapter 7), individual factors (Chapter 9), and the sporting environment (Chapter 10). Overall, in Chapter 7 we showed that peer and media influences are more important than parental influences. However, further studies examining how parental messages are perceived and experienced by adolescents are needed, as this will help us better understand the bidirectional nature of these influences. Adolescent attitudes and behaviours also affect how parents react and respond. In Chapter 8 we mentioned how there are likely to be 'cultural nuances' in body image ideals across different Western countries. However, these are difficult to measure and may be too subtle to detect unless examined qualitatively. Similarly, no conclusions about any body image differences among adolescents from different Western and non-Western countries can be drawn as too few studies have been conducted, and where differences have been found there has been no examination of any of the inter- or intracultural factors that may account for the differences. We highlighted in Chapter 10 that more in-depth studies are needed to fully examine some of the nuances of different sporting environments and how these are experienced by adolescents. We still have a limited understanding of how the sporting environment promotes lower body dissatisfaction but at the same time higher levels of disordered eating.

Adolescents spend a great deal of time in schools. This means that there is great potential for schools to contribute towards the development of body dissatisfaction but also be involved in the implementation of programs to promote positive body image. In Chapter 11, we presented our original research that demonstrates that teachers and schools are willing to take action in this area and that some are already implementing programs and materials that aim to develop self-esteem and promote positive body image. However, almost half of the teachers that responded to our survey indicated that they did not have access to adequate professional development in this area. Many teachers also indicated support for the use of resources and approaches to promote body image that body image experts would consider to be inappropriate as they may cause harm. The development of appropriate, evidence-based resources that teachers will use as intended and the widespread availability of free, just-in-time training for teachers and school professionals in relation to body image will enhance the capacity of schools to promote positive body image.

Programs designed to prevent the development of body dissatisfaction and promote positive body image are critical. Ideally, programs targeted towards individuals would be implemented from an early age, and throughout a range of settings. Developmentally appropriate body image programming could take a media literacy, peer-focused, or cognitive dissonance approach and be integrated into school curricula to ensure that all boys and girls have access to materials and pedagogies that aim to improve their body image. Online programs that feature more targeted information for those who might be more at risk for body image problems, and programs implemented throughout community settings such as girl guides, sporting organisations, and other community groups, would help to support and reinforce these school-based initiatives. Programs need not be lengthy or expensive. Our review presented in Chapter 12 indicated that the average length of effective programs was around four hours. If schools and sporting clubs have the capacity to take a holistic approach, where changes to policy, environment, and ethos are made in addition to the delivery of program content, this would further support efforts to improve body image among adolescents around the world.

Much of the research we have reviewed throughout our book has focused on the development and consequences of the negative aspects of body image and body change strategies, with the emphasis on dissatisfaction with size, weight, shape, appearance, and muscles. In order to further advance knowledge in the field, and to more fully understand adolescents' experiences of body image and identify factors that promote and emerge from it, body image research needs to include the positive dimensions. These include body acceptance and body appreciation (Tylka, 2011). Among adults the research has highlighted the appreciation of the body regardless of actual appearance; acceptance of the body despite weight, body shape, and imperfections; respect of the body by attending to its needs and engaging in healthy behaviours; and protection of the body by rejecting unrealistic media images (Tylka, 2011). Similar research that focuses on these positive aspects of body image among adolescents and how this may have a positive impact on adolescents' lives is now needed.

References

Barter, C., & Renold, E. (2000). "I wanna tell you a story": Exploring the application of vignettes in qualitative research with children and young people. *International Journal of Social Research Methodology, 3,* 307–24.

Devine, D. (2002). Children's citizenship and the structuring of adult-child relationships in primary school. *Childhood, 9,* 303–21.

Lightfoot, J., & Sloper, P. (2002). *Involving young people in health service development. Research Works, 2002–01.* York: Social Policy Research Unit, University of York.

Tylka, T.L. (2011). Positive psychology perspectives on body image. In T.F. Cash & L. Smolak (Eds.), *Body image: A handbook of science, practice, and prevention* (2nd ed., pp. 56–64). New York, NY: Guilford Press.

INDEX